Customer Loyalty and Brand Management

Customer Loyalty and Brand Management

Special Issue Editors

Natalia Rubio
María Jesús Yagüe

MDPI • Basel • Beijing • Wuhan • Barcelona • Belgrade

Special Issue Editors
Natalia Rubio
Autónoma University of Madrid
Spain

María Jesús Yagüe
Autónoma University of Madrid
Spain

Editorial Office
MDPI
St. Alban-Anlage 66
4052 Basel, Switzerland

This is a reprint of articles from the Special Issue published online in the open access journal *Administrative Sciences* (ISSN 2076-3387) from 2018 to 2019 (available at: https://www.mdpi.com/journal/admsci/special_issues/Customer_Loyalty).

For citation purposes, cite each article independently as indicated on the article page online and as indicated below:

LastName, A.A.; LastName, B.B.; LastName, C.C. Article Title. *Journal Name* **Year**, *Article Number*, Page Range.

ISBN 978-3-03921-335-1 (Pbk)
ISBN 978-3-03921-336-8 (PDF)

© 2019 by the authors. Articles in this book are Open Access and distributed under the Creative Commons Attribution (CC BY) license, which allows users to download, copy and build upon published articles, as long as the author and publisher are properly credited, which ensures maximum dissemination and a wider impact of our publications.

The book as a whole is distributed by MDPI under the terms and conditions of the Creative Commons license CC BY-NC-ND.

Contents

About the Special Issue Editors vii

Preface to "Customer Loyalty and Brand Management" ix

Mónica Gómez-Suárez
Examining Customer–Brand Relationships: A Critical Approach to Empirical Models on Brand Attachment, Love, and Engagement
Reprinted from: *Administrative Sciences* **2019**, *9*, 10, doi:10.3390/admsci9010010 1

Silvia Cachero-Martínez and Rodolfo Vázquez-Casielles
Developing the Marketing Experience to Increase Shopping Time: The Moderating Effect of Visit Frequency
Reprinted from: *Administrative Sciences* **2018**, *8*, 77, doi:10.3390/admsci8040077 17

Carmen Berné-Manero, María Gómez-Campillo, Mercedes Marzo-Navarro and Marta Pedraja-Iglesias
Reviewing the Online Tourism Value Chain
Reprinted from: *Administrative Sciences* **2018**, *8*, 48, doi:10.3390/admsci8030048 38

María Francisca Blasco-López, Nuria Recuero-Virto and Sonia San-Martín
Local Food Shopping: Factors Affecting Users' Behavioural E-Loyalty
Reprinted from: *Administrative Sciences* **2018**, *8*, 47, doi:10.3390/admsci8030047 56

Anne Schmitz and Nieves Villaseñor-Román
Do Brands Matter in Unlisted Firms? An Empirical Study of the Association between Brand Equity and Financial Performance
Reprinted from: *Administrative Sciences* **2018**, *8*, 65, doi:10.3390/admsci8040065 76

Andrea Moretta-Tartaglione, Ylenia Cavacece, Giuseppe Russo and Giuseppe Granata
A Systematic Mapping Study on Customer Loyalty and Brand Management
Reprinted from: *Administrative Sciences* **2019**, *9*, 8, doi:10.3390/admsci9010008 88

About the Special Issue Editors

Natalia Rubio is an associate professor in marketing at the Department of Finance and Marketing Research, Autónoma University of Madrid (Spain). Her research interests include brand equity, brand experiences, customer experiences, co-creation through online platforms, multichannel management, and retail marketing. She has published articles in several well-known international journals such as *Food Quality and Preference*; *Cyberpsychology, Behavior, and Social Networking*; *European Journal of Marketing*; *Journal of Service Management*; *Journal of Retailing and Consumer Services*; and *International Journal of Tourism Research*, among others.

María Jesús Yagüe is a full professor in marketing at the Department of Finance and Marketing Research, Autónoma University of Madrid (Spain). Her research interests include a variety of areas related to brand management, brand personality, brand equity, brand identification, customer experiences, tourism brand and retail marketing. She has published papers in several prestigious international journals, such as *Journal of Retailing and Consumer Services*, *International Journal of Hospitality Management*, *European Journal of Marketing*, *Journal of Destination Marketing & Management*, *Journal of Product and Brand Management*, *Complexity*, *European Journal of International Management*, *Computers in Human Behavior*, *Journal of Tourism Research* and *International Journal of Contemporary Hospitality Management*, to name a few.

Preface to "Customer Loyalty and Brand Management"

Loyalty is one of the main assets of a brand (Aaker, 1991; Yoo and Donthu, 2001). It means repeat purchasing of the brand based on strong internal disposition—in other words, repeat purchase behaviour resulting from a preference for that brand. Customers loyal to a brand are customers who return repeatedly to buy the brand because they are emotionally attached and committed to it. These are the customers least tempted by the competition—customers with higher switching costs who are willing to pay a higher price for the brand to which they are loyal.

In today's markets, achieving and maintaining loyal customers has become an increasingly complex challenge for brands due to the widespread acceptance and adoption of diverse technologies by which customers communicate with brands. Customers use different channels (physical, web, apps, social media) to seek information about a brand, communicate with it, chat about the brand and purchase its products. Firms are thus continuously changing and adapting their processes to provide customers with agile communication channels and coherent, integrated brand experiences through the different channels in which customers are present. In this context, understanding how brand management can improve value co-creation and multichannel experience—among other issues—and contribute to improving a brand's portfolio of loyal customers constitutes an area of special interest for academics and marketing professionals.

This Special Issue explores new areas of customer loyalty and brand management, providing new insights into the field. Both concepts have widely evolved over the last decade to encompass such concepts and practices as brand image, experiences, multichannel context, multimedia platforms and value co-creation, as well as relational variables, such as trust, engagement and identification (among others).

In the first paper, Mónica Gómez-Suárez examines the customer–brand relationship through a model that integrates the dimensions of brand attachment, brand love and brand engagement. Her research finds that attachment and engagement are decisive in the brand–customer relationship, and brand love is part of these two dimensions. Brand attachment is the connection between the consumer and a brand that goes beyond mere satisfaction to captivation, affection, bond and friendship. Therefore, brand attachment is built from emotions. When the consumer reaches this emotional state, the consumer considers the brand to have integrated into his/her life, and the consumer identifies with it, likes to show it off socially and engages with it; that is, the consumer wants to choose it and use it in the future. In the opinion of this author, two main drivers can help to develop brand attachment and engagement: consumer experience and coordinated marketing strategies using traditional communication combined with accurate personalization.

The second article by Silvia Cachero-Martínez and Rodolfo Vázquez-Casielles analyses different types of customer experiences at the store and their relationship with consumer engagement and willingness to stay longer in the store. These authors show that customer experiences increase consumer engagement and consumer willingness to extend shopping time. First, the dimensions of experience that strengthen consumer engagement are the intellectual through employees, the social, the pragmatic and the emotional. Second, the dimensions of experience that favour the time in the store and the possible increase in spending are the sensory, the intellectual through design, the pragmatic and the emotional. The research also shows the mediation role of positive emotional experiences between the dimensions of experience (intellectual, sensory, social and pragmatic) and consumer engagement and the stronger influence of positive emotional experiences on consumer engagement in those consumers who visit the store more frequently.

In the third paper, Carmen Berné-Manero, María Gómez-Campillo, Mercedes Marzo-Navarro and Marta Pedraja-Iglesias examine the online tourism value chain. This research provides a comprehensive model of the basic relationships of the quality–satisfaction–loyalty value chain in the online tourism context and analyses the role of the perceived transaction costs relative to the customer's participation in the co-production of the online channel tourism service. The research shows that the basic relationships of the quality–satisfaction–loyalty value chain found in other contexts are valid in B2C tourism online. In addition, the research finds that consumer participation in the service production, present in online channels, influences positively the formation of satisfaction and brand loyalty, which does not solely depend on website perceived quality.

Fourth, María Francisca Blasco-López, Nuria Recuero-Virto and Sonia San-Martín also analyse loyalty in an online context, but in this case, in the online local grocery context. Presently, online grocery shopping accounts for only a small proportion of the e-commerce market (Heng et al., 2018). However, it is expected to grow not only because of the general advantages of online shopping but also because of the increasing demand for specialty foods (Canavan et al., 2007) or the expanding of the slow food movement in response to the modern world's eating habits (Lee et al., 2015; Heng et al., 2018). In addition, regarding local food products, increasing consumer worries related to economic, social, environmental and health issues must be also considered (Pearson et al., 2011). In this context of online local grocery, the research by these authors demonstrates how website features jointly and positively influence perceived user flow and control and improve consumer satisfaction and loyalty.

Fifth, Anne Schmitz and Nieves Villaseñor-Román examine the links between brand equity and financial performance in unlisted (unquoted) firms. These authors underline the scarcity of prior research on this issue in this type of firm (Anees-ur-Rehman et al., 2018) and the importance of marketing managers better assigning marketing efforts towards the construction of a brand equity that improves firm profitability. These authors provide evidence that unlisted firms that invest more resources in brand equity have better financial performance, greater earnings persistence and more future profitability. The positive relationship between brand equity and financial performance is more intense when measured with the model of Aaker (1991) than when modelled with that of Keller (1993), because the brand equity component of perceived quality is mainly related to these positive effects.

Finally, the paper by Andrea Moretta Tartaglione, Ylenia Cavacece, Giuseppe Russo and Giuseppe Granata provides scholars with a systematization and mapping of contributions on the topics of customer loyalty and brand management. This research conducts a bibliometric analysis and a mapping study on 337 publications on customer loyalty and brand management from 2000 to 2018. The authors conclude that customer loyalty is a very complex area of study that includes several interrelated variables as dimensions (i.e., customer attachment, price tolerance, repurchase intentions, repeated purchases, positive word of mouth, etc.), antecedents (i.e., perceived quality, perceived value, customer satisfaction, consumer trust, brand experience, value co-creation, etc.) and consequences (i.e., customer retention, firm performance, customer value, competitive advantage and cost reductions).

In sum, all the papers in the present Special Issue address the complexity of brand management to obtain customer loyalty in actual markets. The relationship quality between the consumer and the brand is comprehensively analysed by Gomez who conceptually and empirically discusses concepts that sometimes have been treated as synonymous in the academic literature and other times have been distinguished (brand attachment, brand love and brand engagement). This Special Issue also analyses the antecedents of customer loyalty, underlining the importance of customer experiences (Cachero-Martínez and Vázquez-Casielles), quality and satisfaction (Berné-Manero et al., and Blasco López et al.,) and customer value co-creation (Berné-Manero et al.). The influence of brand equity on firm financial performance, greater earnings persistence and more future profitability is also evidenced by Schmitz and Villaseñor-Román. Finally, an illustrative analysis of academic research on customer loyalty and brand management from 2000 to 2018 is developed by Tartaglione et al. Together, the papers demonstrate the importance of customer loyalty and how the management of brand marketing strategies related to customer experiences, quality or value cocreation can improve brand equity and consequently influence firm performance and profitability for different sectors in offline and online contexts and in large and small firms. We believe that the present papers represent very well this domain of research, which is continuously expanding. We thank all our colleagues for their contributions.

Conflicts of Interest: The authors declare no conflicts of interest.

Aaker, David A. 1991. Managing Brand Equity. New York: The Free Press.

Anees-ur-Rehman, M., Wong, H. Y., Sultan, P., and Merrilees, B. (2018). How brand-oriented strategy affects the financial performance of B2B SMEs. Journal of Business and Industrial Marketing, 33 (3): 303-315.

Canavan, O., Henchion, M., O'Reilly, S. (2007). The use of the internet as a marketing channel for Irish speciality food. International Journal of Retail and Distribution Management, 35 (2): 178-195.

Heng, Y., Gao, Z., Jiang, Y., & Chen, X. (2018). Exploring hidden factors behind online food shopping from Amazon reviews: A topic mining approach. Journal of Retailing and Consumer Services, 42: 161-168.

Keller, Kevin Lane. 1993. Conceptualizing, measuring, and managing customer-based brand equity. Journal of Marketing 57: 1-22.

Lee, K. H., Packer, J., & Scott, N. (2015). Travel lifestyle preferences and destination activity choices of Slow Food members and non-members. Tourism Management, 46: 1-10.

Pearson, D., Henryks, J., Trott, A., Jones, P., Parker, G., Dumaresq, D., & Dyball, R. (2011). Local food: understanding consumer motivations in innovative retail formats. British Food Journal, 113 (7): 886-899.

Natalia Rubio, María Jesús Yagüe
Special Issue Editors

Article

Examining Customer–Brand Relationships: A Critical Approach to Empirical Models on Brand Attachment, Love, and Engagement

Mónica Gómez-Suárez

Finance and Marketing Department, University Autónoma of Madrid, 28760 Cantoblanco, Spain; monica.gomez@uam.es

Received: 31 October 2018; Accepted: 17 January 2019; Published: 20 January 2019

Abstract: This study establishes the relationship among three concepts (attachment, love, and engagement) that have attracted the interest of both practitioners and researchers lately. Based on the consumer–brand relationship literature, a theoretical model is proposed. Using data obtained from a survey to 320 consumers from Madrid (Spain), the results show that only two constructs actually exist: attachment and active engagement, with love being part of attachment (passion) or engagement (long-term relationship). Thus, emotional attachment must be based on emotions that generate captivation. This admiration activates engagement, turning the consumer into the best brand promoter.

Keywords: brand; consumer; customer; brand love; attachment; engagement; structural equation modeling (SEM)

1. Introduction

Relationships between consumers and brands encompass several dimensions that have attracted the attention of those in marketing research. Terms such as emotional attachment (Thomson et al. 2005), brand love (Carroll and Ahuvia 2006; Batra et al. 2012), or engagement (Brodie et al. 2011; Hollebeek et al. 2014; Vivek et al. 2014) refer, a priori, to different stages of the relationship developed between brands and individuals. They represent close notions, sharing certain features, and describe both the degree of connection and the intensity of the consumer–brand relationship. Although they share some traits, they might be different constructs in terms of their meaning, their dimensionality, items employed to define them, and the link between them.

The purpose of this paper is to shed light into these relationships, delimiting their definitions and measurement. In order to do so, the main objective of this study is to establish the links—and boundaries—between these three related concepts, by examining their relationships. A second objective, derived from the first one, is to provide the readers with a better measurement of the constructs "underlying" attachment, love, and engagement.

Therefore, the current study posed the following research questions (RQ):

(1) Where is the conceptual border between the three notions that allude to the consumer affection toward brands? That is,

   a. Do they represent the same concept or are they different? (RQ1)
   b. Which are the items that define each construct? (RQ2)

(2) Are these concepts properly measured? (RQ3)
(3) Are they multidimensional or unidimensional? (RQ4)

The contribution of this study is threefold. First, it theoretically elucidates the understanding of consumer–brand relationships. Second, it generates a model that comprises the entire process of moving from attachment to engagement. This model is used to test a framework to provide further evidence of the (dis)similarity of the constructs. Third, the findings of this paper could also aid managers to use efficient communication strategies, not only based on the emotions, but also supported by values that produce a viral activation among consumers. Then, attachment supposes a real bond to the brand that transforms loyal consumers into brand promoters.

The remainder of this paper is organized as follows. First, a review of the relevant literature is provided. By defining briefly the three terms and establishing the controversial arguments and evidence in the literature, the reader will understand if these dimensions are the same or are different. Next, the studies that developed empirical analyses are examined, focusing especially on measurement. Then, an empirical model with data from a survey of 320 consumers in Spain with structural equation modeling (SEM) is tested. This improved measurement of the links between the constructs is needed to define managerial implications. The last section is devoted to the discussion, limitations, and possible directions for future research.

2. Background: The Conceptual Border between Attachment, Love, and Engagement

Three related notions were identified in the literature survey: emotional attachment, brand love, and customer engagement. Criticism regarding recent consumer–brand relationship concepts in the marketing literature, especially in the case of brand love (Rossiter 2012; Moussa 2015), highlights the importance of establishing the boundaries between attachment, love, and engagement. This conceptual delimitation is relevant, since the different terms may constitute either antecedents or consequences of different conceptual models that have been researched separately except for four recent studies (Bergkvist and Bech-Larsen 2010; Wallace et al. 2014; Sarkar and Sreejesh 2014; Vernuccio et al. 2015).

Most likely, the problem that creates the relative terminological confusion is that the concepts originate from different pre-existing theories in diverse fields. For instance, the conceptual development of brand love arose from social psychology (Batra et al. 2012). In contrast, consumer engagement comes from the expanded domain of relationship marketing and the service-dominant logic perspective (Brodie et al. 2011; Hollebeek et al. 2014). Hence, the research tradition that shapes their theoretical frameworks and main definitions has not converged.

2.1. Definitions

Thomson et al. (2005) provided the seminal empirical work on emotional attachment to brands (Grisaffe and Nguyen 2011). According to the first authors, emotional attachment is an "emotion-laden target-specific bond between a person and a specific object" (p. 78). Attachments vary in strength, and stronger attachments are associated with stronger feelings of connection, affection, and passion (Thomson et al. 2005).

Brand love represents the intimate experience of very positive emotion toward a particular brand. Nevertheless, there are two main notions for brand love in the literature. On the one hand, Carroll and Ahuvia (2006, p. 81) define it as "the degree of passionate emotional attachment a satisfied consumer has for a particular trade name". On the second hand, Batra et al. (2012, p. 2) provide a more complete definition: "a higher-order construct including multiple cognitions, emotions, and behaviors, which consumers organize into a mental prototype". The first definition is based on the idea that brand love is platonic in nature, and typically focuses on aspirational brands that represent a lifestyle. The second suggests that brand love must be based not only on passion, but also on a long-term relationship (Batra et al. 2012; Albert and Merunka 2013). Thus, it refers to an ongoing relationship over an extended period of time (Gómez-Suárez et al. 2016). These two different conceptualizations have led to diverse conceptual and empirical models.

The third concept, customer engagement, is also considered in the literature as an ongoing relationship between a brand and a customer. According to Romero (2017), marketing researchers study customer engagement from two different perspectives: a psychological perspective, encompassing cognitive, emotional, and behavioral elements (Brodie et al. 2011); and from a behavioral point of view, focusing on customer engagement behavioral manifestation such as word-of-mouth or co-creation. The lack of consensus pertaining to the definition of focal engagement-based concepts (Hollebeek 2013) provides different definitions. For instance, focusing on the psychological perspective, Brodie et al. (2011, p. 3) define customer engagement as "a multidimensional concept comprising cognitive, emotional, and/or behavioral dimensions, [which] plays a central role in the process of relational exchange". By contrast, Vivek et al. (2014, p. 401) state that it is "the level of the customer's (or potential customer's) interactions and connections with the brand or firm's offerings or activities" (Vivek et al. 2014, p. 401).

2.2. Boundaries between the Concepts: Are These Dimensions the Same or Are They Different?

For Moussa (2015), the concepts of brand love and brand attachment are not only composed of the same constituent elements, but are the same concept, being both "the two facets of the same single penny" (p. 79). According to this author, the two terms are distinctly delimited from a non-stop race between academics who have transferred concepts from interpersonal relationship theories into the branding literature as a consequence of the "publish or perish" mechanism, so that hardly a year goes by without some reinventions or retouching of the proposed conceptualizations for both.

Unlike Moussa, some researchers have observed some differences between brand love and attachment. Hwang and Kandampully (2012, p. 101) recognized that both are conceptually similar, and distinguished the two constructs based on intensity: "brand love necessitates the intensity of emotional responses towards an object, while emotional attachment does not necessarily require such intensity". Bergkvist and Bech-Larsen (2010, p. 504) also considered brand love as "a facet or dimension of broader constructs such as brand relationship quality or emotional attachment", with love being "generally regarded as quantitatively different from liking, that is, love is not extreme liking but rather a construct that is different from, but related to, liking" (p. 506).

By contrast, the differences between attachment and engagement are more evident. Vivek (2009, p. 32) claimed that "attachment is an affective construct strongly associated with ownership or possession of objects or products, and so is different from customer engagement. However, attachment could lead to engagement in several situations".

Regarding the brand love and engagement relationship, there has been a fragmented interpretation depending on the research context in which they have been supported. This issue especially arises when analyzing some antecedents of both concepts. According to Gómez-Suárez et al. (2016), different labels refer to the same concepts. For instance, the concepts of self-expression or self-congruity—derived from branding theories—have nearly the same meaning as identity, derived from identification theory.

2.3. Measurement: An Overview of Past Empirical Studies

In order to understand the nature of these three concepts, analyses of past studies were carried out by examining 46 empirical studies. These studies, classified by countries, methods, sample, dimensions, and main constructs, are offered in the Appendix A (Tables A1–A4).

In general, the limitations of the previous studies were due to the method by which the data were obtained. The collection method in most studies was a convenience sample, often including students (18 studies). In some cases, the sample size was very small or had biases regarding age or sex. Mainly, the studies were carried out in a single country with the United States (14 studies) being the most frequently analyzed. If the research was qualitative, the authors recognized the lack of validity without no subsequent quantitative endorsement. If it was an experiment, they required that, in later works, the brand, product, or service not be fictitious. In the case of developing several methods, as in a large part of the studies, the online selection of the sample produced a bias by sex or a number of classification variables.

Regarding dimensionality, although most of the studies that analyzed a single construct proposed a single dimension, the most recent empirical models were multidimensional. This was the case of the attachment models proposed by Fedorikhin et al. (2008), Grisaffe and Nguyen (2011), and Jimenez and Voss (2014). The engagement model was proposed by Javornik and Mandelli (2012) and the brand love models were proposed by Carroll and Ahuvia (2006), Hwang and Kandampully (2012), Rageh and Spinelli (2012), Fetscherin (2014), Huber et al. (2015), Dalman et al. (2017), Delgado-Ballester et al. (2017), and Algharabat (2017). However, the five papers that combined love and engagement (Bergkvist and Bech-Larsen 2010; Wallace et al. 2014; Sarkar and Sreejesh 2014; Vernuccio et al. 2015; Loureiro et al. 2017) treated the concepts as unidimensional constructs.

3. Conceptual Proposal

Following the definitions and models tested in empirical study, the three concepts (attachment, love, and engagement) appear to be multidimensional and reflect different constructs. Most of them reflect affective, cognitive, and behavioral dimensions. Nevertheless, they differ both in the breadth of the term and in the degree of connection with the brand. Therefore, exploring how many dimensions exist in each case and the relationships among them is a key issue for empirical analyses. The proposed model implied by these relationships is shown in Figure 1.

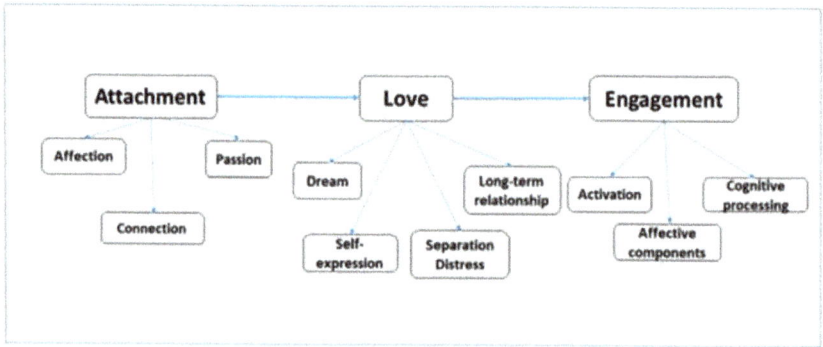

Figure 1. Conceptual proposal.

Based upon the literature review explained before and the theoretical framework proposed, our main research hypotheses are as follows.

H1. *Brand attachment reflects on affection, passion and connection (Thomson et al. 2005; Malär et al. 2011; Zhou et al. 2012).*

Previous studies have proposed a direct and positive relationship between brand attachment and brand love, being attachment an antecedent of love. Then:

H2. *Brand attachment is an antecedent of brand love, being these two constructs positively related (Albert et al. 2008; Bergkvist and Bech-Larsen 2010; Hwang and Kandampully 2012).*

By integrating all the diverse results obtained in the precedent empirical models (Carroll and Ahuvia 2006; Albert et al. 2008; Batra et al. 2012; Rauschnabel and Ahuvia 2014; Gómez-Suárez et al. 2016), brand love could be derived into six dimensions (passion, emotional bonding, separation distress, self-expression), dream, and long-term relationship. However, brand love measure in these past studies seemed to overlap a number of other constructs related to emotional attachment. Thus, in order to minimize the risk of overlap with other brand-related constructs, passion and emotional bonding dimensions were included in the attachment construct, as an antecedent of brand love, being the hypotheses:

H3. *Brand love is reflected into four dimensions: dream, self-expression, separation distress and long-term relationship (Albert et al. 2008; Batra et al. 2012).*

H4. *Brand love is an antecedent of brand engagement, being these constructs positively related (Bergkvist and Bech-Larsen 2010; Sarkar and Sreejesh 2014; Loureiro et al. 2017).*

Regarding the components of engagement, when comparing dimensions and items, there were some similarities between some affective components. For instance, happiness or being proud, on the scale provided by Hollebeek et al. (2014), may be similar to positive emotional connection or positive attitude valence on the scale used by Batra et al. (2012). Activation, the time and effort devoted to the brand, on the scale used by Hollebeek et al. (2014), had a similar meaning to the long-term relationship variables on the scale used by Batra et al. (2012) or by Albert et al. (2008). Vivek et al.'s scale (2014) also included items related to enthused participation reminiscent of the anticipated separation distress by Batra et al. (2012) or social connection, which directly refers to the attachment scale by Thomson et al. (2005). For this research, Hollebeek et al. (2014) model is chosen, but refining some of the items (see Appendix B Table A5). Therefore, the hypothesis is:

H5. *Engagement is reflected into three dimensions: cognitive processing, affective components and activation (Hollebeek et al. 2014).*

4. Research Methods

First, a pilot sample (27 respondents) was used to ensure the wording of the questionnaire was clear, after which some adjustments were made. This pre-test served to clarify the meaning of some confusing items, to analyze incoherent answers, and to test the validity of the scales. Data were collected from a survey of non-student adult participants. Similarly, to the study by Carroll and Ahuvia (2006), a cross-sectional survey of non-student adults, ages 21 and up, was carried out. Students in the last year of postgraduate study in marketing with training in market research approached to residents in Madrid (Spain) to complete a ten-minute self-administered questionnaire. These students were given extensive instructions that stressed the importance data purity (e.g., each respondent was to complete the questionnaire independently). They were also trained to meet pre-set quotas and perform adequate fieldwork. The sample was chosen through a careful stratified process according to sex, age, and occupation. Thus, no bias was produced by these sociodemographic variables. The fieldwork was conducted in January 2016. This process produced complete questionnaires from 320 adult consumers.

The questionnaire was created based on the literature review, and all measurement items were adapted from existing instruments. In order to avoid common method bias, the items and questions were prepared to be simple and concise (not including unfamiliar terms or complex syntax). The physical distance between measures was also considered, so that all items of the same construct were not right next to each other.

Common method variance (CMV) was also examined by making some previous estimations with the data. First, we carried out the procedure suggested by Hair et al. (2014) to check the absence of outliers. According to this procedure, we standardized each variable and analyzed their descriptive measures. The minimum and the maximum do not surpass the threshold value (4) for samples larger than 80 cases. Second, we connected each indicator to single construct in confirmatory factor analysis (i.e., factor that captures the potential common method variance) instead of separate ones, this estimation led to a significant decrease in the model's fit (MacKenzie and Podsakoff 2012). Therefore, CMV did not appear to be a significant problem in the present study.

There was a key previous question. Respondents named a brand for which they felt affection. The approach was similar to the brand elicitations in Thomson et al. (2005). Participants provided self-described reasons for this affection. No constraints on the elicitation were imposed. Respondents had the freedom to choose whatever brand they desired from any product category, without regard to preconceived classifications (e.g., goods vs. services; family brands vs. product item brands).

Afterwards, they had to describe why they chose that brand, then rating their degree of agreement with a series of items related to the three concepts.

The constructs were measured using pre-developed instruments from the marketing literature. Appendix B Table A5 provides a list of all the items. The respondents marked their responses on a Likert-type question format (where 1 = strongly disagree; 7 = strongly agree).

5. Results

Regarding descriptive results, the respondents mentioned 78 different brands. The most mentioned brands were Apple (21), Coca Cola (20), Zara (18), Nike (9), and Hacendado, Mercadona's private label for groceries (9). In terms of product category, the most mentioned was textile (20.8%), followed by food (16.5%). Other categories with a high number of mentions were electronics (11.5%), beverages (10.7%), cosmetics (9.7%), and cars (6.9%).

The purification process was based on a sequence of principal components analysis (PCA) with oblimin rotation. This process was undertaken to study the relationships between the different elements of each construct and to determine the items to be included in the confirmatory analyses (CFA). The accumulated variance of the final PCA model was 73.7%. Descriptive statistics (mean and standard deviation) and PCA results are presented in Table 1. Communality and reliability examinations—Cronbach's alpha—indicated that the final number of items to be included in the CFA model was 11. The dimensions relating to separation distress, self-expression, cognitive processing, and affective engagement did not fulfill the required criteria, either for communality or for reliability. Consequently, they were not included in the next confirmatory model. The PCA model included three factors: attachment (with five items from the connection and affection dimensions), passion (with three items from the dream and passion dimensions), and engagement (three items, two from the activation dimension—engagement, and one from long-term relationship—love).

Next, sequential CFA were run in order to determine psychometric properties and an accurate goodness of fit. These tests were performed using Amos 22.0. (Armonk, NY, USA), according to a maximum likelihood procedure. After four estimations, the achieved final model with three dimensions (attachment, passion, and engagement) lacked discriminant validity (all results can be provided to the readers upon request). Two procedures to test discriminant validity were used: the square inter-construct correlation and the average variance extracted (AVE) comparison (Fornell and Larcker 1981) (Table 2); and a comparison of the goodness of fit indexes for two models—free correlations and correlations restricted to the unit (Anderson and Gerbing 1988) (Table 3). Both showed a lack of discriminant validity for the passion and attachment constructs that appeared to participate in the same dimension.

Table 1. Descriptive and principle components analysis (PCA) results.

Items	Descriptive Measure			Component		
	Mean	SD	Variation Coef.	Attach.	Engage	Love
I feel care for this brand (AFF3)	4.33	1.99	0.46	0.920		
I feel friendship for this brand (AFF2)	4.01	1.88	0.47	0.898		
I feel affection for this brand (AFF1)	4.73	1.83	0.39	0.857		
I feel attached to this brand (CON3)	4.40	2.02	0.46	0.713		
I feel bonded to this brand (CON2)	4.49	1.93	0.43	0.685		
Whenever I am choosing among various products, it is the brand that I use (AC2)	6.12	1.18	0.19		0.862	
It is one of the brands I use the most (AC3)	5.68	1.54	0.27		0.782	
It is the brand that I will use in the future (PS7)	6.16	1.17	0.19		0.780	
It is a brand that surprises me (PS2)	4.78	1.80	0.38			0.897
It is a brand that makes me dream (PS3)	3.63	2.01	0.55			0.606
I feel captivated for this brand (PAS4)	4.15	1.97	0.47			0.548
Accumulated Variance				47.558	16.639	9.505
Cronbach's Alpha				0.918	0.720	0.779

Table 2. Discriminant validity procedure 1 based on Fornell and Larcker (1981).

	Attachment	Passion	Engagement
Attach	0.778 (*)		
Passion	0.788 (**)	0.767 (*)	
Engagement	0.389 (**)	0.359 (**)	0.743 (*)

Note: (*) root-square of AVE; (**) inter-construct correlation.

Table 3. Discriminant validity procedure 2 based on Anderson and Gerbing (1988).

	Goodness of Fit Indexes
Non-restricted model	$X^2 = 14.388$; df = 10; $X^2/df = 1.439$ GFI = 0.965; AGFI = 0.995; NFI = 0.985; CFI = 0.990; RMSEA = 0.037
Restricted Model	$X^2 = 14.966$; df = 11; $X^2/df = 1.363$ GFI = 0.987; AGFI = 0.967; NFI = 0.984; CFI = 0.996; RMSEA = 0.034

Note: df = degrees of freedom; GFI = Goodness of Fit Index; AGFI: Adjusted Goodness of Fit Index; NFI = Normed Fit Index; CFI = Comparative Fit Index; RMSA = Root Mean Square Error of Approximation. Note: $X^2 = 18.88$; df = 7; X2/df = 1.69 GFI = 0.988; AGFI = 0.965; NFI = 0.986; CFI = 0.987; RMSEA = 0.047.

An alternative CFA model was then tested (Table 4). This model had two related dimensions: attachment and engagement. Therefore, the model joined the initial two constructs from attachment and love into a single dimension. To fulfill convergent validity, the item "surprised" from the passion dimension was not included. Next, attachment, a first-order unidimensional construct, comprised four items from those initially proposal by Thomson et al. (2005): two from affection, one from connection, and one from passion. Table 3 shows the parameters and the psychometric properties of this model.

Table 4. Alternative model. Loads, reliability, and validity measures.

Item	Li	Critical Ratio	p-Value	Composite Reliability	AVE	Alfa
I feel affection for this brand (AFF1)	0.160	-	-	0.848	0.584	0.872
I feel friendship for this brand (AFF2)	0.724	18.239	***			
I feel bonded to this brand (CON2)	0.879	12.312	***			
I feel captivated for this brand (PAS4)	0.726	11.623	***			
It is the brand that I use (AC2)	0.705	-	-	0.709	0.550	0.701
It is the brand that I will use in the future (PS7)	0.776	5188	***			

Note: *** significant at 1% level.

The final structural model is shown in Table 5. Attachment ($\lambda = 0.404$) positively and directly influenced engagement. In addition, attachment was reflected in AFF1 affection ($\lambda = 0.716$), AFF2 friendship ($\lambda = 0.724$), bonded CON2 ($\lambda = 0.879$), and PAS4 captivated ($\lambda = 0.726$). Engagement was reflected in the items AC2 ("Whenever I am choosing among various products, it is the brand that I use"; $\lambda = 0.705$), and PS7 ("It is the brand that I will use in the future"; $\lambda = 0.776$).

Table 5. Global model estimation: structural parameters.

Construct/Item		Construct	Estimate
ENGAGEMENT	<—	ATTACHMENT	0.406
AFF1_1	<—	ATTACHMENT	0.716
AFF2_1	<—	ATTACHMENT	0.724
CON2_1	<—	ATTACHMENT	0.879
PAS4_1	<—	ATTACHMENT	0.726
AC2_1	<—	ENGAGEMENT	0.705
PS7_1	<—	ENGAGEMENT	0.776

Note: $X^2 = 11.88$; d.f. = 7; $X^2/d.f. = 1.69$ GFI = 0.988; AGFI = 0.965; NFI = 0.986; CFI = 0.987; RMSEA = 0.047.

6. Discussion and Implications

To the best of our knowledge, this study is the first attempt to integrate three different dimensions proposed in the past literature to understand the consumer–brand relationship: attachment, love, and engagement. A better conceptualization of the phenomenon was provided to delimit these terms, providing a simple and integrative scheme.

Related to the research hypotheses, Table 6 summarizes the main results of our empirical model. Following this table, summarized answers to the research questions are as follows. The conceptual border between the three concepts is not as clear as it initially appeared. In order to answer RQ1—do these dimensions represent the same concept or are they different?—the alternative model shows that there are two dimensions (and not three) that comprised the consumer–brand relationship: attachment and active engagement. Brand love is not a dimension, being actually part of the two other related constructs: attachment and engagement. Passion participates in the attachment dimension, and long-term relationship participates in the engagement dimension. Related to RQ2, whose items define each construct, the number of items is less than expected. Attachment reflects in four items (affection, friendship, bond, captivation) and engagement (activation) reflects in two items (chosen and used, using in the future). Therefore, in relation to RQ3, the three concepts have not been properly measured in the past. When integrating all the dimensions, some constructs and items are not included in the final alternative model. Regarding to RQ4, the two final constructs were both unidimensional instead of multidimensional.

Table 6. Research hypotheses decision and explanation.

Hypotheses	Accepted/Rejected	Explanation
H1: Brand attachment reflects on affection, passion, and connection	Partially	Attachment is a unidimensional construct that reflects into four items related to affection, connection (friendship and bond) and passion (captivation)
H2: Brand attachment is an antecedent of brand love, with these two constructs being positively related	Rejected	Brand love takes part in the attachment construct
H3. Brand love is reflected into four dimensions: dream, self-expression, separation distress, and long-term relationship	Rejected	Brand love also takes part in engagement, being a long-term relationship represented in the activation items
H4: Brand love is an antecedent of brand engagement, with these constructs being positively related	Partially	
H5. Engagement is reflected into three dimensions: cognitive processing, affective components, and activation	Partially	

From a managerial point of view, brand managers need to be aware of the importance of understanding certain traits of their target audience to guide the design of those activities aimed at developing affection and a more effective administration of the emotional bond with brands. Therefore, the manufacturers of leading brands must show values and benefits related to the items that help reinforce the affective bond, such as passion or friendship.

The emotional attachment that the consumer can feel towards a brand is represented then by a connection that goes beyond the mere satisfaction of the client and that is built from emotions that generate captivation. For all this, it is convenient that leader companies reinforce the positive values of their brands and, as far as possible, arouse positive and lasting feelings in the consumer. For instance, Coca-Cola associated its brand with happiness, and Danone with the nostalgia of childhood. More recently, the global campaigns of Apple are based on this kind of captivation claim.

When it is possible to reach this state of connection, the consumer considers that the brand has integrated into their life, identifies with it and its values, and likes to show it socially. To achieve these affective bonds with their customers, companies must be willing to offer exclusive experiences, in order to make position themselves as market benchmarks.

In our view, two main drivers can help to develop a strong link between attachment and engagement: consumer experience and coordinated communication strategies, using traditional mass campaigns combined with an accurate personalization.

The sense of captivation is more difficult to develop in mass-market products. However, a brand that provides happiness, pleasure, or positive emotions is probably creating this sensation. These intrinsic rewards are commonplace among brands that adapt to the customer through offers or personalized communication. The brand adopts a dimension of uniqueness based on communication that gives the consumer something else, for instance, offering exclusive care, personalized information, and even a sense of romance. This strategy is particularly intense in the fashion market for luxury brands (Chanel, Dior, Louis Vuitton, Armani, etc.)

Finally, the framework proposed for the consumer–brand relationship is based on the global Marketing 4.0 perspective that emerged by the end of 2016. Its goal is to help organizations reach and engage consumers more fully than in previous years by analyzing shifts in consumers' behaviors (Kotler et al. 2017). Thus, Marketing 4.0 emphasizes the need to consider, simultaneously, the "new" and the "old" marketing, to turn consumers into brand main promoters (Martínez-Ruiz et al. 2017).

The case of Toyota can be used to illustrate this new perspective. Its re-positioning in Europe is based on this kind of connection between the brand and its potential customers. Toyota cars, widely recognized for their reliability, were not leaders in the European markets because this attribute was not appealing for consumers. In 2017, the company decided to change their differentiation pattern by focusing on two different attributes: mobility and ecological motors. Communication managers in Spain decide to risk with a very different message "Drive as you think", emphasizing the bond with the consumer based on ecological values: Toyota hybrid cars help to conserve the planet. Some ads were even risking the sale of their brand since they urge drivers to park the Yaris Hybrid car and take the bus. This campaign—appealing to emotions and connecting with the new millennial consumer—has been a great success, activating the consumers' wish for this brand. Those loyal to the brand before changed from gasoline to hybrid Toyota cars. Those new in the market chose this brand or will choose it in the future. The global ad campaign in Spain is winning advertisement prizes, and the social networks made the slogan viral, with very positive comments that showed the consumers' admiration. This produced a multiplying presence of Toyota everywhere, with news in traditional media (magazines, newspapers, or TV). This finally has turned into sales, since half of the hybrid models were sold by Toyota in 2018. In market share terms, this brand has occupied the first place in sales, surpassing Volkswagen, the traditional leader in the Spanish market.

7. Limitations and Future Research

The present study has several limitations, specifically in its exploratory nature, the use of a small sample, and the need to establish a better control of different possible segments a priori. Although participants were consumers, non-student adults, and carefully chosen through a stratification process, the sample was chosen by convenience; therefore, caution should be taken when generalizing the results. In addition, the final model lost many initial items in the purification process through PCA and CFA, in order to fulfill all the requirements for psychometric properties. The reduction in the number of items may seem drastic, but this was the only method that could possibly reproduce an accurate statistical SEM model. Furthermore, as the study was conducted among consumers in Spain, it should be tested further, using participants from a variety of cultures and locations, to enhance the validity and reliability of the results. However, studies on consumer–brand relationships have been completed in cultural environments that differ from the Spain. Thus, considering the cultural determinants, this research provides new empirical evidence about the Spanish context.

Future studies could further employ qualitative and quantitative methods that enhance the robustness and generalizability of the findings, such as in-depth interviews, longitudinal studies, or experiments. For instance, the last method will allow the comparison of different segments, such as groups of "traditional" and "social media" consumers, both in high/low involvement consumption contexts. Maybe these groups perceive attachment or engagement differently, and a new model could better explain their perceptions.

Furthermore, there is a need to investigate the managerial relevance related to the identification of actionable variables for these constructs. Self-congruity or identification could represent antecedents for attachment. Further research could assess the relative strength of the constructs that compose the output of the process, such as word-of-mouth, loyalty, trust, and commitment. Such an assessment would provide both academic researchers and practitioners with valuable results.

Funding: This research was funded by the Spanish Ministry of Economy and Competitiveness research project (ECO 2015-69103-R). The study was also conducted under the framework of the research group TECHNOCOM (Consumer Behavior and Technology). The author is grateful to Francisco Palma, Communications General Manager in Toyota, who provided the example to develop the final illustration of the empirical model, following Marketing 4.0 paradigm, in the Forum "Education and Commercial Communication II" organized by the Master in Marketing Management Coordination, December 15, 2019. Economics and Business Faculty. Universidad Autónoma de Madrid.

Conflicts of Interest: The author declares no conflict of interest. The funders had no role in the design of the study; in the collection, analyses, or interpretation of data; in the writing of the manuscript, or in the decision to publish the results.

Appendix A

Table A1. Summary of past empirical studies for emotional attachment.

Author	Country	Method	Sample	Dimensions	Main Constructs
Thomson et al. (2005)	USA	Survey and experiment (5 studies)	Students (Study 1 = 68; Study 2 = 120; Study 3 = 75; Study 4 = 184; Study 5 = 175)	Multidimensional	Emotional attachment Three dimensions: affection, connection, and passion
Fedorikhin et al. (2008)	USA	Experiment. 2 × 3 between-subject design	Consumers ($n = 70$)	Unidimensional	Emotional attachment
Park et al. (2010)	USA	Survey	Students (Study 1 = 108; Study 2 = 141)	Multidimensional	Brand attachment and brand attitude strength
Grisaffe and Nguyen (2011)	USA	Qualitative, brand elicitation, code development	579 students and acquaintances	Unidimensional	Emotional attachment
Malär et al. (2011)	Switzerland	E-mail survey. 2 studies	Students (Study 1 = 1329; Study 2 = 890)	Multidimensional	Emotional attachment Three dimensions: affection, connection and passion
Zhou et al. (2012)	China	Online survey	586 car club members	Multidimensional	Emotional attachment Three dimensions: affection, connection and passion
So et al. (2013)	Malaysia	Survey with random systematic mall-intercept	282 consumers	Multidimensional	Emotional attachment
Jimenez and Voss (2014)	USA	Survey	Students (Study 1 = 149, Study 2 = 119)	Unidimensional	Emotional attachment

Table A2. Summary of past empirical studies for brand love.

Author	Country	Method	Sample	Dimensions	Main Constructs
Pawle and Cooper (2006)	USA	Storytelling, beta-test, visual images	300 individuals	Multidimensional	Mystery, passion, intimacy
Carroll and Ahuvia (2006)	USA	Survey administrated by students	334 non-student adults	Unidimensional	Brand love
Albert et al. (2008)	France	Internet survey; not directly asking for love but through images identification	843 individuals	Multidimensional	Passion, duration of the relationship, self-congruity, dreams, memories, pleasure, attraction, uniqueness, beauty, trust, declaration of affect
Bergkvist and Bech-Larsen (2010)	Australia	Survey	Students: Study 1 = 158; Study 2 = 135	Unidimensional	Brand love
Pang et al. (2009)	China	Experiment	100 students	Multidimensional	Passion, intimacy, commitment
Patwardhan and Balasubramanian (2011)	USA	Survey	99 students; 112 students	Multidimensional	Brand romance
Rageh and Spinelli (2012)	UK	Survey	250 students	Unidimensional	Brand love
Batra et al. (2012)	USA	Three studies: 70 structures telephone interviews; 18 in-depth interviews and survey	Main study: 268 undergrad students	Multidimensional	Passion-driven, self-brand integration, positive emotional connection, anticipated separation distress, long-term relationship, positive attitude valence, certainty, and confidence
Long-Tolbert and Gammoh (2012)	USA	Experiment	210 students	Multidimensional	Brand love (passion, intimacy, decision commitment)
Hwang and Kandampully (2012)		Online survey	210 students	Unidimensional	Brand love, emotional attachment
Rageh and Spinelli (2012)	UK	Survey	250 students	Unidimensional	Brand love
Albert and Merunka (2013)	France	Survey: online panel	1505 consumers	Multidimensional	Idealization, intimacy, dream, pleasure, memories and unicity, passion, and affection
Fetscherin (2014)	USA/Japan	Survey	180 students USA and 225 in Japan	Unidimensional	Interpersonal love/parasocial love
Rauschnabel and Ahuvia (2014)	Germany	Online survey	1092 internet users	Multidimensional	Brand love (Batra et al. 2012 dimensions)

Table A2. Cont.

Author	Country	Method	Sample	Dimensions	Main Constructs
Wallace et al. (2014)	Ireland	Survey	265 students (Facebook users)	Unidimensional	Brand love
Sarkar and Sreejesh (2014)	India	Survey	320 car owners	Unidimensional	Brand love
Huber et al. (2015)	Germany	Survey: Online questionnaire	175	Unidimensional	Passion
Vernuccio et al. (2015)	Internet (no country)	Facebook survey	20 Facebook fans' pages	Unidimensional	Social engagement, social identity
Dalman et al. (2017)	Internet (no country)	mTurk Survey	339 buyers	Unidimensional	Brand love
Delgado-Ballester et al. (2017)	Spain	Survey online panel	256 panelists	Unidimensional	Single measure (general indicator)
Algharabat (2017)	Jordan	Online survey	400 students	Unidimensional	Brand love

Table A3. Summary of past empirical studies for engagement.

Author	Country	Method	Sample	Dimensions	Main Constructs
Algesheimer et al. (2005)	Germany	Web-based survey	529 participants in car clubs	Multidimensional	Utilitarian, hedonic, social
Hollebeek (2011)	New Zealand	In-depth interviewing/focus group	14 informants	Multidimensional	Cognitive, emotional, behavioral
Brodie et al. (2011)	New Zealand	Qualitative-ethnographic	427 posts	Multidimensional	Cognitive, emotional, behavioral
Gummerus et al. (2012)	Finland and Sweden	Survey	276 usable responses	Multidimensional	Community and transactional engagement behaviors
Goldsmith and Goldsmith (2012)	USA	Online survey	132 American college students	Multidimensional	Specific brand engagement, brand engagement with self-concept
Javornik and Mandelli (2012)	Switzerland	Survey and focus groups	66 participants in the survey and 6 in the focus group	Unidimensional	Behavioral engagement: willingness of customers to engage
Hollebeek (2013)	New Zealand	Dual-depth interviewing/focus group	14 informants	Na	Conceptual association between engagement and customer value
Hollebeek and Chen (2014)	Internet (no specific country)	Ethnography	141 posts for Apple; 11 posts for Samsung	Multidimensional	Immersion, passion, activation
Vivek et al. (2014)	USA	Survey	247 students	Multidimensional	Conscious activation, enthused participation, social connection
Hollebeek et al. (2014)	New Zealand	Survey	194 students; 554 consumers	Multidimensional	Cognitive processing, affection, activation

Table A4. Summary of past empirical studies for both brand love and engagement.

Author	Country	Method	Sample	Dimensions	Main Constructs
Bergkvist and Bech-Larsen (2010)	Australia	Survey	Students: Study 1 = 158; Study 2 = 135	Unidimensional	Brand love and engagement
Wallace et al. (2014)	Ireland	Survey	265 students (Facebook users)	Unidimensional	Brand love and online customer engagement
Sarkar and Sreejesh (2014)	India	Survey	320 car owners	Unidimensional	Brand love and engagement
Vernuccio et al. (2015)	Internet (no country)	Facebook survey	20 Facebook fans' pages	Unidimensional	Social engagement, social identity
Loureiro et al. (2017)	Germany	Survey panel sampling Qualtrics	201 panelists	Unidimensional	Brand love and online customer engagement

Appendix B

In order to measure brand attachment, the scale suggested by Thomson et al. (2005) is used. This study uses a 10-item scale with three first-order dimensions of affection, connection, and passion. Hence, in the present study, these constructs are antecedents of brand love. The scale for brand love was adapted from the studies by Albert et al. (2008) and Batra et al. (2012). As previously mentioned in Section 2, passion is part of attachment dimension and long-term relationship is part of engagement. The scale proposed by Hollebeek et al. (2014) served to measure engagement.

Table A5. Dimensions, sub-dimensions, items, and authors.

Dimension	Sub-Dimension	Short	Item	Description	Authors
Attachment	affection	AFF1	affection	I feel affection for this brand	Thomson et al. (2005)
Attachment	affection	AFF2	friendship	I feel friendship for this brand	Thomson et al. (2005)
Attachment	affection	AFF3	care	I feel care to this brand	Thomson et al. (2005)
Attachment	connection	CON1	connected	I feel connected to this brand	Thomson et al. (2005)
Attachment	connection	CON2	bonded	I feel bonded to this brand	Thomson et al. (2005)
Attachment	connection	CON3	attached	I feel attached to this brand	Thomson et al. (2005)
Attachment	passion	PAS1	peaceful	I feel peaceful when I use this brand	Thomson et al. (2005)
Attachment	passion	PAS2	love	I feel love for this brand	Thomson et al. (2005)
Attachment	passion	PAS3	delighted	I am delighted when I use this brand	Thomson et al. (2005)
Attachment	passion	PAS4	captivated	I feel captivated for this brand	Thomson et al. (2005)
Attachment	passion	PS6	passion	I feel passion for this brand	Batra et al. (2012)
Love	dream	PS1	mythical	It is a mythical brand	Albert et al. (2008)
Love	dream	PS2	surprises	It is a brand that surprises me	Albert et al. (2008)
Love	dream	PS3	dream	It is a brand that makes me dream	Albert et al. (2008)
Love	separation	PS10	separation	I feel bad if I cannot use this brand	Batra et al. (2012)
Love	self-expression	PS9	sense	It is a brand that makes sense to my life	Batra et al. (2012)
Love	self-expression	SBC1	reflects	It is a brand that reflects what I am	Batra et al. (2012)
Love	self-expression	SBC1	personality	It is a brand that reflects my personality	Batra et al. (2012)
Love	long-term	PS5	committed	It is a brand I feel committed to	Albert et al. (2008)
Love	long-term	PS8	invest	It is a brand that I am willing to invest on it	Batra et al. (2012)
Love	long-term	PS4	longtime	It is a brand that I use long time ago	Albert et al. (2008)
Love	long-term	PS7	use future	It is the brand I think I will use in the future	Albert et al. (2008)
Engagement	activation	AC1	lot of time	I spend a lot of time using this brand	Hollebeek et al. (2014)
Engagement	activation	AC2	chosen	Whenever I am choosing among various products, it is the brand that I use	Hollebeek et al. (2014)
Engagement	activation	AC3	use the most	It is one of the brands I use the most	Hollebeek et al. (2014)
Engagement	affective	AF2	happy	Using this brand makes me happy	Hollebeek et al. (2014)
Engagement	affective	AF3	feel good	I feel good when I use this brand	Hollebeek et al. (2014)
Engagement	affective	AF4	proud	I'm proud to use this brand	Hollebeek et al. (2014)
Engagement	cognitive	CP1	makes me think	Using this brand gets me to think about it	Hollebeek et al. (2014)
Engagement	cognitive	CP2	think a lot	I think about this brand a lot when I am using it.	Hollebeek et al. (2014)
Engagement	cognitive	CP3	learning	Using this brand stimulates my interest to learn more about it	Hollebeek et al. (2014)

References

Albert, Noel, and Dwight Merunka. 2013. The role of brand love in consumer-brand relationships. *Journal of Consumer Marketing* 30: 258–66. [CrossRef]

Albert, Noel, Dwight Merunka, and Pierre Valette-Florence. 2008. When consumers love their brands: Exploring the concept and its dimensions. *Journal of Business Research* 61: 1062–75. [CrossRef]

Algesheimer, René, Utpal M. Dholakia, and Andreas Hermann. 2005. The Social Influence of Brand Community: Evidence from European Car Clubs. *Journal of Marketing* 69: 19–34. [CrossRef]

Algharabat, Raed Salah. 2017. Linking social media marketing activities with brand love. *Kybernetes* 46: 1801–19. [CrossRef]

Anderson, James C., and David W. Gerbing. 1988. Structural Equation Modeling in Practice: A Review and Recommended Two-Step Approach. *Psychological Bulletin* 103: 411–23. [CrossRef]

Batra, Richard, Aaron Ahuvia, and Rajeev P. Bagozzi. 2012. Brand love. *Journal of Marketing* 76: 1–16. [CrossRef]

Bergkvist, Lars, and Tino Bech-Larsen. 2010. Two studies of consequences and actionable antecedents of brand love. *Journal of Brand Management* 17: 504–18. [CrossRef]

Brodie, Roderick J., Linda D. Hollebeek, Biljana Jurić, and Ana Ilić. 2011. Customer Engagement: Conceptual Domain, Fundamental Propositions & Implications for Research in Service Marketing. *Journal of Service Research* 14: 252–71.

Carroll, Barbara A., and Aaron C. Ahuvia. 2006. Some antecedents and outcomes of brand love. *Marketing Letters* 17: 79–89. [CrossRef]

Dalman, M. Deniz, Mari W. Buche, and Junhon Min. 2017. The Differential Influence of Identification on Ethical Judgment: The Role of Brand Love. *Journal of Business Ethics*, 1–17. [CrossRef]

Delgado-Ballester, Elena, Maria Palazón, and Jenny Pelaez-Muñoz. 2017. This anthropomorphised brand is so loveable: The role of self-brand integration. *Spanish Journal of Marketing—ESIC* 21: 89–101. [CrossRef]

Fedorikhin, Alexander, C. Wang Park, and Matthew Thomson. 2008. Beyond fit and attitude: The effect of emotional attachment on consumer responses to brand extensions. *Journal of Consumer Psychology* 18: 281–91. [CrossRef]

Fetscherin, Marc. 2014. What type of relationship do we have with loved brands? *Journal of Consumer Marketing* 31: 430–40. [CrossRef]

Fornell, Claes, and David F. Larcker. 1981. Evaluating structural equation models with unobservable variables and measurement error. *Journal of Marketing Research* 18: 39–50. [CrossRef]

Goldsmith, Ronald E., and Elizabeth B. Goldsmith. 2012. Brand Personality and Brand Engagement. *American Journal of Management* 12: 11–20.

Gómez-Suárez, Mónica, Luis Enrique Alonso, and Sara Campo. 2016. Exploring the link between brand love and engagement through a qualitative approach. *Journal of Business Environment* 8: 367–84. [CrossRef]

Grisaffe, Douglas B., and Hieu P. Nguyen. 2011. Antecedents of emotional attachment to brands. *Journal of Business Research* 64: 1052–59. [CrossRef]

Gummerus, Johanna, Veronica Liljander, Emil Weman, and Mina Pihlström. 2012. Customer engagement in a Facebook brand community. *Management Research Review* 35: 857–77. [CrossRef]

Hair, Joseph F., William C. Black, Barry J. Babin, and Rolph E. Anderson. 2014. *Multivariate Data Analysis*, 7th ed. Essex: Pearson.

Hollebeek, Linda D. 2011. Exploring Customer Brand Engagement: Definition and Themes. *Journal of Strategic Marketing* 19: 555–73. [CrossRef]

Hollebeek, Linda D. 2013. The customer engagement/value interface: An exploratory investigation. *Australasian Marketing Journal* 21: 17–24. [CrossRef]

Hollebeek, Linda D., and Tom Chen. 2014. Exploring positively- versus negatively-valenced brand engagement: A conceptual model. *Journal of Product & Brand Management* 23: 62–74

Hollebeek, Linda D., Mark S. Glynn, and Roderick J. Brodie. 2014. Customer brand engagement in social media: Conceptualization, scale development and validation. *Journal of Interactive Marketing* 28: 149–65. [CrossRef]

Huber, Frank, Frederik Meyer, and David A. Schmid. 2015. Brand love in progress—The interdependence of brand love antecedents in consideration. *Journal of Product & Brand Management* 24: 567–79.

Hwang, Jiyoung, and Jay Kandampully. 2012. The role of emotional aspects in younger consumer-brand relationships. *Journal of Product & Brand Management* 21: 98–108.

Javornik, A., and A. Mandelli. 2012. Behavioral perspectives of customer engagement: An exploratory study of customer engagement with three Swiss FMCG brands. *Journal of Database Marketing & Customer Strategy Management* 19: 300–10.

Jimenez, Fernando R., and Kevin E. Voss. 2014. An alternative approach to the measurement of emotional attachment. *Psychology and Marketing* 31: 360–70. [CrossRef]

Kotler, Philip, Hermawan Kartajaya, and Iwan Setiawan. 2017. *Marketing 4.0: Moving from Traditional to Digital*. Hoboken: John Wiley and Sons.

Long-Tolbert, Silvia J., and Bashar S. Gammoh. 2012. In good and bad times: The interpersonal nature of brand love in service relationships. *Journal of Services Marketing* 26: 391–402. [CrossRef]

Loureiro, Sandra M. C., Taghjana Gorgus, and Hans R. Kaufmann. 2017. Antecedents and outcomes of online brand engagement. *Online Information Review* 41: 985–1005. [CrossRef]

MacKenzie, Scott B., and Phillip M. Podsakoff. 2012. Common Method Bias in Marketing: Causes, Mechanisms, and Procedural Remedies. *Journal of Retailing* 88: 542–55. [CrossRef]

Malär, Lucia, Hailer Krohmer, Wayne D. Hoyer, and Bettina Nyffenegger. 2011. Emotional Brand Attachment and Brand Personality: The Relative Importance of the Actual and the Ideal Self. *Journal of Marketing* 75: 35–52. [CrossRef]

Martínez-Ruiz, Maria Pilar, Mónica Gómez-Suárez, Ana I. Jiménez-Zarco, and Alicia Izquierdo-Yusta. 2017. Editorial: From Consumer Experience to Affective Loyalty: Challenges and Prospects in the Psychology of Consumer Behavior 3.0. *Frontiers in Psychology* 8: 2224. [CrossRef]

Moussa, Salim. 2015. I may be a twin but I'm one of a kind. *Qualitative Market Research: An International Journal* 18: 69–85. [CrossRef]

Pang, Jun, Hean T. Keh, and Siqing Peng. 2009. Effects of advertising strategy on consumer-brand relationships: A brand love perspective. *Frontiers of Business Research in China* 3: 599–620. [CrossRef]

Park, C. Whan, Deborah J. MacInnis, Joseph Priester, Andreas B. Eisingerich, and Dawn Iacobucci. 2010. Brand Attachment and Brand Attitude Strength: Conceptual and Empirical Differentiation of Two Critical Brand Equity Drivers. *Journal of Marketing* 74: 1–17. [CrossRef]

Patwardhan, Hemant, and Shiva K. Balasubramanian. 2011. Brand romance: A complementary approach to explain emotional attachment toward brands. *Journal of Product & Brand Management* 20: 297–308.

Pawle, John, and Peter Cooper. 2006. Measuring emotion. Lovemarks, the future beyond brands. *Journal of Advertising Research* 46: 38–48. [CrossRef]

Rageh, Ismail Ahmed, and Gabriella Spinelli. 2012. Effects of brand love, personality and image on word of mouth. *Journal of Fashion Marketing and Management: An International Journal* 16: 386–98. [CrossRef]

Rauschnabel, Philipp A., and Aaron C. Ahuvia. 2014. You're so lovable: Anthropomorphism and brand love. *Journal of Brand Management* 21: 372–95. [CrossRef]

Romero, Jaime. 2017. Customer engagement behaviors in hospitality: Customer based antecedents. *Journal of Hospitality Marketing & Management* 26: 565–84.

Rossiter, John R. 2012. A new C-OAR-SE-based content-valid and predictively valid measure that distinguishes brand love from brand liking. *Marketing Letters* 23: 905–16. [CrossRef]

Sarkar, Abhigyan, and S. Sreejesh. 2014. Examination of the roles played by brand love and jealousy in shaping customer engagement. *Journal of Product & Brand Management* 23: 24–32.

So, Jing T., Andrew G. Parsons, and Sheau-Fen Yap. 2013. Corporate branding, emotional attachment and brand loyalty: The case of luxury fashion branding. *Journal of Fashion Marketing and Management* 17: 403–23.

Thomson, Mathew, Deborah J. MacInnis, and C. Whang Park. 2005. The ties that bind: Measuring the strength of consumers' emotional attachment to brands. *Journal of Consumer Psychology* 15: 77–91. [CrossRef]

Vernuccio, Maria, Margheritta Pagani, Camilla Barbarossa, and Alberto Pastore. 2015. Antecedents of brand love in online network-based communities. A social identity perspective. *Journal of Product & Brand Management* 24: 706–19.

Vivek, Shiri D. 2009. A Scale of Consumer Engagement. Ph.D. dissertation, The University of Alabama, Tuscaloosa, AL, USA.

Vivek, Shiri D., Sharon E. Beatty, Vivek Dalela, and Robert M. Morgan. 2014. A Generalized Multidimensional Scale for Measuring Customer Engagement. *The Journal of Marketing Theory and Practice* 22: 401–20. [CrossRef]

Wallace, Elaine, Isabel Buil, and Leslie de Chernatony. 2014. Consumer engagement with self-expressive brands: Brand love and WOM outcomes. *Journal of Product & Brand Management* 23: 33–42.

Zhou, Zhimin, Qiyuan Zhang, Chenting Su, and Nan Zhou. 2012. How do brand communities generate brand relationships? Intermediate mechanisms. *Journal of Business Research* 65: 890–95. [CrossRef]

© 2019 by the author. Licensee MDPI, Basel, Switzerland. This article is an open access article distributed under the terms and conditions of the Creative Commons Attribution (CC BY) license (http://creativecommons.org/licenses/by/4.0/).

Article

Developing the Marketing Experience to Increase Shopping Time: The Moderating Effect of Visit Frequency

Silvia Cachero-Martínez [1,*] and Rodolfo Vázquez-Casielles [2]

[1] Cátedra Fundación Ramón Areces de Distribución Comercial, University of Oviedo, 33006 Oviedo, Spain
[2] Business Administration, University of Oviedo, 33006 Oviedo, Spain; rvazquez@uniovi.es
* Correspondence: cacherosilvia@uniovi.es; Tel.: +34-985-102-847

Received: 25 October 2018; Accepted: 26 November 2018; Published: 30 November 2018

Abstract: In the retail sector, the creation of shopping experiences becomes increasingly important to obtain a competitive advantage, and to meet consumers' needs and desires. Knowing how to design and apply these experiences can stimulate consumer engagement and their intention to spend more time at the retailer. Under this premise, the objective of this research is to analyze the relationship between different shopping experience dimensions, consumers' engagement, and their willingness to spend more time at the retailer. Using survey methodology on a sample of 527 consumers, the results show that shopping experiences stimulate the consumers' engagement and their predisposition to spending more time at the store. In addition, a moderating effect of visit frequency to the retailer is observed, such that the higher this is, the more intense the relationship between experience dimensions and consumer engagement will be.

Keywords: shopping experience; retail; consumer engagement; shopping time; shopping frequency

1. Introduction

The retail sector, one of the most dynamic in the economy (IBM 2012), must know how to adapt to the new market's demands. It faces increasingly demanding consumers, who demand unique products and services, and who have shared loyalty (Alfaro 2012). In addition, consumers do not demand only products or services, but they also want to live unique and unrepeatable experiences during the shopping. Given this new scenario of distribution, retailers have had to update both their offers and their ways of doing things, in order to offer a differentiated product and service, and thus seek the engagement and loyalty of their customers. For this, as the study by Deloitte (2016) indicates, it is necessary to design strategies that are focused on the "shopping experience", identifying those factors or dimensions that "create" experiences, defining how they will be implemented, and developing ongoing actions to revitalize and to surprise the customer with these shopping experiences. These new strategies provoke the situation in which the consumer goes to the retail establishment, not only to shop for a product or service, but also to enjoy the act of shopping itself (Krishna 2013).

Most consumers initially engage with a retailer for rational reasons, such as the value that it brings, or comfort. As the frequency of visits increases, feelings begin to emerge, due to the commitment or engagement that is acquired with the retailer. In this process, the experiences formed during shopping play a fundamental role (Homburg et al. 2017). Understanding how consumers experience emotions caused by marketing stimuli raises various implications in the design of the retailer's offer. Retailers need to develop action procedures that allow them to manage what they can offer in marketing experiences (Alfaro 2012).

Shopping experience research relates these experiences to satisfaction, relegating consumer behavior to the background, and not identifying that marketing actions are what lead to loyal and committed customers (Brun et al. 2017). Tsaur et al. (2007) examine whether experiences of experiential marketing have positive effects on consequent visitors' behaviors. They affirm that the experiences of experiential marketing have positive effects on emotions. Furthermore, emotions also have a positive effect on the behavioral intention, through the mechanism of satisfaction. No studies have been found that directly relate shopping experiences with engagement and shopping time. In this paper, the authors analyzed different experience dimensions, and their relationship with consumer engagement and with the predisposition to extend consumer shopping time, which is the main contribution of this research. This will allow the store manager to identify the aspects to be modified in its strategy, in order to obtain more engagement from customers who wish to stay longer in the store, thus creating deeper relationships that distinguishing the store from the competition. Grewal et al. (2017) highlight the importance of the study of engagement as an area of great interest in retailing.

This article contributes to the management literature of retail companies in two ways. In the first place, the knowledge of the type of experiences at the store is extended, analyzing the relationship between different dimensions of experience (sensory, intellectual, social, pragmatic, and emotional), consumer engagement, and willingness by the consumer to extend their shopping time. Secondly, the empirical research expands on existing knowledge, analyzing the moderating effect of visit frequency to the retailer. This is to understand whether a greater frequency of visits increases the positive influence of the experience dimensions on the engagement, intensifying not only the attitudinal loyalty, but also other shopping behaviors from the desire to spend more time in the store.

In the following sections, we comment on the relevant literature on the subject, and propose various hypotheses. Later we describe the research methodology and the results of the estimation of our causal model. Finally, we carry out a discussion on the theoretical and managerial implications, as well as the conclusions of the study.

2. Literature Review

In the marketing literature, different dimensions of customer experience have been analyzed. In different studies, four dimensions of experience are identified (Pine et al. 1999; Schmitt 1999, 2003; Gentile et al. 2007; Brakus et al. 2009; Grewal et al. 2009; Verhoef et al. 2009; Cachero and Vázquez 2017): sensory experience, intellectual experience, social experience, and pragmatic experience. Furthermore, Holbrook and Hirschman (1982) were the first to introducing emotions (e.g., happiness, enjoyment) as a component of consumer behavior, and to recognize emotional experience as a fundamental aspect of consumption (Bagozzi et al. 1999; Arnold and Reynolds 2003). In this paper we propose a hierarchical structure of the experience dimensions (Schmitt 1999), in line with the cognitive-affective approach of Ajzen and Fishbein (1980). As a background of emotional experience, we identify other dimensions of experience (Gentile et al. 2007; Brakus et al. 2009; Verhoef et al. 2009): sensory experience, intellectual experience, social experience, and pragmatic experience.

2.1. Sensory Experience

This is a dimension of experience that includes the senses of consumers, and that affects their perception, judgment, and behavior (Smith and Wheeler 2002). The empowerment of the consumer senses has been used in the retail sector for a long time; what has changed is the way of doing it: before, sensory experience was developed unconsciously, and today, planning by the retailer is maximum, either because sensory experience affects the consumer's perception of the store (Helkkula 2011), or the consumer's perception of the brand (Moreira et al. 2017).

The retailer is looking for absolute well-being, both for the consumer and for the people who work there. For this, it affects different environmental factors that it modifies based on the sensory experience that it wants to offer. Thus, the lighting varies, the layout of the product, the design, the smells, the color, the music, etc. Sensory-based stores have experienced great developments; they are shops where the brand is played, smelled, and heard. Table 1 presents the most relevant studies related to the sensory experience.

Table 1. Relevant studies related to sensory experience.

Sense	Author	Descriptions
Visual	Sachdeva and Goel (2015); Orth and Wirtz (2014); Kahn (2017); Wedel and Pieters (2015); Zielke (2011); Tantanatewin and Inkarojrit (2016)	This type of experience focuses on colors, shapes, distance, article size, lighting, or digital merchandising. It is the most direct way to provide information to consumers, either offline, online, or through advertising exhibitions, attracting them to the shop and trying to get the consumer to remember and "record" in their mind. Designing a good visual experience is decisive for a retailer, given that 90% of the information received by the brain is visual. The most studied factor is the impact of color as a trigger in the decision to shop and choose a brand.
Scent	Spence et al. (2014); Krishna (2013)	The stimulation of smell is a marketing tool of great potential, since it allows the retailer to generate affective states, promote a product, positioning a brand, or to assign "exclusive aromas" to a retailer and to differentiate it from the competition. In addition, it is also used to stimulate impulse-buying at store. For the scent experience to produce greater positive effects, there needs to be congruence between the smell, the desired environment for a retailer, the product offered, and/or the profile of the target buyer.
Auditory	Zaltman and Puccinelli (2000); Wiener and Chartrand (2014)	The sense of hearing is constantly active, making it an interesting point of attention for retailers who wish to apply sensory marketing to their store. It is not just about experiencing the sound, but trying to create, through music and the voice, a link with the consumer, facilitating the representation of the brand in the consumers' minds, and creating associations that activate emotions and experiences. The review of the literature places special emphasis on the use of music as a tool to create the store image in the consumer's mind, as well as the identity of the brand. In addition, it can help to change the mood and to create sensations that help customers to extend their shopping time.
Taste	Lawton (2016); Krishna (2013)	The sense of taste has been studied in the field of food and beverage products. The responses to different flavors are programmed genetically, instead of being learned or linked to experience, but they are highly influenced by the rest of the senses, so that taste can be considered as a mix of the rest of the senses, since these can affect the perception of the consumer's taste. This raises many possibilities of action to retailers that offer food and drink products, since they can link their products with certain scents to modify the behavior of consumers.
Tactile	George (2015); Gallace and Spence (2014); Ackerman et al. (2010)	Touching a product is fundamental when generating consumer information, given that the integration of these tactile perceptions in their behavior facilitates the purchase decision. Being able to touch the products and to experiment with them, intentionally or not, makes the customer–product relationship much closer, thus favoring the possibility of purchase. Although we have tactile sensors in all parts of our body, marketing research has focused on the hands as a primary source of the perceptual system: they are the "outer brain" of a person.
Multisensory	Krishna et al. (2010); Spence and Gallace (2011); Spence et al. (2014); Krishna (2006); Krishna and Morrin (2008); Spence (2012)	The review of the literature recognizes and identifies different sensory modalities, since consumers rarely process information using only one sense. There are, therefore, multisensory interactions, whose responses are more positive than if only one of the senses was used. Thus, the study of these interactions is of great interest, since they can facilitate consumer perceptions, attitudes, and preferences.

2.2. Intellectual Experience

Intellectual experience occurs when the retailer's merchandising strategy (intellectual experience through design) and/or interaction with employees (intellectual experience with employees) stimulates the consumer's curiosity and invites them to think and imagine (Schmitt 1999). Consumer curiosity is achieved when a seller evokes mystery during shopping (Menon and Soman 2002). Some academics say that the induction of curiosity produces positive results for the retailer (Hill et al. 2016). An emerging tool for retailers is augmented reality (Scholz and Smith 2016), with a promising future (Javornik 2016). It consists of combining the real world with the virtual world through a computer process, enriching the visual experience and provoking curiosity (Carmigniani and Furht 2011).

2.3. Social Experience

This type of experience refers to the consumer himself and his social context, his relationships with other consumers (Ferguson et al. 2010), and with the employees. From the research of Tauber (1972), the literature suggests that shopping is a social experience, so that relationships with the group are determinants of many of their behaviors.

2.4. Pragmatic Experience

The pragmatic experience implies that the consumer is motivated by the utility, value, functionality, efficiency, convenience, and usability of things, and not by their appearance, aesthetics, or social context. It refers to heuristic rules and election criteria linked to savings, acquiring products or services that are practical and of recognized quality, as well as the speed and efficiency of the actions of information search and purchase at the retailer (Walsh et al. 2011). For example, to stimulate the pragmatic experience, a retailer can offer an assortment of well-known brands with a price-quality ratio and better promotions than those of the competition. The objective is to attract a group of consumers who are interested in obtaining detailed information on prices and promotions, ensure that there is sufficient stock of the promoted products, or that the quality of the products is maintained during promotion periods. The retailer can also offer an assortment range that meets the needs of customers, all types of guarantees and complementary services (changes, returns, home delivery) or discounts, as well as allowing customers to verify the utility and practical value of some products.

3. Research Model and Hypotheses

In line with the review literature, the objective of this research is to analyze the relationship between different shopping experience dimensions, consumers' engagement, and their willingness to spend more time at the retailer (see Figure 1). This section discusses our key research variables and their hypothesized relationships.

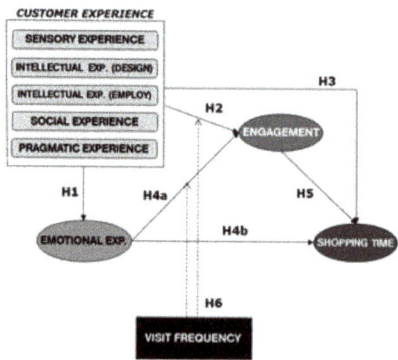

Figure 1. Conceptual model exploring customer experience, engagement, and shopping time.

3.1. Effects of Experience Dimensions (Sensory, Intellectual, Social, and Pragmatic)

The store stimuli linked to sensory experience are not only a source of emotional experience (Kaltcheva and Weitz 2006; Walsh et al. 2011; Nasermoadeli et al. 2013), but can also encourage consumer engagement (Gentile et al. 2007; Iglesias et al. 2011), attitudinal loyalty (Brakus et al. 2009; Iglesias et al. 2011), and other shopping behaviors such as extension in shopping time (e.g., wishing to spend more time in the establishment because of the good sensory environment that is enjoyed in the shop: smells, lighting, appropriate music, etc.). Thus, the following hypotheses are formulated:

Hypothesis 1a. *Favorable perceptions of sensory experience have a positive influence on consumers' positive emotional experience.*

Hypothesis 2a. *Favorable perceptions of sensory experience have a positive influence on consumer engagement.*

Hypothesis 3a. *Favorable perceptions of sensory experience are positively related to extended shopping time.*

In relation to intellectual experience, the retailer needs to consider the process of reflection and surprise that he wishes to invoke via the shop design, novelty in the presentation and testing of products, leisure activities, and interaction with employees. The offer with original and creative products that lead the consumer to imagine, combined with the stimulation of creativity by retailers, for example through the creation of augmented reality experiences, can generate emotional experiences, engagement, attitudinal loyalty, and other shopping behaviors such as extended shopping time (Foroudi et al. 2016). Thus:

Hypothesis 1b. *Favorable perceptions of intellectual experience (through design) have a positive influence on consumers' positive emotional experiences.*

Hypothesis 2b. *Favorable perceptions of intellectual experience (through design) have a positive influence on consumer engagement.*

Hypothesis 3b. *Favorable perceptions of intellectual experience (through design) are positively related to extended shopping time.*

Hypothesis 1c. *Favorable perceptions of intellectual experience (through employees) have a positive influence on consumers' positive emotional experience.*

Hypothesis 2c. *Favorable perceptions of intellectual experience (through employees) have a positive influence on consumer engagement.*

Hypothesis 3c. *Favorable perceptions of intellectual experience (through employees) are positively related to extended shopping time.*

The design of social experiences by the retailer is a strategy desired by the consumer because it provides various non-monetary benefits (Borges et al. 2010). One of them would be to have the opportunity to go shopping with family/friends, and to obtain information about new products/services or trends that reflect attitudes and lifestyles. Other experiences that the consumer wants are to go shopping to find new friends, meet other people, or simply to see people. In addition, the social experience offers the opportunity to interact with other consumers who share interests, and to go to a place where reference groups can meet.

Going shopping today is a social act, a time of enjoyment in the company of friends or family (Mangleburg et al. 2004), and where a closer relationship with employees is expected (Chang et al. 2011), which encourages the positive emotional experience. Being advised, understood, and heard by employees are aspects that are highly valued by consumers, so that these actions can awaken the positive emotions of the consumer during shopping, with a consequent increase in their engagement. In addition, improving social interactions in the retailer results in higher levels of consumer loyalty and other shopping behaviors such as extended shopping time (Penz and Hogg 2011; Nasermoadeli et al. 2013). All of these lead to the following hypotheses:

Hypothesis 1d. *Favorable perceptions of social experience have a positive influence on consumers' positive emotional experiences.*

Hypothesis 2d. *Favorable perceptions of social experience have a positive influence on consumer engagement.*

Hypothesis 3d. *Favorable perceptions of social experience are positively related to extended shopping time.*

At many times, the client may experience emotions that are derived from pragmatic experience (Spinelli et al. 2015). The present study considers that functional purchases, apparently utilitarian, such as searching for good prices, promotions, or products, can be pleasant, and therefore influence the emotional experience. This is due to non-monetary reasons, including for example, the hedonic benefits provided by non-monetary promotions, or even the emotions derived from getting a good product at a good price (Alba and Williams 2013).

The creation of pragmatic experiences positively influences the positive emotional experience (derived from getting a product at a better price, or finding a product with less effort), in the engagement (derived from the continuous relationship with the retailer looking for his products of quality or its promotions), loyalty (derived from having carried out an effective, convenient and useful purchase, which encourages re-living that process or extending it), and other shopping behaviors such as extended shopping time (Walsh et al. 2011). Therefore, the following hypotheses are proposed:

Hypothesis 1e. *Favorable perceptions of pragmatic experience have a positive influence on consumers' positive emotional experiences.*

Hypothesis 2e. *Favorable perceptions of pragmatic experience have a positive influence on consumer engagement.*

Hypothesis 3e. *Favorable perceptions of pragmatic experience are positively related to extended shopping time.*

3.2. Consequences of Emotional Experience

The review of the literature confirms that having positive emotional experiences is a desired factor for consumers (Li et al. 2009); thus, in recent years, the emotional components in decision-making have become more relevant (Quartier et al. 2014; Adam et al. 2015; Pérez and Bosque 2015; Kim et al. 2016; Ladhari et al. 2017). Currently, retailers have begun to develop experience-marketing strategies as a way to express the values that represent the company. What they seek is to generate emotions and feelings in the consumer, such that the links with these feelings are deeper (Mishra et al. 2016), and engagement is encouraged (Johnson et al. 2008).

Beatty et al. (2012) propose an analysis with three components of commitment: affective commitment, calculated commitment, and normative commitment. This research has considered the positive dimension of commitment, i.e., affective commitment (Gilliand and Bello 2002), where the consumer is faithful to the retailer due to different relational benefits: benefits of special treatment (with extra services, sensory experiences, and intellectual experiences), social benefits (personal and friendly links between consumers and employees), and trust benefits.

The affective commitment is configured in the literature as a continuous relationship between a distributor or between a brand and a consumer (Hollebeek 2011). This commitment is the result of the emotional bond between both (Brodie et al. 2011; Claffey and Brady 2014), and it plays a key role in long-term relationships (Bowden 2009; Mollen and Wilson 2010), leading to deeper relationships and the creation of a real engagement. So, it raises:

Hypothesis 4a. *Favorable perceptions of emotional experience have a positive influence on consumer engagement.*

It is interesting for retailers to investigate the relationship between shopping experiences and attitudinal loyalty (Srivastava and Kaul 2014), to select strategies that are linked to experience marketing, and to obtain loyal customers. The model proposed in this research studies the effect of positive emotional experience on an indicator of shopping behavior: predisposition to extend shopping time. The time that consumers spend today to make their purchases has decreased significantly. It is interesting to investigate whether the consumers that are emotionally linked to a retail store or a brand are really willing to invest a greater part of their time in the act of shopping in it. It is to be expected that consumers who are emotionally linked to a retailer have more loyalty (Foroudi et al. 2016; Srivastava and Kaul 2014), as well as more predisposition to extend their shopping time (Andreu et al. 2006). For all these reasons, it is proposed that:

Hypothesis 4b. *Favorable perceptions of emotional experience are positively related to extended shopping time.*

Finally, this research raises the possible relationship between the consumer engagement and the predisposition to extend shopping time, from the review of literature that analyze the link between engagement and other indicators of loyalty and shopping behavior (Evanschitzky et al. 2006; Hsu et al. 2010). Engagement is the indicator of the consumer's desire to maintain the relationship (Geyskens et al. 1996). A consumer engagement, is one that manifests a sense of belonging towards the retailer (De Ruyter et al. 2001), and where the consumer is more likely to want to extend their time of purchase at the retailer. This leads us to propose the following hypothesis:

Hypothesis 5. *Consumer engagement is positively related to extended shopping time.*

3.3. Moderating Effect of Visit Frequency

Presumably, those consumers who visit the retailer more, whether or not they make purchases there, are looking for the shopping experience that it offers, and because the memory of that experience remains in their mind, creating value and providing satisfaction (Tsiotsou 2006). The frequency of shopping should indicate that the consumer is engaged and is loyal to the brand, but other factors must be evaluated. There are studies, such as Roy's (1994), which relate more frequent visits with hedonic motivations and less frequent visits with functional motivations (for example, going to the retailer only when there are promotions). Traditionally, shopping frequency has also been linked to security, closer relationships, and excitement and enjoyment during the purchase (Swinyard 1998).

Shopping experiences can influence consumer engagement to a greater extent if they visit the retailer with some frequency. One of the reasons that may be due to the consumer visiting the store regularly is due to the memory of the shopping experience, and through which he has created a certain level of commitment with the retailer. As the consumer–retailer relationship matures and becomes more personal and close, as a result of a greater number of visits, the amount of information available and the trust in the shop or brand increases (Gill et al. 1998). In addition, more frequent shoppers tend to be more hedonic-oriented. Consumers who have a hedonic orientation are pursuing an activity that they do not "have to do", and that they find personally gratifying. These consumers desire to derive richer and fuller experiences from the activity, which facilitates a greater engagement (Kaltcheva and Weitz 2006; Vieira and Torres 2014). Therefore, it is expected that for those consumers who visit the establishment more frequently, the effect of the shopping experience on the engagement is greater. Thus, it is proposed that:

Hypothesis 6. *As the frequency of the visit to the retailer increases, the positive influence of the experience dimensions on the consumer engagement increases.*

As a conclusion to this section, Figure 1 summarizes all of the hypotheses that are previously proposed and justified.

4. Research Methodology

4.1. Research Scope

In order to contrast the hypotheses, the present investigation focused on nine retail sectors: clothing store and fashion; shoes; cosmetics and perfumery; jewelry; sports; electronics; decoration; bookstores and toys. For these sectors, retail brands offer different types of shopping experiences: sensory, intellectual, social, and pragmatic. Each interviewee indicated his opinion of a retailer, which he had visited in the last two weeks. The sample was 527 consumers from several cities in Spain. Its distribution was made by age and sex levels. Table 2 details the technical data of the study.

Table 2. Research data.

Survey type	Structured questionnaire
Universe	Customers of offline stores that have recently made a purchase in the sectors selected for the study
Geographical scope	Spain
Sampling procedure	By sex and age
Sampling size	527 valid surveys
Sampling error	±4.27%
Desire level of confidence	95%; p = q = 0.5

4.2. Research Design and Measurement Scales

At the methodological level, work has been subdivided into two stages. The first one consists of the identification of the dimensions of the experience that are present in the retail sector, and the second analyzes the relationships between those dimensions of experience and consumer engagement and attitudinal loyalty (using shopping time as an indicator).

For the data collection, a questionnaire was prepared so that a sample of consumers could indicate their opinion on different dimensions of the shopping experience, and factors related to the engagement with the retailer, and with shopping time. The format of the scales was the following: the positive emotional experience was measured with a Likert scale that reflected the intensity of those emotions, from "1-Not at all" to "7-Extremely", and the rest of the concepts were measured with Likert scales whose answers varied from "1—Total Disagreement" to "7—Total Agreement". The scales have been elaborated from the review of the literature: Cachero and Vázquez (2017) for the dimensions of the experience; Walsh et al. (2011), Curth et al. (2014) and Vivek et al. (2014) for engagement; and Andreu et al. (2006) for the predisposition to extend shopping time, adapting these scales to the retail sector.

5. Data Analysis

An approach comprising confirmatory factor analysis (CFA), structural equation modeling (SEM), and multi-group analysis was adopted.

First, CFA was run to check the reliability and validity of the variables (Hair et al. 2010).

Second, to examine the effects of the experience dimensions (sensory, intellectual, social, and pragmatic), consequences of emotional experience, and the mediating effect of positive emotional experience, EQS 6.2 software was used, applying the Structural Equation Model (SEM-covariances). The estimation method used was that of the robust maximum likelihood (ML Robust). In addition to its use in similar research, the choice of this software focused on its advantages. SEM-covariances allow us to estimate multiple and cross-referenced dependency relationships among diverse variables and constructs, and they have the capacity to represent concepts that are not observed in these relationships, considering the measurement error in the estimation process (Hair et al. 2010). Finally, it is a flexible technique that allows for the comparison of alternative models that represent the same situation and selection of the ideal one, as well as rectifying the initial model to find an improved one.

Third, to test for the moderating effect of visit frequency on the relationships between customer experience (sensory, intellectual, social, pragmatic, emotional) and engagement, a multi-group analysis was run, which compared differences in coefficients of the corresponding structural paths for the individuals with a high frequency of visits, and for individuals with a low frequency of visits to retailers.

6. Results

6.1. Research Reliability and Measurement Scales

To demonstrate the reliability and validity of the measurement model, a confirmatory factorial analysis was carried out, from which satisfactory overall adjustment results were obtained, with content validity (standardized loading factors greater than 0.6) (Table 3). The Cronbach's alpha coefficients were all above 0.7, the composite reliability was greater than 0.7, and the Average Variance Extracted (AVE) was close to or greater than 0.5, confirming the convergent validity. There was also discriminant validity, given that the confidence intervals of all the correlations between the concepts analyzed did not contain the unit value, and its squared value did not exceed the AVE of the measurement scales considered (Table 4). The psychometric properties were adequate, so we continued with the estimation of the structural model.

Table 3. Analysis of the reliability and validity of the proposed model.

Factors	λ Stand.	CR	AVE	α Cronbach
Positive Emotional Experience		0.946	0.746	0.945
Happy	0.878			
Excited	0.877			
Entertaining	0.828			
Animated	0.880			
Enthusiastic	0.904			
Surprised (favorably)	0.811			
Sensory Experience		0.894	0.587	0.891
Temperature is suitable, activating the shopping experience	0.684			
Cleanliness and good condition, stimulating the shopping experience	0.816			
Lighting is motivating, making the shopping experience pleasant	0.849			
Color of the walls and floor provide a shopping experience in a pleasant environment	0.853			
Music (tempo, volume, and type) provides a very pleasant shopping experience	0.692			
Smells provides a very pleasant shopping experience	0.680			
Intellectual Experience (Design)		0.904	0.574	0.903
Design (furniture, decoration and equipment) stimulates consumer curiosity	0.784			
Section design stimulates the shopping experience and interactions with the product	0.761			
Communication materials (display) stimulate imagination and consumer creativity	0.761			
Store layout stimulates curiosity	0.828			
Shop-window offers an attractive presentation (artistic, creative)	0.719			
Store has a pleasant entry (spacious and inviting)	0.727			
Outside of the store design invites you to enter	0.717			

Table 3. Cont.

Factors	λ Stand.	CR	AVE	α Cronbach
Intellectual Experience (Employees)		0.868	0.628	0.869
Employees are always willing to help (provide information, support decision-making) and answer all customer questions	0.882			
Employees have great knowledge of what they sell and the experiences that the products provide	0.902			
There are enough employees to offer personalized services and to explain the experiences provided by the use of products	0.749			
Payment for the items purchased is fast, avoiding negative experiences	0.600			
Social Experience		0.808	0.587	0.797
Shopping at this store gives me the opportunity to experience the feeling of status (interactions with other customers)	0.760			
Shopping at this store allows me to obtain information and experiences on trends that are consistent with my lifestyle	0.862			
Going to this store allows me to spend a pleasant time with my family/friends	0.663			
Pragmatic Experience		0.743	0.492	0.866
Price	0.764			
Product	0.684			
Promotion	0.651			
Engagement		0.932	0.822	0.931
I am very proud to be a customer of this store	0.899			
I feel like I identify with the values and objectives of this company	0.920			
I am loyal to this company because I like the relationship that I have with it	0.900			
Extended Shopping Time		0.839	0.635	0.837
Spending more time searching for information in this store is a good idea	0.768			
If I had more time I would extend my stay in the store	0.791			
The time I've spent in this store has been worth it	0.830			

Overall fit of the structural model: S-BX^2(532) = 1513.6040, $p < 0.001$. BBNFI = 0.860, BBNNFI = 0.893, CFI = 0.904, IFI = 0.905, RMSEA = 0.051, SRMR = 0.050. AVE = Average Variance Extracted; CR = Composite Reliability; BBNFI = Bentler-Bonett Normed Fit Index; BBNNFI = Bentler-Bonnet Non-Normed Fit Index; CFI = Confirmatory Fit Index; IFI = Incremental Fit Index; RMSEA = Root Mean Square Error of Approximation; SRMR = Standardized Root Mean Square Residual.

Table 4. Discriminant validity analysis of the proposed model.

	1	2	3	4	5	6	7	8
1. Positive emotional experience	**0.746** [A]							
2. Sensory experience	0.047 [B]	**0.587**						
3. Intellectual (design) experience	0.090	0.448	**0.574**					
4. Intellectual (employees) experience	0.052	0.121	0.160	**0.628**				
5. Social experience	0.150	0.315	0.480	0.336	**0.587**			
6. Pragmatic experience	0.109	0.260	0.320	0.329	0.357	**0.492**		
7. Engagement	0.259	0.072	0.123	0.202	0.316	0.277	**0.822**	
8. Extended shopping time	0.386	0.059	0.149	0.145	0.300	0.304	0.425	**0.635**

[A]: The data in the table that appears in bold and on the diagonal is the AVE of each concept. [B]: The data below the diagonal of the table correspond to the squared correlations between pairs of constructs.

6.2. Estimation of the Structural Model

Table 5 and Figure 2 shows the results of the structural model, obtained with EQS 6.2. The goodness indices of the adjustment are adequate (BBNNFI = 0.894, IFI = 0.929, CFI = 0.929, RMSEA = 0.052). It is observed that the positive emotional experience is affected by the sensory experience (H1a: $\beta 1a = 0.056$), the intellectual design (H1b: $\beta 1b = 0.132$), the social experience (H1d: $\beta 1d = 0.264$), and the pragmatic experience (H1e: $\beta 1e = 0.140$). Regarding the engagement, the variables that directly and positively influence it are the intellectual experience with employees (H2c: $\beta 2c = 0.178$), the social experience (H2d: $\beta 2d = 0.229$), the pragmatic experience (H2e: $\beta 2e = 0.226$), and the positive emotional experience (H4a: $\beta 4a = 0.346$). Finally, the shopping time is modified directly and positively by the sensory experience (H3a: β3a = 0.109), the intellectual experience through design (H3b: β3b = 0.120), the pragmatic experience (H3e: β3e = 0.130), and the positive emotional experience (H4b: β4b = 0.238). In addition, this shopping time is also directly and positively influenced by consumer commitment (H5: β5 = 0.662).

Table 5. Results of the structural equation model analyses.

Structural Relationships	Standardized Coef.	t-Value
H1a: Sensory experience → Positive emotional experience	0.056	1.948 *
H1b: Intellectual experience (design) → Positive emotional experience	0.132	3.045 ***
H1c: Intellectual experience (employees) → Positive emotional experience	ns	ns
H1d: Social experience → Positive emotional experience	0.264	5.398 ***
H1e: Pragmatic experience → Positive emotional experience	0.140	2.764 **
H2a: Sensory experience → Engagement	ns	ns
H2b: Intellectual experience (design) → Engagement	ns	ns
H2c: Intellectual experience (employees) → Engagement	0.178	4.510 ***
H2d: Social experience → Engagement	0.299	6.671 ***
H2e: Pragmatic experience → Engagement	0.226	4.515 ***
H3a: Sensory experience → Shopping time	0.109	3.053 **
H3b: Intellectual experience (design) → Shopping time	0.120	3.536 ***
H3c: Intellectual experience (employees) → Shopping time	ns	ns
H3d: Social experience → Shopping time	ns	ns
H3e: Pragmatic experience → Shopping time	0.130	3.154 **
H4a: Positive emotional experience → Engagement	0.346	6.932 ***
H4b: Positive emotional experience → Shopping time	0.238	5.518 ***
H5: Engagement → Shopping time	0.662	11.571 ***

* $p < 0.05$; ** $p < 0.01$; *** $p < 0.01$; ns: not significant.

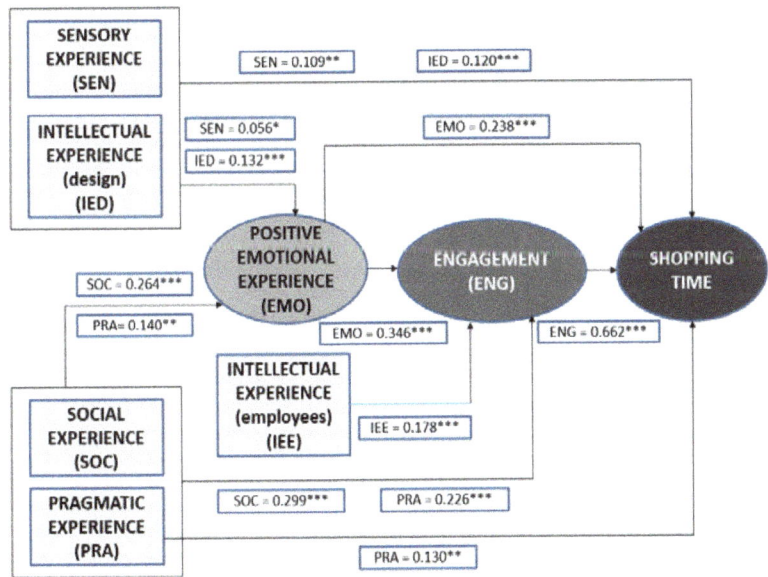

Figure 2. Significant relationships between all of the variables studied. * $p < 0.05$; ** $p < 0.01$; *** $p < 0.01$.

6.3. The Mediating Effect of Positive Emotional Experience

Once the structural model has been proposed, it is considered relevant that the mediating effect of the positive emotional experience in relation to experience dimensions–engagement is analyzed. In order to assess these mediating effects, the B-K method is a good alternative (Baron and Kenny 1986; Iacobucci 2008). However, although this method has been extensively applied for years, there is some criticism towards it, and many statistics recommend that other methods are applied (Preacher and Hayes 2004, 2008; Hayes 2013). Thus, two general approaches can be adopted to analyze mediation models: the regression approach, and the structural equation model (SEM) approach. The regression approach is used when the variables are observable indicators for which it is assumed that there is no measurement error. The most popular alternative is the macro/interface Process for SPSS that uses re-sampling methods (e.g., bootstrap procedure) to calculate the variance of the indirect effect or mediation. The SEM approach is more complex, but more recommendable, and it is used when any of the variables are a non-observable or latent variable, which is assumed to be free of measurement error, and is studied by using multiple indicators of the construct. In this paper, we used the structural equations approach (SEM), since each of the dimensions of experience and engagement are latent constructs with multiples indicators. In this way, we also controlled the measurement errors.

For each of the relationships between Customer Experience (X), Emotional Experience (Y), and Engagement (Z), the SEM approach allowed us to develop three stages (Holmbeck 1997, p. 602):

In the first stage, a partial model is calculated (unrestricted model), in which the direct and indirect effects are included among all the variables X, Y, and Z. The path coefficients obtained must be significant, and the value of χ^2 with respect to the degrees of freedom required must be greater than 0.05.

In the second stage, several restricted models are calculated (models of total mediation), such that the paths X → Y are restricted to zero (that is, this parameter is omitted). The coefficients paths obtained must be significant, and the value of χ^2 with respect to the degrees of freedom required must be greater than 0.05.

In the third stage, a difference test χ^2 is calculated. The objective is to verify the improvement of the fit of one model with respect to another alternative model. The adjustment of a model against its alternative is considered to be acceptable when the probability of the value of the test χ^2 with respect to the degrees of freedom required is significant ($p < 0.05$). In this case, if the restricted models improve the adjustment of the unrestricted model, it can be affirmed that there is a partial mediation of the emotional experience.

Figure 2 and Table 6 summarize the mediating effects that have been significant after applying the three stages of the SEM approach. Taking these results into account, the analyses showed that positive emotional experience presents (a) an effect of total mediation between sensory experience and engagement; (b) an effect of total mediation between the intellectual experience through design and engagement; (c) an effect of partial mediation between social experience and engagement; and (c) an effect of partial mediation between pragmatic experience and engagement.

Table 6. Analysis of the mediating effect of positive emotional experience in the relationship between experiences–engagement.

Relationship between Factors	Significant Effect	Mediation of Positive Emotional Experience
Sensory experience → Engagement	Only indirect (through positive emotions)	Total
Intellectual experience (design) → Engagement	Only indirect (through positive emotions)	Total
Intellectual experience (employees) → Engagement	YES (only direct)	No
Social experience → Engagement	YES (direct) YES (indirect) (through positive emotions)	Partial
Pragmatic experience → Engagement	YES (direct) YES (indirect) (through positive emotions)	Partial

Table 7 summarizes the direct and indirect effects for each consumer experience dimension. The dimensions with the greatest influence on engagement are social experience (0.390) and positive emotional experience (0.346).

Table 7. Direct and indirect effects of type of experience on engagement.

Type of Experience	Effect of Each Type of Experience on Engagement		
	Direct	Indirect	Totals
Sensory	NO	Sensory → Positive emotional experience Positive emotional experience → Engagement (0.056)(0.346) = 0.019	0.019
Intellectual (design)	NO	Intellectual (design) → Positive emotional experience Positive emotional experience → Engagement (0.132)(0.346) = 0.046	0.046
Intellectual (employees)	0.178	NO	0.178
Social	0.299	Social → Positive emotional experience Positive emotional experience → Engagement (0.264)(0.346) = 0.091	0.390
Emotional	0.346	NO	0.346
Pragmatic	0.226	Pragmatic → Positive emotional experience Positive emotional experience → Engagement (0.140)(0.346) = 0.048	0.274

6.4. The Moderating Effect of Visit Frequency

To analyze the moderating effects of the visit frequency, a distinction was made between individuals with a high frequency of visits (those who visited the establishment weekly or several times a month) and individuals with a low frequency of visits (several times a year or less), obtaining the causal parameters for both groups, and later testing the difference between said coefficients gamma and beta in LISREL notation, using an adequate moderation test (Baron and Kenny 1986). A multisample analysis was carried out, following the two methodological stages proposed by Jaccard et al. (1996).

The first stage involves a "multi-group solution". Using the EQS 6.2 software, parameters are estimated for each group of individuals, and a measure of the goodness of the fit of the model for both groups considered simultaneously. To study the differences between the groups it is more appropriate to perform the analysis in terms of non-standardized regression coefficients, due to the possible differences between the groups in the standard deviations of their constructs (Jaccard et al. 1996).

In the second stage, in order to check if there are significant differences between the causal parameters, the model was re-estimated by introducing (as a null hypothesis) the restriction that the coefficients in the structural model are the same in both groups (Iglesias and Vázquez 2001). In this second stage, and thanks to the Lagrange multiplier test (lmtest), it is possible to analyze if there are significant differences between the parameters of both subsamples. That is to say, the goal is to verify whether the elimination of the restrictions produces a significant change in the X^2 statistic. This would lead to a rejection of the equality restriction in the parameters, since its elimination would significantly improve the adjustment of the model.

The multi-group solutions of the first stage are summarized in Table 8, and the results of the second stage in Table 9. For those consumers with a high frequency of visits (weekly or several times a month), the social, pragmatic, and positive emotional experiences have a greater influence on engagement than for those consumers with low frequency of visits (several times a year or less). If consumers are very engaged with the company, it is logical to think that they will be the ones who visit the retailer more, because of the engagement that they have with it. This makes them value more positively the experiences that are developed in the store, especially those that are related to the emotional bond.

Table 8. Multi-group analysis: shoppers with high versus low visit frequencies.

Causal Relationships	High Visit Frequency (N = 206)	Low Visit Frequency (N = 321)
	β (t-Student)	β (t-Student)
Sensory experience → Engagement	NS	NS
Intellectual experience (design) → Engagement	NS	NS
Intellectual experience (employees) → Engagement	0.210 (3.571)	0.175 (3.159)
Social experience → Engagement	0.377 (5.190)	0.254 (4.533)
Pragmatic experience → Engagement	0.284 (3.458)	0.166 (2.746)
Positive emotional experience → Engagement	0.353 (4.213)	0.302 (5.322)
Fit of Goodness	BBNNFI = 0.873; CFI = 0.892; RMSEA = 0.053	

NS: not significant.

Table 9. Hypothesis test result in a multi-group analysis.

Causal Relationships	df	χ^2 Differences between High and Low Visit Frequency	p-Value
Sensory experience → Engagement	1	0.049	0.825
Intellectual experience (design) → Engagement	1	0.144	0.704
Intellectual experience (employees) → Engagement	1	1.107	0.293
Social experience → Engagement	1	4.666	0.033
Pragmatic experience → Engagement	1	3.847	0.050
Positive emotional experience → Engagement	1	5.400	0.023

7. Discussion

The consumer of today seeks to enjoy himself during shopping. We are faced with a consumer who is much more demanding than just a decade ago, given that the pace of life has changed; a customer who may not often even have time to make purchases. That is why the retailer, must allow the consumer to "get away from it all", making him enjoy the escape from his daily routine, in the time dedicated to shopping. The generation of experiences at the store facilitates this task for retailers. A unique and an unrepeatable shopping process can encourage the creation of a special bond with the consumer, which leads to more loyal customers and encourages them to devote a greater part of their time to shopping. In this way retailers, can get real fans instead of just customers (Alfaro 2012). Therefore, it is relevant to identify which types of experiences involve engagement (Brun et al. 2017), in order to stimulate this type of experience.

The literature published up to now and applied to the retail sector identifies and analyzes different dimensions of the experience, but not its direct influence on consumer engagement and on their willingness to extend their shopping time. This research reveals which of these dimensions of experience have a greater impact on consumer behavior. To do this, experiences at the store have been defined as a subjective perception of a retailer's commercial strategies. These experiences manifest themselves in a variety of dimensions that can be grouped into different categories: sensory, intellectual (through design and through employees), social, pragmatic, and emotional. Summarizing, the generation of experiences is complex, and it involves the presence of more than one dimension. The most important thing is to identify what types of experiences the consumer values, to be able to gain loyal and engaged customers.

8. Conclusions

The results of empirical research suggest that the dimensions of experience that can increase consumer engagement are the intellectual through employees, and the social, the pragmatic, and the emotional. Examples include creating spaces where customers can interact with employees, to demonstrate the uses of the product, organizing events at the store to encourage interaction between consumers with the same interests, offering quality products and efficiency in information search actions, or encouraging the generation of positive emotions in the retailer.

Thus, it is clear how important it is today to carry out experiential marketing activities, given that it influences not only the level of consumer engagement, but also the willingness to extend the shopping time. This is especially relevant nowadays. Given that the consumer has little time to make his purchases, it is essential to design a store that appeals to him, and that makes him want to spend more time in the retail store. Analyzing the predisposition to extend shopping time, it is observed that the dimensions of experience that lead to this type of predisposition are the sensory, the intellectual through design, the pragmatic, and the emotional. If the retailer seeks to increase consumer shopping time in order to achieve a possible increase in spending, this type of experience should be encouraged, to enable the customer to feel good, and for them to enjoy the act of purchasing. Examples include designing the store with sensory factors (such as an identifiable product or store smell, or type of music, according to the target customer), in a functional way for the consumer, so that they can shop for desired products without much effort, appealing to the emotions through these factors. These emotions can be stimulated through the creation of elements of sensory and intellectual experiences through design, and of social and pragmatic experiences. For example, designing stores so that consumers can interact with the products and encourage creativity and imagination when using them; encouraging consumers to come to the store to obtain information about new products or trends that reflect their lifestyle; or by making customers feel good about buying a cheaper product or a better-value-for-money product. An interesting option to improve this study would be to measure positive emotional experiences in the moment when those emotions are experienced. Nowadays, this is possible thanks to neuromarketing techniques, such as the eye tracking used in the Shopper Lab, which recreates shopping environments stimulating the development of different shopping experiences.

As a complement, we have analyzed the relationships between the dimensions of the shopping experience and consumer engagement by consumer segments, depending on the level of visit frequency to the store (high frequency or low frequency). The conclusions obtained indicate that positive emotional experience has a stronger influence on engagement in those consumers who visit the establishment more often. This may be due to the fact that the promotion of favorable affective states activates consumer engagement with the company, and the desire to return to it. Traditionally, consumer engagement has been linked to the experience of positive emotions at the store, and this study confirms this relationship, noting that it is greater for customers who visit the retailer more frequently. In addition, the social experience and the pragmatic experience also influence consumer engagement to a greater extent for these customers who visit the retail store more often. The idea that the consumer is a social being is confirmed, and that those activities of a social nature that the store can organize leads to higher levels of engagement. It is that feeling of belonging to a social group that is greater when visiting the retailer more frequently (to look for a social experience with family, friends, and other consumers with the same tastes). We must also mention the importance of offering a pragmatic experience when designing strategies to increase levels of consumer engagement, given that it is a dimension of the experience that draws the attention mainly of consumers who most frequently visit the retail store. Thus, attention should be paid to the functionality and quality of the offer, so that the consumer continues to frequently visit the store with the desire to find that kind of experience.

Managerial Implications

This study serves as support for decision-making by managers of retail companies, mainly when the consumer seeks shopping experiences. In the first place, stimulating the senses of consumers enhances their emotions in the retail store. Being able to manipulate the products offered by the retailer, and allowing users to interact with them, can be a source of emotion creation. Creating a pleasant shopping environment, e.g., in olfactory and visual terms, allows consumers to have a pleasant time. Enjoyment in the retail store with friends and family affects the sensations experienced by the consumer, since their comments can affect and alter emotions. From this perspective, the visual and design elements are very important for making a purchase attractive: augmented reality or platforms like Pinterest are some examples. In addition, the use of different screens and omnichannel technologies in physical stores helps create a visual experience that also intervenes in the shopping process.

What types of experiences are those that lead the consumer to increase their engagement with a particular retailer? The human being is a social being. For that reason, the interactions with the employees and with other consumers of the store are crucial. This is where experiences take on special relevance. It is about creating experiences that allow the consumer to interact with other customers, e.g., organizing book signings, records, sponsored concerts, lectures on new uses of certain products, or workshops/test centers and co-innovation. Knowing and developing those activities and services that will really surprise and interest the consumer can promote their engagement, willingness to extend their shopping time, and loyalty, turning the consumer into a true fan of the retailer.

The results of this research invite retailers to create emotional experiences, since these are the ones that most greatly influence consumer engagement. However, intellectual experiences through employees, and social and pragmatic experiences also affect that engagement. Currently, consumption has become a form of leisure, so that purchases are increasingly emotional, and consumers more often tend to want to enjoy the act of receiving information and/or purchasing a product. Also, this positive emotional experience also encourages the consumer to extend their shopping time, along with the creation of sensory experiences (stores that smell, allow touch, etc.) and pragmatic (oriented to the functionality of the store, the assortment and quality of the offer). Nowadays, getting the consumer to extend his shopping time is a challenge for the retailers' strategies, and for this, it is essential to achieve the emotional engagement of the consumer. On the other hand, the retailer should know the frequency by which their customers come to the store, in order to invest their resources in designing those strategies that have more impact on consumer engagement. This is possible nowadays, for example, through geolocation from apps installed on the consumers' smartphone. Encouragement to download the app of the retailer can be a tactic that can be developed, in order to obtain detailed factors such as the number of visits and their duration, including the route that is made within the store.

Although digital technologies have simplified the shopping process, tangible experiences are very valuable for consumers. That is why retailers must transform themselves from a simple place where the product is sold, to a more experimental, more sensory-rich space. Those retailers that do not bet on the marketing of experiences will be disadvantaged in terms of competitiveness and the possibilities of protecting themselves against falls in margins and prices. It is necessary to link customers through shopping experiences so that the price is not the most relevant factor, but rather the favor of the consumer towards the recommendation of the retailer, its products/brands/services, and above all, the achievement of consumer engagement. The retail store of the future will have to call hearts, not minds, since in a world of increasingly similar products and services, it will be the experience that makes the retailers different, and therefore, the factor that will bring them to market success.

Author Contributions: Conceptualization, S.C.-M. and R.V.-C.; Formal analysis, S.C.-M. and R.V.-C.; Investigation, S.C.-M.; Methodology, S.C.-M.; Software, S.C.-M.; Validation, S.C.-M. and R.V.-C.; Writing—original draft, S.C.-M. and R.V.-C.; Writing—review & editing, S.C.-M.

Funding: This research received no external funding.

Acknowledgments: The authors are grateful to Cátedra Fundación Ramón Areces de Distribución Comercial (www.catedrafundacionarecesdcuniovi.es) for their valuable support to develop this empirical research.

Conflicts of Interest: The authors declare no conflict of interest.

References

Ackerman, Joshua M., Christopher C. Nocera, and John A. Bargh. 2010. Incidental haptic sensations influence social judgments and decisions. *Science* 328: 1712–15. [CrossRef] [PubMed]

Adam, Marc T., Jan Krämer, and Marius B. Müller. 2015. Auction fever! How time pressure and social competition affect bidders' arousal and bids in retail auctions. *Journal of Retailing* 91: 468–85. [CrossRef]

Ajzen, Icek, and Martin Fishbein. 1980. *Understanding Attitudes and Predicting Social Behaviour*. Upper Saddle River: Prentice-Hall.

Alba, Joseph W., and Elanor F. Williams. 2013. Pleasure principles: A review of research on hedonic consumption. *Journal of Consumer Psychology* 23: 2–18. [CrossRef]

Alfaro, Elena. 2012. *El ABC Del Shopping Experience. Cómo Generar Experiencias Para Vender MÁS*. Madrid: Wolters Kluwer España.

Andreu, Luisa, Enrique Bigné, Ruben Chumpitaz, and Valérie Swaen. 2006. How does the perceived retail environment influence consumers' emotional experience? Evidence from two retail settings. *The International Review of Retail, Distribution and Consumer Research* 16: 559–78. [CrossRef]

Arnold, Mark J., and Kristy E. Reynolds. 2003. Hedonic shopping motivations. *Journal of Retailing* 79: 77–95. [CrossRef]

Bagozzi, Richard P., Mahesh Gopinath, and Prashanth U. Nyer. 1999. The role of emotions in marketing. *Journal of the Academy of Marketing Science* 27: 184–206. [CrossRef]

Baron, Reuben M., and David A. Kenny. 1986. The moderator-mediator variable distinction in social psychological research: Conceptual, strategic, and statistical considerations. *Journal of Personality and Social Psychology* 51: 1173–82. [CrossRef] [PubMed]

Beatty, Sharon E., Kristy E. Reynolds, Stephanie M. Noble, and Mary P. Harrison. 2012. Understanding the relationships between commitment and voice: Hypotheses, empirical evidence, and directions for future research. *Journal of Service Research* 15: 296–315. [CrossRef]

Borges, Adilson, Jean-Charles Chebat, and Barry J. Babin. 2010. Does a companion always enhance the shopping experience? *Journal of Retailing and Consumer Services* 17: 294–99. [CrossRef]

Bowden, Jana L. 2009. The process of customer engagement: A conceptual framework. *Journal of Marketing Theory & Practice* 17: 63–74.

Brakus, J. Joško, Bernd H. Schmitt, and Lia Zarantonello. 2009. Brand experience: What is it? How is it measured? Does it affect loyalty? *Journal of Marketing* 73: 52–68. [CrossRef]

Brodie, Roderick, Linda Hollebeek, Biljana Juric, and Ana Ilić. 2011. Customer engagement: Conceptual domain, fundamental propositions, and implications for research. *Journal of Service Research* 14: 252–71. [CrossRef]

Brun, Isabelle, Lova Rajaobelina, Line Ricard, and Bilitis Berthiaume. 2017. Impact of customer experience on loyalty: A multichannel examination. *The Service Industries Journal* 37: 317–40. [CrossRef]

Cachero, Silvia, and Rodolfo Vázquez. 2017. Living positive experiences in store: How it influences shopping experience value and satisfaction? *Journal of Business Economics and Management* 18: 537–53. [CrossRef]

Carmigniani, Julie, and Borko Furht. 2011. Augmented reality: An overview. In *Handbook of Augmented Reality*. Edited by Borko Furht. New York: Springer, pp. 3–46.

Chang, Hyo-Jung, Molly Eckman, and Ruoh-Nan Y. Yan. 2011. Application of the Stimulus Organism-Response model to the retail environment: The role of hedonic motivation in impulse buying behavior. *The International Review of Retail, Distribution and Consumer Research* 21: 233–49. [CrossRef]

Claffey, Ethel, and Mairead Brady. 2014. A model of consumer engagement in a virtual customer environment. *Journal of Customer Behaviour* 13: 325–46. [CrossRef]

Curth, Susane, Sebastian Uhrich, and Martin Benkenstein. 2014. How commitment to fellow customers affects the customer-firm relationship and customer citizenship behavior. *Journal of Services Marketing* 28: 147–58. [CrossRef]

De Ruyter, Ko, Luci Moorman, and Jos Lemmink. 2001. Antecedents of commitment and trust in customer–supplier relationships in high technology markets. *Industrial Marketing Management* 30: 271–86. [CrossRef]

Deloitte. 2016. Digital and Asociación DEC. I Estudio Nacional Sobre el Nivel de "Operativización" de la Experiencia de Cliente. Available online: https://www2.deloitte.com/es/es/pages/operations/articles/OCX-estudio-operativizacion-experiencia-cliente.html (accessed on 12 May 2018).

Evanschitzky, Heiner, Gopalkrishnan R. Iyer, Hilke Plassmann, Joerg Niessing, and Heribert Meffert. 2006. The relative strength of affective commitment in securing loyalty in service relationships. *Journal of Business Research* 59: 1207–13. [CrossRef]

Ferguson, Ronald J., Michéle Paulin, and Jasmin Bergeron. 2010. Customer sociability and the total service experience: Antecedents of positive word-of-mouth intentions. *Journal of Service Management* 21: 25–44. [CrossRef]

Foroudi, Pantea, Zhongeqi Jin, Suraksha Gupta, TC Melewar, and Mohammad M. Foroudi. 2016. Influence of innovation capability and customer experience on reputation and loyalty. *Journal of Business Research* 69: 4882–89. [CrossRef]

Gallace, Alberto, and Charles Spence. 2014. *In Touch with the Future: The Sense of Touch from Cognitive Neuroscience to Virtual Reality*. Oxford: Oxford University Press.

Gentile, Chiara, Nicola Spiller, and Giuliano Noci. 2007. How to sustain the customer experience: An overview of experience components that co-create value with the customer. *European Management Journal* 25: 395–410. [CrossRef]

George, Miriam. 2015. Haptics: The new wave of tactics for customer experience. *International Journal of Information & Futuristic Research* 2: 2606–11.

Geyskens, Inge, Jan B. E. Steenkamp, Lisa K. Scheer, and Nirmalya Kumar. 1996. The effects of trust and interdependence on relationship commitment: A trans-Atlantic study. *International Journal of Research in Marketing* 13: 303–17. [CrossRef]

Gill, Michael J., William B. Swann Jr., and David H. Silvera. 1998. On the genesis of confidence. *Journal of Personality and Social Psychology* 75: 1101. [CrossRef]

Gilliand, David I., and Daniel C. Bello. 2002. Two sides to attitudinal commitment: The effect of calculative and loyalty commitment on enforcement mechanisms in distribution channels. *Journal of the Academy of Marketing Science* 30: 24–43. [CrossRef]

Grewal, Dhruv, Michael Levy, and Vijay Kumar. 2009. Customer experience management in retailing: An organizing framework. *Journal of Retailing* 85: 1–14. [CrossRef]

Grewal, Dhruv, Anne L. Roggeveen, and Jens Nordfält. 2017. The future of retailing. *Journal of Retailing* 93: 1–6. [CrossRef]

Hair, Joseph F., William C. Black, Barry J. Babin, Rolph E. Anderson, and Ronald L. Tatham. 2010. *Multivariate Data Analysis: A Global Perspective*, 7th ed. Upper Saddle River: Pearson Prentice Hall.

Hayes, Andrew F. 2013. *Introduction to Mediation, Moderation and Conditional Process Analysis. A Regression Based Approach*. New York: The Guilford Press.

Helkkula, Anu. 2011. Characterising the concept of service experience. *Journal of Service Management* 22: 367–89. [CrossRef]

Hill, Krista, Paul W. Fombelle, and Nancy J. Sirianni. 2016. Shopping under the influence of curiosity: How retailers use mystery to drive purchase motivation. *Journal of Business Research* 69: 1028–34. [CrossRef]

Holbrook, Morris B., and Elizabeth C. Hirschman. 1982. The experiential aspects of consumption: Consumer fantasies, feelings, and fun. *Journal of Consumer Research* 9: 132–40. [CrossRef]

Hollebeek, Linda. 2011. Demystifying customer brand engagement: Exploring the loyalty nexus. *Journal of Marketing Management* 27: 785–807. [CrossRef]

Holmbeck, Grayson N. 1997. Toward terminological, conceptual and statistical clarity in the study of mediators and moderators: Examples from the child-clinical and pediatric psychology literatures. *Journal of Consulting and Clinical Psycholog* 65: 599–610. [CrossRef]

Homburg, Christian, Danijel Jozic, and Christina Kuehnl. 2017. Customer experience management: Toward implementing and evolving marketing concept. *Journal of the Academy of Marketing Science* 45: 377–401. [CrossRef]

Hsu, Chieng-Lu, Chia-Chang Liu, and Yuan-Duen Lee. 2010. Effect of commitment and trust towards micro-blogs on consumer behavioral intention: A relationship marketing perspective. *International Journal of Electronic Business Management* 8: 292–303.

Iacobucci, Dawn. 2008. *Mediation Analysis*. London: Sage.

IBM. 2012. Retail 2020: Reinventando la Distribución Minorista (UNA VEZ MÁS). Available online: https://www-05.ibm.com/services/es/bcs/pdf/REW03013-ESES-01_HR.pdf (accessed on 6 November 2017).

Iglesias, Víctor, and Rodolfo Vázquez. 2001. The moderating effects of exclusive dealing agreements on distributor satisfaction. *Journal of Strategic Marketing* 9: 215–31. [CrossRef]

Iglesias, Oriol, Jatinder J. Singh, and Joan M. Batista-Foguet. 2011. The role of brand experience and affective commitment in determining brand loyalty. *Journal of Brand Management* 18: 570–82. [CrossRef]

Jaccard, James, Choi K. Wan, and Jim Jaccard. 1996. *Lisrel Approaches to Interaction Effects in Multiple Regression*. Thousand Oaks: Sage.

Javornik, Ana. 2016. Augmented reality: Research agenda for studying the impact of its media characteristics on consumer behaviour. *Journal of Retailing and Consumer Services* 30: 252–61. [CrossRef]

Johnson, Mark S., Eugene Sivadas, and Ellen Garbarino. 2008. Customer satisfaction, perceived risk and affective commitment: An investigation of directions of influence. *Journal of Services Marketing* 22: 353–62. [CrossRef]

Kahn, Barbara E. 2017. Using visual design to improve customer perceptions of online assortments. *Journal of Retailing* 93: 29–42. [CrossRef]

Kaltcheva, Velitchka D., and Barton A. Weitz. 2006. When should a retailer create an exciting store environment? *Journal of Marketing* 70: 107–18. [CrossRef]

Kim, Sooyun, Geebum Park, Yeonjoo Lee, and Sunmee Choi. 2016. Customer emotions and their triggers in luxury retail: Understanding the effects of customer emotions before and after entering a luxury shop. *Journal of Business Research* 69: 5809–18. [CrossRef]

Krishna, Aradhna. 2006. Interaction of senses: The effect of vision versus touch on the elongation bias. *Journal of Consumer Research* 32: 557–66. [CrossRef]

Krishna, Aradhna. 2013. *Customer Sense: How the 5 Senses Influence Buying Behavior*. New York: Palgrave Macmillan.

Krishna, Aradhna, and Maureen Morrin. 2008. Does touch affect taste? The perceptual transfer of product container haptic cues. *Journal of Consumer Research* 34: 807–18. [CrossRef]

Krishna, Aradhna, Ryan Elder, and Cindy Caldara. 2010. Feminine to smell but masculine to touch? Multisensory congruence and its effect on the aesthetic experience. *Journal of Consumer Psychology* 20: 410–18. [CrossRef]

Ladhari, Riadh, Nizar Souiden, and Beatrice Dufour. 2017. The role of emotions in utilitarian service settings: The effects of emotional satisfaction on product perception and behavioral intentions. *Journal of Retailing and Consumer Services* 34: 10–18. [CrossRef]

Lawton, Stuart. 2016. Exploring the meal experience: Customer perceptions of dark-dining. In *Food Science, Production, and Engineering in Contemporary Economies*. IGI Global: Hershey, pp. 225–44.

Li, Jiunn-Ger T., Jai-Ok Kim, and So Young Lee. 2009. An empirical examination of perceived retail crowding, emotions, and retail outcomes. *The Service Industries Journal* 29: 635–52. [CrossRef]

Mangleburg, Tamara F., Patricia M. Doney, and Terry Bristol. 2004. Shopping with friends and teens' susceptibility to peer influence. *Journal of Retailing* 80: 101–16. [CrossRef]

Menon, Satya, and Dilip Soman. 2002. Managing the power of curiosity for effective web advertising strategies. *Journal of Advertising* 31: 1–14. [CrossRef]

Mishra, Prashant, Madhupa Bakshi, and Ramendra Singh. 2016. Impact of consumption emotions on WOM in movie consumption: Empirical evidence from emerging markets. *Australasian Marketing Journal* 24: 59–67. [CrossRef]

Mollen, Anne, and Hugh Wilson. 2010. Engagement, telepresence and interactivity in online consumer experience: Reconciling scholastic and managerial perspectives. *Journal of Business Research* 63: 919–25. [CrossRef]

Moreira, António C., Nuno Fortes, and Ramiro Santiago. 2017. Influence of sensory stimuli on brand experience, brand equity and purchase intention. *Journal of Business Economics and Management* 18: 68–83. [CrossRef]

Nasermoadeli, Amir, Kwek C. Ling, and Farshad Maghnati. 2013. Evaluating the impacts of customer experience on purchase intention. *International Journal of Business and Management* 8: 128–38. [CrossRef]

Orth, Ulrich R., and Jochen Wirtz. 2014. Consumer processing of interior service environments: The interplay among visual complexity, processing fluency, and attractiveness. *Journal of Service Research* 17: 296–309. [CrossRef]

Penz, Elfriede, and Margaret Hogg. 2011. The role of mixed emotions in consumer behavior: Investigating ambivalence in consumers' experiences of approach-avoidance conflicts in online and offline settings. *European Journal of Marketing* 45: 104–32. [CrossRef]

Pérez, Andrea, and Ignacio R. Del Bosque. 2015. An integrative framework to understand how CSR affects customer loyalty through identification, emotions and satisfaction. *Journal of Business Ethics* 129: 571–84. [CrossRef]

Pine, B. Joseph, Joseph Pine, and James H. Gilmore. 1999. *The Experience Economy: Work Is Theatre & Every Business a Stage*. Brighton: Harvard Business Press.

Preacher, Kristopher J., and Andrew F. Hayes. 2004. SPSS and SAS procedures for estimating indirect effects in simple mediation models. *Behavior Research Methods, Instruments & Computers* 36: 717–31.

Preacher, Kristopher J., and Andrew F. Hayes. 2008. Asymptotic and resampling strategies for assessing and comparing indirect effects in multiple mediator models. *Behavior Research Methods* 40: 879–91. [CrossRef] [PubMed]

Quartier, Katelijn, Jan Vanrie, and Koenraad Van Cleempoel. 2014. The Mediating Role of Consumers' Perception of Atmosphere on Emotions and Behavior. A Study to Analyze the Impact of Lighting in Food Retailing. Available online: www.academia.edu/download/13148766/final2_1.pdf (accessed on 15 May 2017).

Roy, Abhik. 1994. Correlates of mall visit frequency. *Journal of Retailing* 70: 139–61. [CrossRef]

Sachdeva, Ishita, and Sushma Goel. 2015. Role of store atmospherics on customer experience. *International Journal of Multidisciplinary Approach & Studies* 2: 72–83.

Schmitt, Bernd. 1999. Experiential marketing. *Journal of Marketing Management* 15: 53–67. [CrossRef]

Schmitt, Bernd H. 2003. *Customer Experience Management: A Revolutionary Approach to Connecting with Your Customers*. Hoboken: John Wiley & Sons.

Scholz, Joachim, and Andrew N. Smith. 2016. Augmented reality: Designing immersive experiences that maximize consumer engagement. *Business Horizons* 59: 149–61. [CrossRef]

Smith, Shaun, and Joe Wheeler. 2002. *Managing the Customer Experience: Turning Customers into Advocates*. London: Pearson Education.

Spence, Charles. 2012. Managing sensory expectations concerning products and brands: Capitalizing on the potential of sound and shape symbolism. *Journal of Consumer Psychology* 22: 37–54. [CrossRef]

Spence, Charles, and Alberto Gallace. 2011. Multisensory design: Reaching out to touch the consumer. *Psychology & Marketing* 28: 267–308.

Spence, Charles, Nancy M. Puccinelli, Dhruv Grewal, and Anne L. Roggeveen. 2014. Store atmospherics: A multisensory perspective. *Psychology & Marketing* 31: 472–88.

Spinelli, Sara, Camila Masi, Gian Paolo Zoboli, John Prescott, and Erminio Monteleone. 2015. Emotional responses to branded and unbranded foods. *Food Quality and Preference* 42: 1–11. [CrossRef]

Srivastava, Mala, and Dimple Kaul. 2014. Social interaction, convenience and customer satisfaction: The mediating effect of customer experience. *Journal of Retailing and Consumer Services* 21: 1028–37. [CrossRef]

Swinyard, William R. 1998. Shopping mall customer values: The national mall shopper and the list of values. *Journal of Retailing and Consumer Services* 5: 167–72. [CrossRef]

Tantanatewin, Warakul, and Vorapat Inkarojrit. 2016. Effects of color and lighting on retail impression and identity. *Journal of Environmental Psychology* 46: 197–205. [CrossRef]

Tauber, Edward M. 1972. Why do people shop? *Journal of Marketing* 36: 46–49. [CrossRef]

Tsaur, Sheng-Hshiung, Yi-Ti Chiu, and Chih-Hung Wang. 2007. The visitors behavioral consequences of experiential marketing: An empirical study on Taipei Zoo. *Journal of Travel & Tourism Marketing* 21: 47–64.

Tsiotsou, Rodoula. 2006. Using visit frequency to segment ski resorts customers. *Journal of Vacation Marketing* 12: 15–26. [CrossRef]

Verhoef, Peter C., Katherine N. Lemon, Ananthanarayanan Parasuraman, Anne Roggeveen, Michael Tsiros, and Leonard A. Schlesinger. 2009. Customer experience creation: Determinants, dynamics and management strategies. *Journal of Retailing* 85: 31–41. [CrossRef]

Vieira, Valter A., and Claudio V. Torres. 2014. The effect of motivational orientation over arousal-shopping response relationship. *Journal of Retailing and Consumer Services* 21: 158–67. [CrossRef]

Vivek, Shiri D., Sharon E. Beatty, Vivek Dalela, and Robert M. Morgan. 2014. A generalized multidimensional scale for measuring customer engagement. *Journal of Marketing Theory and Practice* 22: 401–20. [CrossRef]

Walsh, Gianfranco, Edward Shiu, Louise M. Hassan, Nina Michaelidou, and Sharon E. Beatty. 2011. Emotions, store-environmental cues, store-choice criteria, and marketing outcomes. *Journal of Business Research* 64: 737–44.

Wedel, Michel, and Rik Pieters. 2015. The buffer effect: The role of color when advertising exposures are brief and blurred. *Marketing Science* 34: 134–43. [CrossRef]

Wiener, Hillary J., and Tanya L. Chartrand. 2014. The effect of voice quality on ad efficacy. *Psychology & Marketing* 31: 509–17.

Zaltman, Gerald, and Nancy Puccinelli. 2000. *Strategic Use of Music in Marketing: A Selective Review [Case Study]*. Boston: Harvard Business School Publishing.

Zielke, Stephan. 2011. How store lightning influences store atmosphere, price and quality perceptions and shopping intention. Paper present at the European Marketing Academy Conference, Ljubljana, Slovenia, May 24–27.

 © 2018 by the authors. Licensee MDPI, Basel, Switzerland. This article is an open access article distributed under the terms and conditions of the Creative Commons Attribution (CC BY) license (http://creativecommons.org/licenses/by/4.0/).

Article

Reviewing the Online Tourism Value Chain

Carmen Berné-Manero *, María Gómez-Campillo, Mercedes Marzo-Navarro and Marta Pedraja-Iglesias

Marketing Department, University of Zaragoza, Facultad de Economía y Empresa, 2, 50005 Zaragoza, Spain; mgc@unizar.es (M.G.-C.); mmarzo@unizar.es (M.M.-N.); mpedraja@unizar.es (M.P.-I.)
* Correspondence: cberne@unizar.es; Tel.: +34-976-761-000

Received: 18 July 2018; Accepted: 16 August 2018; Published: 22 August 2018

Abstract: The booking purchase process in B2C tourism online from the perspective of the quality-satisfaction-loyalty value chain has scarcely been investigated. The measurement models of the variables are not unified and essential variables, as transaction costs, need more research in order to achieve a comprehensive model of the digital tourist purchase process. This research is aimed at solving this gap through the proposal of a theoretical structural model, which is tested for the Spanish context. The results show that the measurement of website-perceived quality must include utilitarian and hedonic aspects, which can provide a competitive advantage to acquire and retain customers. Perceived quality and transaction costs determine customer's satisfaction and, ultimately, repurchase intentions or brand loyalty. Prices are found as mediator variables fostering the effect of quality on satisfaction, and non-monetary costs act as a cause of satisfaction. The online B2C tourism business must implement efficient internal and external processes to justify perceived costs.

Keywords: B2C tourism online; online booking purchases; re-purchase intentions; satisfaction; transaction costs; value chain; website quality

1. Introduction

The latest research literature on tourism studies the evolution of virtual channels as a result of the intensive application of Information Technology and Communication (ICT). Since the establishment of Internet use initiated in the 90s (Oskan and Zandberg 2016), major changes have been observed in the consumers' purchase process. The relevance of paying attention to this evolution and consequences is that the customer purchase is implicit in the company's service-profit chain (Heskett et al. 2008).

The results of B2C tourism online companies depend on the successful accomplishment of the customers' purchasing process and on the right decisions in the distribution channels regarding the acquisition and retention of customers (end consumers in consumer markets). The emergence of online tourism channels has decreased the gap between providers and consumers (Ponte et al. 2015). The growing co-production or participation of the consumer in the production and distribution processes is considered as an initial stage of a continuum towards co-creation, which aims at the creation of innovations based on the collaboration of the client (Shaw et al. 2011). Consumers are essential as co-producers in the online tourism purchase processes, and companies need to ensure a suitable interaction with them and to adapt the characteristics of the service as much as possible. This task covers the whole process from the first electronic contact (website quality), to the purchase decision (website quality and satisfaction), and the effects on customer retention to the brand (loyalty).

This customer-centred strategic perspective follows the basic quality-satisfaction-loyalty chain, a sequence of the purchasing process that explains the results of an online tourism agent from the customer point of view. In the first phase of search and assessment, consumers gain a perception of the quality of the company's products (Kim and Lee 2005); when a consumer chooses a certain e-provider, the process leads to a second phase of co-production that, when completed, results in a certain satisfaction level (e.g., Kim et al. 2011; Hung et al. 2014) or dissatisfaction (Amin and Nasharuddin 2013), and ultimately in some degree of loyalty in terms of intention to repurchase or in actual repetition behaviour (e.g., Ali et al. 2012; Ryu et al. 2012; Betancourt et al. 2017). There is some relevant research integrating the search-purchase-consumption process regarding the traditional service sector channels (e.g., Grewal et al. 1998; Olsen 2002; Darsono and Junaedi 2006; Helgesen et al. 2010; Ho et al. 2017). In particular, authors like Anderson et al. (1994); González et al. (2007); Yüksel et al. (2010); Chen and Chen (2010); Chen and Xiao (2013); Deng et al. (2013), and Gallarza et al. (2013), have provided interesting contributions to this knowledge area regarding the traditional tourism service distribution. However, there is not enough research that addresses the cause-effect relationships value chain in the case of the online purchasing process (Grissemann and Stokburger-Sauer 2012). The models are usually specified in the case of a particular level of the online distribution channel; they present some changes in the cause-effect structure, and they do not consider all the basic variables. The role of perceived transaction costs is particularly forgotten. Moreover, the measurement models of the variables are not unified.

Perceived quality is the most extensively researched by itself (see Law et al. 2010) but not so much as an antecedent of satisfaction (Hao et al. 2015), and rarely of loyalty (Park et al. 2007). Recently, Ali (2016) recognized the importance of investigating the complete sequence of website quality-satisfaction-loyalty and provided a model that confirms this structure of relationships for the hotel context.

The most striking lack is the shortage of research on the effect of the transaction costs—other than prices—incurred by the customer in the purchase process on his/her loyalty intentions. Due to the higher level of participation of customers required in the online purchase process, the transaction costs incurred by customers other than the price paid for the final product could have a significant role in determining the intentions to repurchase or brand loyalty.

These antecedents warn of the importance to deepen the research in order to provide a better understanding of the e-booking purchase process and a comprehensive model focused on the electronic B2C tourism. Thus, this research endeavours to cover the limitations observed through analysing the dynamics of the online tourism channel from the point of view of digital tourism customers and in accordance with the quality-satisfaction-loyalty scheme of the website. From the literature review of the relationships between the three milestones involved and from exploring the role of transaction costs within the value chain, the ultimate goal of this research is to provide an integral model of the relationships between the basic variables involved in the process of purchasing online tourist reservations. Thus, there are two research questions that summarize our research interests:

- Do the basic relationships of the quality-satisfaction-loyalty value chain validated in other contexts, work in the same way in online tourism?
- What is the role of the perceived transaction costs (relative to the customer's participation in the co-production of the online channel tourism service) in the value chain?

To tackle these questions, the first section of this work reviews the research literature to make clear the prior contributions and to justify the hypotheses and a theoretical model. The second section describes the empirical setting and the data collection procedure. The third section presents the results. From these results, useful conclusions and management implications are drawn as well as future research lines.

2. Literature Antecedents and Theoretical Model

The most common case in online purchase of tourism services is that the consumer purchases the right to use a tourism service in advance. The online tourism channel is where the purchase process takes place, separated to a great extent in time and space from the final product experience. This separation brings the need to evaluate the booking purchase process per se. However, the crucial role of customer evaluation of the three steps in the purchase process—perceived quality, satisfaction and repurchase—is not encompassed with the attention paid in the context of online tourism purchase research.

2.1. The Online Tourism Quality-Satisfaction-Loyalty Value Chain

From the point of view of the customers, the performance indicators of a company in the market follow the quality-satisfaction-loyalty basic framework. In the current context of study, this framework regards the digital tourist purchase process that explains the results sequence of an online tourism agent (online tourism brand).

Before deciding on an online booking purchase, consumers try to match their quality expectations with the perceived quality of the product-service offered by online tourism agents, including suppliers, searchers, meta-searchers and online travel agencies as retailers. Balanced perceptions could lead them to make the decision to purchase with the consequent effects on the results of a market-oriented company (Grissemann and Stokburger-Sauer 2012).

A website is the main communication channel between service suppliers and consumers (Ali 2016). Ruiz-Mafe et al. (2018) affirm that when booking tourism products in an online community, consumers are generally unable to make valued judgements prior to purchase because of the lack of information regarding product quality. Nevertheless, when it deals with customers which purchase through the website of a touristic provider or an intermediary, the website quality is evaluated by the user through different attributes. Perceived quality is a parameter used to evaluate the performance of tourism organizations, destinations, hotels and travel agencies (Hao et al. 2015). Website quality captures the users' evaluation of whether a website's features meet their needs and reflects the overall excellence of the website (Chang and Chen 2008). Wang et al. (2015) compare the website as an online store where users need to rely on its attributes to reach a purchase decision. Perceived quality in the e-commerce context—mainly focused on the website used for a purchase—has been stated as a multi-dimensional construct (Ahn et al. 2007). However, there is not a unanimously accepted version but different contributions including different dimensions and measurement scales of the variable.

In this regard, the research has been mainly targeted at identifying the utilitarian quality which have been confirmed as essential to explain the website quality perceived by users. Different dimensions have been identified, mainly regarding easy-of-use, information quality and customer service (e.g., Kaynama and Black 2000; Madu and Madu 2002; Kim and Lee 2004; Kim et al. 2005; Park et al. 2007). Usability, functionality and security-privacy have been confirmed by Ali (2016) as utilitarian dimensions of hotel website quality.

The hedonic quality has received less attention (Vázquez et al. 2009). First approaches used indirect measurements such as the website design (García and Garrido 2013), a utilitarian attribute that leads back to visual appeal (Park and Gretzel 2007), the level of sociability perceived by users (Barnes and Vidgen 2014) and more recently, the perceived flow (Ali 2016), defined as the development of a pleasant experience, and validated as a mediator variable between utilitarian quality and satisfaction, not as a dimension of website quality. There is a parallelism of these website indicators with the e-store or e-channel attributes identified in other online contexts of study (Ganesh et al. 2010; Betancourt et al. 2017). Nevertheless, the hedonic elements might have increased their importance for digital consumers. The increasing experience and continuous learning of online operations, as well as a more relevant role as a co-producer, are potential determinants to boost pleasant online purchase experiences of the e-customer. Since Park et al. (2007) did not confirm the direct indicators of visual appeal as a determinant of company results, more recent references have provided some advances in this sense. Analysing the online airline tickets purchase context, Llach et al. (2013) find the hedonic dimension of the website quality in the hotel context as a determinant of perceived value. They define hedonic quality as an intrinsic value derived from the enjoyment in searching information and purchasing. The hedonism is measured through five indicators regarding enjoyment visiting the page, using the information provided, as well as finding the possibility to interact with other users.

Although the authors do not propose a second-order variable, their results are enlightening because the hedonic variable and the functional dimension of hotel website quality (based on E-S-QUAL model by (Parasuraman et al. 2005)) were correlated. Ali et al. (2016) extend this model and achieve to confirm the website perceived quality as a second-order latent variable reflected in functional and hedonic dimensions. Ozturk et al. (2016) validate a model that includes utilitarian and hedonic value of the mobile use as direct causes of reuse intentions. The hedonic aspects are measured through three indicators, related to fun and pleasantness in the use of the mobile device.

The second milestone of the value chain is the customer's satisfaction. This is defined as an attitude that deals with an evaluation of the (dis) confirmation of expectations inherent in a product acquisition and/or consumption experience (Oliver 2010). The definition of customer satisfaction varies throughout the marketing literature; however, all definitions agree that the satisfaction implies the necessary presence of a goal that the consumer wants to achieve (Ali et al. 2016).

In the tourism context, satisfaction is considered to be one of the most important results of all marketing activities of market-oriented companies (Kandampully and Suhartanto 2000). Dealing with traditional touristic distribution, contributions such as González et al. (2007); Yüksel et al. (2010); Chen and Xiao (2013) and Deng et al. (2013) relate service quality to expectations, satisfaction and loyalty. In the online context, works such as those by Kim and Lee (2005); Park and Gretzel (2007); and Hao et al. (2015) relate the assessment of the website quality to greater satisfaction with the experience. Llach et al. (2013) discover a positive link between website quality and perceived value, defined according Zeithaml (1988) as the customer judgment or evaluation of the service offered comparing advantages or utility obtained from a product/service and sacrifices or perceived costs. This is a definition close to that of satisfaction, which also requires customer experience (purchase interaction) with the service. Ali (2016) confirms the role of perceived flow as a mediator of the relationship between website quality, satisfaction and hotel rebooking intention.

To the extent that the user perceives a higher quality of an online tourism distribution service, it can be expected to cause an increase in the level of satisfaction with the service.

Moving onto the relationship structure of the chain, the relevance of pursuing the customer's satisfaction is that it leads directly to repeat behaviour and benefits (Ali et al. 2012; Ryu et al. 2012). In addition, it increases the probability of positive recommendations (Oliver 2010). In several research contexts of online distribution channels, it has been shown that greater satisfaction leads to greater intentions of repeated purchases (e.g., Finn et al. 2009; Chiu et al. 2014; Betancourt et al. 2017). Within the context of online tourism, the study of this relationship is a more recent concern, and the results are not conclusive. Even though the relationship between satisfaction and loyalty is postulated as positive, in the model by Bai et al. (2008), the satisfaction of visitors with travel websites is not a mediating variable of the intention to make an online purchase, but there is a direct relationship between the perceived quality of a website and the desire to purchase trips online. The satisfaction measurement deals with the decision to visit a travel website and not with a purchase experience, and the variable for the intention to purchase is related to the virtual travel purchase in general. Kim et al. (2011) find a positive relationship between satisfaction and loyalty. However, once again, the loyalty variable is measured as the intention to purchase at the online tourism channel in general versus a physical store, not as loyalty intention to a brand or company. Amaro and Duarte (2015) call attention to the potential of satisfaction with online purchases of trips to explain the intention to continue using the online option for purchasing trips. They find that attitude and perceived control, which are similar to perceived utility and ease of use according to the authors, are the main determinants of the intention to purchase trips online, which would confirm an attribute relationship between website quality and loyalty. This research does not include the satisfaction variable, and the purchase intention variable is not linked to a specific brand or company. Ali (2016) and Ali et al. (2016) are the only references found in which satisfaction is considered a direct variable of loyalty intentions, particularly in the context of a hotel reservation intention.

Taking into account the revised contributions, it is expected that the higher the customer's satisfaction with the shopping experience provided by an online tourism brand, the greater the customer's intentional loyalty.

Proving that the repurchase of online tourism services is determined by digital tourist' satisfaction is essential; satisfaction and loyalty increments through co-production and co-creation drive higher switching costs (including search costs), which reduce the likelihood to change the provider or the brand of the customer (Jackson 1985). This drives the success of retention strategies and reinforces the long-term survival of the company.

Hypothesis H1. *The greater the quality (utilitarian and hedonic) of an online tourism service, the greater the satisfaction with the e-purchasing experience maintained with the online tourist brand.*

Hypothesis H2. *The greater the customer's satisfaction with the booked online tourist company, the greater the loyalty intentions towards the brands.*

2.2. The Role of Perceived Costs

Mainly due to the increase of consumer participation in online tourism production and distribution processes, the perceived transaction costs from the point of view of the digital consumer may influence notably the relationships between the principal variables pertaining to the value chain, and provide better understanding of the online purchase processes.

In the context of the value chain, transaction costs can play a relevant role as moderating or mediating variables in determining the level of customer satisfaction. According the definition of satisfaction, they would complement the task of the perceived quality. The satisfaction level evaluation requires quantifying a feeling after enjoying a service, that is, a comparison between the benefits received and the costs that are paid (Cronin and Taylor 1992; Berné et al. 1996). Therefore, the perceived transaction costs derived from making an online purchase might be relevant in determining the satisfaction level of an online tourism consumer.

Co-production processes imply the contribution to productivity by means of the consumer participation in the production and distribution of products; particularly in the context of e-commerce, this practice allows for closer relations with consumers (Stockdale 2007). The point is that this new connected, informed and active consumer—announced by Prahalad and Ramaswamy (2004, 2013)—with an intensive role as co-producer, might have to bear higher costs as an operand resource, according to Goods Dominant Logic, and as an operant resource according to Services Dominant Logic (Vargo and Lusch 2004, 2008). The reduction of costs could be an essential trigger for co-creation (Etgar 2006, 2008), and a process aimed at co-creation can lead to lower costs borne by the company, due to the participation of the customer (Ahn et al. 2007).

Shaw et al. (2011) point out that the experiences are the core of the tourism industry and the consumer is the centre of development through co-production processes; thus, providing co-creation opportunities in a consistent way with involvement levels of customer, the experience can be improved and a more consistent competitive advantage can be achieved. Therefore, the digital tourists may prefer higher levels of participation even if they increase their non-monetary costs in exchange for lower prices.

The resources, interests and expectations of both providers and consumers have to be integrated in order to obtain mutual benefits, as a positive effect on market share (Chathoth et al. 2013). In this line, it is essential to analyse the role played by perceived transaction costs in the online booking purchase process.

Transaction costs might be monetary, pertaining to the price of the service, and non-monetary, pertaining to time and effort costs. In our research context, they are perceived costs basically related to the time and the efforts made by the consumer in the purchase process. The Internet allows the consumers to use the distribution services at any time and place when searching and purchasing a particular product (Betancourt et al. 2016). Hann and Terwiesch (2003) discussed greater cognitive effort and time opportunity when making online purchase decisions, and suggested that the non-monetary costs could turn out to be much more important in co-production activities. Accepting that consumer participation is very dynamic and relevant in online tourism services, another reason arises to consider the role of transaction costs. Nevertheless, despite some contributions, the inclusion of costs in research models has been scarcely considered within the context of online B2C tourism.

Price has a relevant role making purchase decisions (Krishnamurthi and Raj 1988). Price sensitivity has been related to customer satisfaction, so companies with higher satisfaction ratings can set higher prices (e.g., Zeithaml et al. 1996; Cronin et al. 2000). The customers usually consider price as a cue in their expectations of the service performance, which shapes their attitude and behaviour as well (Han and Ryu 2012). Although perceived quality and monetary costs show a positive relationship according to the laws of economics (the greater product quality the greater product price), there is evidence about a negative relationship between costs and customer's satisfaction. In that way, higher perceived costs will drive lower satisfaction. In this line, Jiang and Rosenbloom (2005) observe that favourable price perceptions have direct and positive effects on overall customer satisfaction and on customer intention to return. Han and Ryu (2009) state that customers' perceptions of a reasonable price intervene as a moderator variable to enhance the impact of quality on their satisfaction.

While it is generally accepted that online commerce reduces the transaction costs (Bunduchi 2005), we have not much more knowledge about its role in the value chain. Cho and Agrusa (2006) considered the monetary costs (price) within the specific context of online travel agencies, although the research was limited to studying the variable as a determinant of the website perceived quality. Authors recognize that the price influences the purchaser perceptions both positively and negatively. In their model, price is shown as a determinant of easy-of-use and utility dimensions of the website, and the consumer involvement degree is a mediator variable of the relation. These website quality dimensions determine the attitudes toward online travel agencies, which in turn determine e-satisfaction.

In the same way, Kim et al. (2011) model the transaction costs as antecedents of satisfaction of Korean buyers of online tourism services. In particular, they confirm the monetary transaction costs as direct determinants of satisfaction and also as determinants of indirect effects on trust and loyalty through the satisfaction variable. However, they do not find a direct effect by costs on trust. In comparison with the transaction costs of offline transactions, online monetary costs are positively related to satisfaction. In a hotel context, Ye et al. (2011) find that the perceived price has a determinant effect on quality and a negative impact on the perceived value. Analysing the Spanish online travel agencies, García and Garrido (2013) found a moderate correlation between prices (in monetary units) and some attributes of website (simplicity, clarity and customer service). Authors interpret this result as a greater power of the online channel in order to compare prices. The online environment facilitates comparing prices and consequently, the sensitivity to the price of the customer could increase (Cho and Agrusa 2006).

Regarding the non-monetary costs and their role in the quality-satisfaction-loyalty value chain, there is a lack of knowledge. It is recognized that different type of costs are implicit in the assessment of the perceived quality of a service (Cho and Agrusa 2006), and it is accepted the purchase effort as the perceived difficulty and time costs consumers experience when purchasing a product using a specific channel (Verhoef et al. 2007). Nevertheless, not much more contributions have been found in this respect. The hypothesis will be formulated for overall online perceived costs, and it will defend them as covariates of the level of satisfaction in comparison to other alternatives.

Hypothesis H3. *The lower the perceived costs of an online tourism transaction with respect to other (offline and online) alternatives, the greater the satisfaction of the customer.*

The relationships postulated through the formulated hypotheses are included in a theoretical model of the electronic tourist purchasing process (e-TPP model), which involves latent variables of different orders (Figure 1).

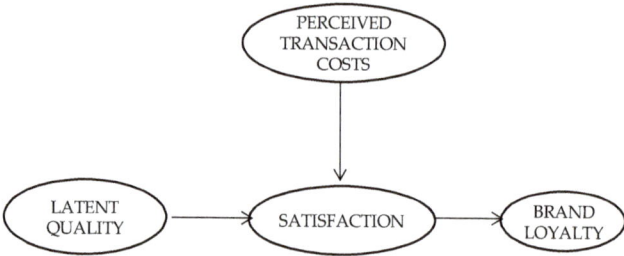

Figure 1. E-TPP structural theoretical model.

3. Research Methods

A structured questionnaire was developed to obtain the necessary information for testing the working hypotheses and the proposed theoretical model. The target population for this study was limited to those Spanish online tourism services purchasers who have had an online tourism purchase experience over the last twelve months.

3.1. Measures

Specific information was requested about the user's experience with the company where they made their last online tourism purchase. The opinion questions were measured through semantic differential scales of 11 points, from 0 for the least favourable option to 10 for the most favourable option regarding the specific proposal (completely adequate, very easy, much less expensive, much less effort, completely satisfactory, yes-always).

The measurement of the perceived quality of a website included the indicators most commonly used in the literature, three of which referred to utilitarian quality (ease of use, information provided by the page, and customer service) and one to hedonic quality (attractiveness of the website). This latter criterion was measured through an overall measure, on a points-scale from very unattractive to very attractive, according Sauro (2015).

Thus, the perceived quality of a website is postulated as a second-order latent variable. Satisfaction is considered a first-order latent variable, measured through one indicator of satisfaction with the last transaction conducted and another indicator of accumulated experience. The perceived transaction costs were measured through three indicators, two of them regarding relative prices (monetary costs) and the third regarding the effort perceived by the user (non-monetary). Loyalty was measured with one item on the recommendation of the service and another on the intention to repeat the purchase (Table 1).

Table 1. Criteria, indicators and prior references.

Criteria, Items	Prior References *
Ease-of-use P1. Ease of access to the web page. P2. Possibility offered by the company to combine tourism products in a single order. P3. Perceived clarity (ease of identification) about the company's products and services on its web page. P4. Preciseness (absence of ambiguity) of the definition of the products and services on the company's web page. P5. Purchase payment modes offered through the online service. P6. Task of consumers in the event that they may have combined products in the last transaction or in other, previous transactions with the same company to get the desired combination. P7. Time used to finalise the purchase.	Kaynama and Black (2000); Donthu (2001); Jeong and Lambert (2001); Madu and Madu (2002); Kim and Lee (2004); Kim et al. (2005); Park et al. (2007); Verhoef et al. (2007, buying time); Seiders et al. (2007, accessibility); Jaiswal et al. (2010); Ganesh et al. (2010, ease of payment); Ali (2016, usability)
Information attributes P8. The information provided by the company, online, for making the purchase. P9. ... provided by the company's web page about the characteristics of the contracted tourism service. P10. ... from the web page about the variety of the online tourism products-services offered by the company.	Kaynama and Black (2000); Jeong and Lambert (2001); Madu and Madu (2002); Kim and Lee (2004); Kim et al. (2005); Park et al. (2007); Verhoef et al. (2007); Ganesh et al. (2010) (merchandise variety); Hung et al. (2014); Ali (2016, functionality)
Customer service P11. Confirmation procedure of the booking-purchase, discounts and/or invoices by the company. P12. ... for cancelling the contracted online tourism service. P13. Customer service and/or complaints and claims system available on the company's web page. P14. Privacy and security policy followed by the contracted online service with respect to the customer's personal data.	Kaynama and Black (2000); Madu and Madu (2002); Kim and Lee (2004); Kim et al. (2005, security); Park et al. (2007); Jaiswal et al. (2010, privacy, security); Ali (2016, security and privacy)
Visual attraction P15. Attractiveness of the web page where the tourism service has been contracted	Kaynama and Black (2000); Kim et al. (2005); Bauer et al. (2006); Urban et al. (2009); Ganesh et al. (2010); García and Garrido (2013)
Perceived costs P16. Prices of the service contracted online in relation to purchases in offline channels. P17. ... with respect to other, similar online services. P18. Effort made in the online purchasing process versus the offline process.	Kim et al. (2011); García and Garrido (2013); Chiu et al. (2014, monetary savings); Verhoef et al. (2007, search and purchase effort)
Satisfaction P19. Overall satisfaction with the last purchase of tourism services contracted online (satisfaction with the last transaction). P20. Online purchasing experience over time with the last contracted company (accumulated satisfaction).	Arrondo et al. (2002); Berné et al. (2005); Finn et al. (2009, cummulative); Hung et al. (2014, cummulative); Betancourt et al. (2017, cummulative)
Brand/Company loyalty P21. Intention to continue using the same online tourism service. P22. Recommendation of the contracted online service.	Arrondo et al. (2002); Berné et al. (2005); Finn et al. (2009, repurchase); Chiu et al. (2014, repurchase); Betancourt et al. (2017, repurchase)

* References in parentheses use only the contents contained therein.

3.2. Data Collection

A market research company was contracted to distribute the online questionnaire and select a sample (toluna.com) from its e-consumers' panel. The questionnaire is structured in sections according geo-demographic information required and the indicators (Likert scale format) pertaining to the variables included in the model (Table 1). The type of sampling is convenience with quotas, initially requested for an approximation of the specifications observed in literature. The survey conducted by the company attained 408 valid questionnaires, after following a checking process to confirm to the initial requirements. The characteristics of the sample are shown in Table 2.

Table 2. Characteristics of the sample.

Sex	Male	50.7%
	Female	49.3%
Age	18–30	28.2%
	31–55	46.6%
	Over 55	25.2%
Education	Primary education	1.5%
	Secondary education (mandatory)	6.6%
	Higher secondary education	19.1%
	Uncompleted university studies	10.5%
	Higher education (graduated and post-graduated)	51.9%
	Vocational training (post-secondary)	2.2%

Regarding the geographic origin of the respondents, the greatest weight by autonomous community corresponds to Madrid (19.6%), followed by Catalonia (18.1%), Andalucía (14.5%) and the Community of Valencia (10%). This matches the population distribution in Spain.

The companies used the most for the online contracting of tourism services by respondents are Booking (14.5%), eDreams (10.8%), El Corte Ingles (10.3%) and Rumbo (7.1%). Booking, eDreams and Rumbo are the online travel agencies named the most regarding the Spanish context in Sarmiento (2016). Odigeo-eDreams and Bravofly-Rumbo led the top 5 of the Hosteltur' Ranking of Online Agencies. Approximately 22% of respondents have contracted the last online tourism service to a supplier (direct channel for hospitality and transport, mainly).

4. Results

The data analysis was conducted through Exploratory Factorial Analysis (EFA), Principal Components Analysis (PCA), Confirmatory Factorial Analysis (CFA) and Structural Equation Models (SEM). The literature reviewed supports the content validity of the indicators selected. First, we identify the underlying structure for each of the proposed dimensions (EFA-PCA). Subsequently, the measurement models are validated through CFA. Afterwards, the relationships between the dimensions are tested through SEM (SPSS 22 and EQS 6.0).

4.1. Ease-of-Use Measurement Model

After the corresponding PCA with Varimax rotation (PCA-VM) of the first seven indicators (P1 to P7), one component that explains almost the 60% of the variance is obtained. It groups together all the indicators and is called Ease-of-Use (EU) and it refers to the degree of effort that online customers give to the electronic medium (Donthu 2001). It deals with functionality, accessibility of a website, consistency and effective browsing, as well as search capacity and desired products. EU Cronbach's alpha coefficient reaches a value of 0.885 (Nunnally 1978). The estimate of CFA model shows the overall goodness-of-fit statistics and indexes (Table 3). The reliability coefficients of the observed variables take values that exceed 0.5, except for items P1, P2, and P6, whose estimated parameters take values of 0.654, 0.663 and 0.696. These deal with the ease of access and combine products as well as the task of consumers to reach the desired combination. Due to the importance given to these aspects in literature, we decide to keep them in the model. The most relevant services are the ease of product identification. The values taken by the standardized factor loadings comparing the correlations between factors demonstrates the discriminant validity and the convergent validity of the model. CF1 (Fornell and Larcker's coefficient), and CF2 (Omega's coefficient) take values of 0.536 and 0.889, respectively.

4.2. Service Information Measurement Model

Considering P8 to P10, the PCA-VM resulted in a single component that explains 75.5% of the variance. The purchasing experience of customers is increased by the integrity, uniqueness, preciseness and entertainment value of a website, as well as the opportunity for information/content (Kaynama and Black 2000; Aladwani and Palvia 2002; Sigala and Sakellaridis 2004). Thus, service information (SI) can be defined as the degree to which a user believes that the information or content is useful, updated and reliable. Cronbach's Alpha coefficient is 0.862. The corresponding CFA is conducted imposing a restriction on the equality of factor loadings, since this model did not show degrees of freedom (see Table 3). Reliability coefficients of the dimension (CF1and CF2 take values of 0.684 and 0.866, respectively) offer evidence of the reliability and of the convergent validity.

4.3. Customer Service Measurement Model

Customer service is determined through the transmission of an appropriate response to e-mail requests or complaints, as well as order confirmations, which represent an important factor in the assessment of a website by customers (see Yang and Jun 2002; Long and McMellon 2004). The dimension may be defined as the desire or willingness for customer service, thereby providing a quick, streamlined service in an online context. PCA-VM confirms the existence of a factor, Customer Service (CS), which explains 64.1% of the variance and includes P1 to P14. Cronbach's alpha takes a value of 0.805. The estimate of the CFA of the CS model presents adequate values of the R-RMSEA statistic and of the goodness-of-fit indexes (Table 3). CF1 and CF2 take values of 0.517 and 0.808. The procedure for cancelling the tourism service receives the lowest value. However, it is kept due to the importance given to this aspect in the literature. The most relevant variable refers to privacy and security policy with respect to the customer's personal data.

4.4. Perceived Costs Measurement Model

The PCA-VM offers two components that explain 87.82% of the total variance of transaction costs (PC). The first component groups together the indicators pertaining to the monetary costs borne, and the second one the non-monetary costs. These costs are posed in relation to other situations, either in comparison with offline purchases or other online alternative companies. The correlation coefficient takes a value of 0.777.

The two indicators of perceived monetary costs are grouped into a first-order dimension of perceived online monetary costs (MPC) (Table 4); CF1 and CF2 take values of 0.586 and 0.735, respectively. The other dimension corresponds to non-monetary costs (NMPC).

4.5. Satisfaction and Loyalty Measurement Models

Customer's satisfaction (S) is measured considering the satisfaction level with the last transaction (short-term), and the satisfaction with the accumulated experience with the online tourism company (long-term) (e.g., Arrondo et al. 2002; Berné et al. 2005). The underlying dimensional structure for the set of two variables pertaining to the satisfaction, treated through PCA-VM, shows one component that explains 91.94% of the variance. The CFA result shows the adequacy of the identified structure, and the goodness-of-fit statistics and indexes of the model are shown in Table 3.

Similarly, the two variables pertaining to the brand loyalty (L) were subjected to a PCA-VM, and one component that explains 88.56% of the variance was obtained. It concerns attitudinal loyalty through the intention to make repeat purchases with the online tourism operator and the intention to recommend the operator to other users. CFA estimated presents adequate goodness-of-fit statistics and indexes (Table 3). The CF1 and CF2 values are 0.734 and 0.847, respectively, which indicate reliability and convergent validity.

Both satisfaction and brand loyalty are confirmed as first-order dimensions. Reliability coefficients of the observed variables (R^2) exceed 0.7.

Table 3. Measurement Models. Goodness-of-Fit.

	d.f.	Chi-Square S-B	P	R-RMSEA	SRMR	GFI	AGFI	R-BBN	R-CFI
EU	14	29.479	0.009	0.054	0.038	0.957	0.913	0.964	0.981
SI	2	0.6012	0.740	0.0001	0.029	0.996	0.988	0.998	0.999
CS	2	9.455	0.009	0.098	0.040	0.974	0.868	0.966	0.973
PC	2	23.872	0.0001	0.167	0.163	0.933	0.798	0.812	0.823
S	1	0.7593	0.384	0.0001	0.028	0.997	0.992	0.996	0.999
L	1	0.0017	0.967	0.001	0.001	0.999	0.999	0.999	0.999

4.6. e-TPP Model

After confirming the different measurement models, the entire structural model was estimated. The results obtained made it advisable to include a previously non-postulated cause-effect relationship between the monetary costs variable and the latent quality variable. We accepted this, given that quality and monetary costs have been previously related in literature (e.g., Cho and Agrusa 2006; Han and Ryu 2009; Ye et al. 2011). After re-estimating the model, the results led to acceptable goodness of fit. The model explains 83.7% of a customer's level of satisfaction. In turn, satisfaction has a positive impact on a customer's attitude of brand loyalty and explains that attitude by 75.2%. CF1 and CF2 coefficients evidence internal validity (see Table 4 and Figure 2).

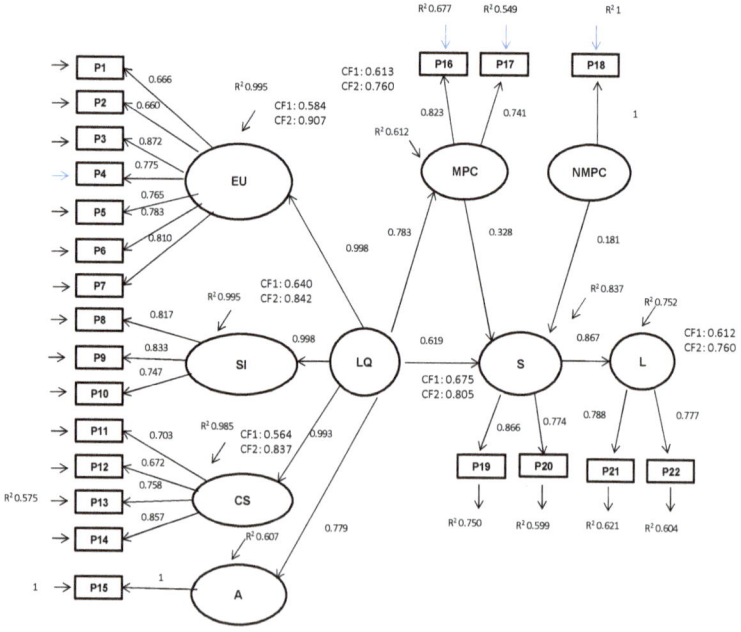

Figure 2. Estimation of the e-TPP Model.

Table 4. e-TPP Model. Goodness-of-Fit.

	d.f.	Chi-Square S-B	P	R-RMSEA	SRMR	GFI	AGFI	R-BBN	R-CFI
e-TPP	202	412.8158	0.000	0.055	0.144	0.860	0.825	0.878	0.933

Satisfaction turns out to be an effect variable of both the website perceived quality and the perceived costs (monetary and non-monetary). The influence by perceived quality is both direct and indirect through monetary costs (parameters values of 0.619 and 0.257, respectively). The satisfaction variable thus becomes a mediating variable of brand loyalty, unlike the results of Bai et al. (2008).

Monetary costs result in a significant parameter of 0.328 regarding the influence on satisfaction, which indicates that lower perceived prices result in greater satisfaction. The non-monetary costs (0.181) have a lower but significant effect on customer's satisfaction.

Consequently, the hypotheses cannot be rejected. The theoretical model thus reveals a large part of the process of forming attitudinal loyalty to an online tourism brand.

5. Conclusions

With respect to the first research question formulated, the results obtained confirm the basic relationships of the quality-satisfaction-loyalty value chain previously found in other study contexts, in the case of B2C tourism online. The e-TTP model explains more than 83% of the satisfaction of digital tourists. While, as a novelty, the value chain is extended, including monetary and non-monetary perceived costs. Monetary perceived costs foster the effect of quality on satisfaction, and non-monetary transaction costs help to determine customer satisfaction. The explanatory power of the model regarding repurchase intentions exceeds 75%. These results give confidence to the comprehensive e-TPP model overcoming some of the limitations of previous models and are in line with Ali (2016) and Ali et al. (2016).

With respect to the second question, this research confirms the important role played by the perceived transaction costs. The consumer participation in the service production, facilitated by online channels, draw a new scenario where the formation of the satisfaction and brand loyalty does not solely involve the website perceived quality. The perceived costs, both monetary and non-monetary, reinforce the customer's satisfaction derived from the relationship maintained with a company, and ultimately, the customer loyalty to the company or brand. It should be noted that the positive relationship between latent quality and monetary costs is contrary to what has been traditionally postulated. The greater the perceived website quality of the tourism service, the greater the perception of a lower price in relation to other channels (online and traditional). Also, the lower perceived price reinforces the customer's satisfaction as well as non-monetary costs. This is relevant because it suggests the existence of an effective win-win dynamic, required according Friesen (2001) to facilitate co-creation by building trust and sharing benefits. The rate presentation might be important as pointed out by Noone and Mattila (2009) and Webb (2016).

Regarding implications, this work provides different measurement models. It is worth highlighting the validated measurement model of the website latent quality in the context of online tourism services purchases. It is reflected in four first-order dimensions: the ease of use, the information provided, the attention perceived by customers through the online environment, and the attractiveness of a website. Even though the attractiveness of a website has less weight in reflecting latent quality than utilitarian dimensions in our research, its valuation by users has a positive influence on the results of the tourism company both in satisfaction and the brand repurchase intentions. It matches the results obtained by Ali et al. (2016) and Ozturk et al. (2016), and is in line with Betancourt et al. (2017) for online private sales clubs, where the attractiveness of the design had an influence on loyalty for the most-satisfied group of customers.

In this sense, future research about perceived website quality should include the hedonic dimension. For practitioners, the hedonic content of the website could be an element of differentiation and an instrument for achieving useful competitive advantages in the acquisition and retention of customers.

Moreover, this research shows that multi-dimensional constructs increases the overall construct understanding (Law et al. 1998), and thereby provides details about its various facets (Petter et al. 2007). Thus, tourism managers can use, with guarantee, the validated instrument to analyse the situation of each website quality dimension in order to identify those aspects that may need improvement. The structure of latent quality can be considered to support decision-making taking into account different types of customers and characteristics of the channel or market where the company is operating.

In addition, the opportunity to interact with a customer must be taken as an advantage ensuring that perceived costs are included in the development of strategies for customer acquisition and retention. The way in which perceived monetary costs are handled can differentiate a company, considering that an improvement in website quality from the user's point of view is not related to the acceptance of higher prices for a tourism service, rather it has the opposite effect. Therefore, a company must find justification for prices through more efficient processes, both internal (such as centralising the control of distribution) and external (such as through the negotiation of commissions or selecting the channels in which commissions are lower). Care must be taken with non-monetary costs by providing efficiency for the user, whose participation in the purchasing process depends on lower effort in the virtual interaction.

Despite the highlighted contributions of this research, some limitations have to be taken into account, thereby serving as proposals for future research. First, our model is tested on a sample of convenience, so that the level of representativeness of the sample can be affected. This situation is addressed using quotas, although the success is dependent on the accuracy of the selection made by the contracted market research company. In addition, despite the high explanatory power of the model, it could be reinforced by adding control variables, such as the personal characteristics of customers and specific conditions of the market under analysis or loyalty of behaviour. On the other hand, given that the study explores a situation that groups together all possible travel contexts, it could be of interest for research to specify online purchasing situations for different purposes. Also, to explore the dimensionality of the hedonic character of the quality of the website in function of the different situations of purchase and the different supports or screens used by customers is an interesting line of future research. In addition, the analysis of the longitudinal databases available to companies should allow them to make comparisons over time as a result of eventual changes in the variables.

In the academic scope, inter-cultural comparisons could offer reinforcement of the theoretical model and offer results that allow justifying the implementation of differentiated marketing strategies. Studying the behaviour of the e-TPP model in different types of online tourism channels is another task for future research. A comparative study of actions in the direct channel and the indirect channels could better illustrate the situation of competition in the sector from the user's point of view. Furthermore, in addition to the online tourism channels observed in this work and in the tourism distribution system, there are channels whose development is currently growing such as the channel consumer-to-consumer (C2C), and social networks, although these are still marginal as a sales channel according Stangl et al. (2016).

In any event, this research contributes a holistic model that goes beyond others by including variables that have been confirmed relevant as mediators of brand loyalty. The confirmed model manages to integrate the phases of the online tourism purchasing process and shows how the development of the business-client interaction is achieving the objectives of both. The work provides a meaningful explanation of the purchasing process and the results of online tourism companies, thus helping to implement strategies to acquire and, above all, retain brand customers.

Author Contributions: Conceptualization, C.B.-M. and M.P.-I.; Methodology, C.B.-M. and M.M.-N.; Validation, M.M.-N.; Investigation, M.G.-C.; Writing-Original Draft Preparation, M.G.-C. and C.B.-M.; Writing-Review & Editing, C.B.-M.; Supervision, C.B.-M. and M.P.-I.

Funding: We acknowledge the support for this research from the Crevalor Research Group and the UZ2018-SOC-04 Research Project.

Conflicts of Interest: The authors declare no conflict of interest.

References

Ahn, Tony, Seewon Ryu, and Ingoo Han. 2007. The impact of web quality and playfulness on user acceptance of online retailing. *Information Management* 44: 263–75. [CrossRef]

Aladwani, Adel M., and Prashant C. Palvia. 2002. Developing and validating an instrument for measuring user-perceived website quality. *Information and Management* 39: 467–76. [CrossRef]

Ali, Faizan. 2016. Hotel website quality, perceived flow, customer satisfaction and purchase intention. *Journal of Hospitality and Tourism Technology* 7: 213–28. [CrossRef]

Ali, Faizan, Abdul Khan, and Fatin Rehman. 2012. An assessment of the service quality using gap analysis: A study conducted at Chitral, Pakistan. *Interdisciplinary Journal of Contemporary Research in Business* 4: 259–66.

Ali, Faizan, Muslim Amin, and Cihan Cobanoglu. 2016. An Integrated Model of Service Experience, Emotions, Satisfaction, and Price Acceptance: An Empirical Analysis in the Chinese Hospitality Industry. *Journal of Hospitality Marketing & Management* 25: 449–75.

Amaro, Suzzane, and Paulo Duarte. 2015. An integrative model of consumers' intentions to purchase travel. *Tourism Management* 46: 64–79. [CrossRef]

Amin, Muslim, and Siti Z. Nasharuddin. 2013. Hospital service quality and its effects on patient satisfaction and behavioural intention. *Clinical Governance: An International Journal* 18: 238–54. [CrossRef]

Anderson, Eugene W., Claes Fornell, and Donald R. Lehmann. 1994. Satisfaction, market share, and profitability: Findings from Sweden. *Journal of Marketing* 58: 53–66. [CrossRef]

Arrondo, Elvira, Carmen Berné, José M. Múgica, and Pilar Rivera. 2002. Modelling of customer retention in multi-format retailing. *The International Review of Retail, Distribution and Consumer Research* 12: 281–96. [CrossRef]

Bai, Billy, Rob Law, and Ivan Wen. 2008. The impact of website quality on customer satisfaction and purchase intentions: Evidence from Chinese online visitors. *International Journal of Hospitality Management* 27: 391–402. [CrossRef]

Barnes, Stuart J., and Richard T. Vidgen. 2014. Technology socialness and website satisfaction. *Technological Forecasting and Social Change* 89: 12–25. [CrossRef]

Bauer, Hans H., Tomas Falk, and Maik Hammerschmidt. 2006. eTransQual: A Transaction Process-Based Approach for Capturing Service Quality in Online Shopping. *Journal of Business Research* 59: 866–75. [CrossRef]

Berné, Carmen, José M. Múgica, and María J. Yagüe. 1996. La gestión estratégica y los conceptos de calidad percibida, satisfacción del cliente y lealtad. *Economía Industrial* 307: 63–74.

Berné, Carmen, José M. Múgica, and Pilar Rivera. 2005. The managerial ability to control the varied behavior of regular customers in retailing: Interformat differences. *Journal of Retailing and Consumer Services* 12: 151–64. [CrossRef]

Betancourt, Rogert R., Raquel Chocarro, Monica Cortiñas, Margarita Elorz, and José M. Mugica. 2016. Channel choice in the 21st century: The hidden role of distribution services. *Journal of Interactive Marketing* 33: 1–12. [CrossRef]

Betancourt, Rogert R., Raquel Chocarro, Monica Cortiñas, Margarita Elorz, and José M. Mugica. 2017. Private sales clubs: A 21st. Century distribution channel. *Journal of Interactive Marketing* 37: 44–56. [CrossRef]

Bunduchi, Raluca. 2005. Business relationship in Internet-base electronic markets: The role of Goodwill trust and transaction costs. *Information Systems Journal* 15: 321–41. [CrossRef]

Chang, Hisn H., and Su W. Chen. 2008. The impact of online store environment cues on purchase intention: Trust and perceived risk as a mediator. *Online Information Review* 32: 818–41. [CrossRef]

Chathoth, Prakash, Levent Altinay, Robert J. Harrington, Fevzi Okumus, and Eric S.W. Chan. 2013. Co-production versus co-creation: A process based continuum in the hotel service context. *International Journal of Hospitality Management* 32: 11–20. [CrossRef]

Chen, Ching-Fu, and Fu-Shian Chen. 2010. Experience quality, perceived value, satisfaction and behavioral intentions for heritage tourists. *Tourism Management* 13: 29–35. [CrossRef]

Chen, Ganghua, and Honggen Xiao. 2013. Motivations of repeat visits: A longitudinal study in Xiamen, China. *Journal of Travel & Tourism Marketing* 30: 350–64.

Chiu, Chao-Min, Eric T. G. Wang, Yu-Hui Fang, and Hsin-Yi Huang. 2014. Understanding customers'repeat purchase intentions in B2C e-commerce: The roles of utilitarian value and perceived risks. *Information Systems Journal* 24: 85–114. [CrossRef]

Cho, Yoon C., and Jerome Agrusa. 2006. Assessing use acceptance and satisfaction toward online travel agencies. *Information Technology & Tourism* 8: 179–95.

Cronin, Joseph J., and Steven A. Taylor. 1992. Measuring service quality: A reexamination and extension. *Journal of Marketing* 56: 55–68. [CrossRef]

Cronin, Joseph, Michael Brady, and Tomas Hult. 2000. Assessing the effects of quality, value and customer satisfaction on consumer behavioral intentions in service environments. *Journal of Retailing* 76: 193–218. [CrossRef]

Darsono, Licen Indahwati, and Marliana C. Junaedi. 2006. An Examination of Perceived Quality, Satisfaction, and Loyalty Relationship: Applicability of Comparative and Noncomparative Evaluation. *Gadjah Mada International Journal of Business* 8: 323–42.

Deng, Wei-Jaw, Ming Lang Yeh, and M. L. Sung. 2013. A customer satisfaction index model for international tourist hotels: Integrating consumption emotions into the American customer satisfaction index. *International Journal of Hospitality Management* 35: 133–40. [CrossRef]

Donthu, Naveen. 2001. Does your web site measure up? *Marketing Management* 10: 29–32.

Etgar, Michael. 2006. Co-production of services: A managerial extension. In *The Service-Dominant Logic of Marketing: Dialog, Debate and Directions*. Edited by Robert Lusch and Stephen Vargo. New York: Sharpe, pp. 128–38.

Etgar, Michael. 2008. A descriptive model of the consumer co-production process. *Journal of the Academy of Marketing Science* 36: 97–108. [CrossRef]

Finn, Adam, Luming Wang, and Tema Frank. 2009. Attribute perceptions, customer satisfaction and intention to recommend e-services. *Journal of Interactive Marketing* 23: 209–20. [CrossRef]

Friesen, Bruce G. 2001. Co-creation: When 1 and 1 make 11. *Consulting to Management* 12: 28–31.

Gallarza, Martina, Irene Gil, and Francisco Moreno. 2013. The quality-value-satisfaction-loyalty chain: Relationships and impacts. *Tourism Review* 68: 3–20. [CrossRef]

Ganesh, Jaishankar, Kristy E. Reynolds, Michael Luckett, and Nadia Pomirleanu. 2010. Online shopper motivations, and e-store attributes: An examination of online patronage behavior and shopper typologies. *Journal of Retailing* 86: 106–15. [CrossRef]

García, Franciso, and Pablo Garrido. 2013. Agencias de viaje online en España: Aplicación de un modelo de análisis de sedes web. *Revista de Investigación en Turismo y Desarrollo Local* 6: 1–15.

González, María E. A., Lorenzo Comesaña, and José A. F. Brea. 2007. Assessing tourist behavioral intentions through perceived service quality and customer satisfaction. *Journal of Business Research* 60: 153–60. [CrossRef]

Grewal, Dhruv, Kent B. Monroe, and Ram Krishnan. 1998. The effects of price-comparison advertising on buyer's perceptions of acquisition value, transaction value, and behavioral intentions. *Journal of Marketing* 62: 49–59. [CrossRef]

Grissemann, Ursula S., and Nicola E. Stokburger-Sauer. 2012. Customer co-creation of travel services: The role of company support and customer satisfaction with the co-creation performance. *Tourism Management* 33: 1483–92. [CrossRef]

Han, Heesup, and Kisang Ryu. 2009. The roles of the physical environment, price perception, and customer satisfaction in determining customer loyalty in the restaurant industry. *Journal of Hospitality and Tourism Research* 33: 487–510. [CrossRef]

Han, Heesup, and Kisang Ryu. 2012. Key factors driving customers' word-of-mouth intentions in full-service restaurants: The moderating role of switching costs. *Cornell Hospitality Quarterly* 53: 96–109. [CrossRef]

Hann, Il-Horn, and Christian Terwiesch. 2003. Measuring the frictional costs of online transactions: The case of a name-your-own-price channel. *Management Science* 49: 1563–79. [CrossRef]

Hao, Jing-Xing, Yan Yu, Rob Law, and Davis K. C. Fong. 2015. A genetic algorithm-based learning approach to understand customer satisfaction with OTA websites. *Tourism Management* 48: 231–41. [CrossRef]

Helgesen, Oyvind, Jon I. Havold, and Erik Nesset. 2010. Impacts of store and chain images on the "quality-satisfaction-loyalty process" in petrol retailing. *Journal of Retailing and Consumer Services* 17: 109–18. [CrossRef]

Heskett, James L., Thomas O. Jones, Gary W. Loveman, Earl W. Sasser, and Leonard A. Schlesinger. 2008. Putting the service-profit chain to work. *Harvard Business Review* 86: 118–29.

Ho, Enoch, Elaine Principi, Charissa P. Cordon, Yavra Amenudzie, Krista Kotwa, Sarah Holt, and Maura MacPhee. 2017. The synergy tool: Making important quality gains within one healthcare organization. *Administrative Sciences* 7: 32. [CrossRef]

Hung, Shin-Yuan, Charlie Chen, and Ning-Hung Huang. 2014. An integrative approach to understanding customer satisfaction with e-service of online stores. *Journal of Electronic Commerce Research* 15: 40–57.

Jackson, Barbara B. 1985. *Winning and Keeping Industrial Customers: The Dynamics of Customer Relationship*. Lexington: Lexington Books.

Jaiswal, Anand A., Rakesh Niraj, and Pingali Venugopal. 2010. Context-general and context-specific determinants of online satisfaction and loyalty for commerce and content sites. *Journal of Interactive Marketing* 24: 222–38. [CrossRef]

Jeong, Miyoung, and Carolyn U. Lambert. 2001. Adaptation of an information quality framework to measure customers' behavioral intentions to use lodging websites. *International Journal of Hospitality Management* 20: 129–46. [CrossRef]

Jiang, Pingjun, and Bert Rosenbloom. 2005. Customer intention to return online: Price perception, attribute-level performance, and satisfaction unfolding over time. *European Journal of Marketing* 39: 150–74. [CrossRef]

Kandampully, Jan, and Dwi Suhartanto. 2000. Customer loyalty in the hotel industry: The role of customer satisfaction and image. *International Journal of Contemporary Hospitality Management* 12: 346–51. [CrossRef]

Kaynama, Shohreh, and Christine Black. 2000. A proposal to assess the service quality of online travel agencies: An exploratory study. *Journal of Professional Service Marketing* 21: 63–88. [CrossRef]

Kim, Woo G., and Hae Y. Lee. 2004. Comparison of web service quality between online travel agencies and online travel suppliers. *Journal of Travel & Tourism Marketing* 17: 105–16.

Kim, Seong-Seop, and Choong-Ki Lee. 2005. Push and pull relationships. *Annals of Tourism Research* 29: 257–60. [CrossRef]

Kim, Lisa H., Dong J. Kim, and Jerrold K. Leong. 2005. The effect of perceived risk on purchase intention in purchasing airline tickets online. *Journal of Hospitality & Leisure Marketing* 13: 33–53.

Kim, Myung-Ja, Namho Chung, and Choong-Ki Lee. 2011. The effect of perceived trust on electronic commerce: Shopping online for tourism products and services in South Korea. *Tourism Management* 32: 256–65. [CrossRef]

Krishnamurthi, Lakshman, and S. P. Raj. 1988. A Model of Brand Choice and Purchase Quantity Price Sensitivities. *Marketing Science* 7: 1–20. [CrossRef]

Law, Kenneth S., Wong Chi-Sum, and William H. Mobley. 1998. Toward a taxonomy of multidimensional constructs. *Academy of Management Review* 23: 741–55. [CrossRef]

Law, Rob, Shanshan Oi, and Dimirtios Buhalis. 2010. Progress in tourism management: A review of website evaluation in tourism research. *Tourism Management* 31: 297–313. [CrossRef]

Llach, Josep, Frederic Marimon, María M. Alonso-Almeida, and Merce Bernardo. 2013. Determinants of online booking loyalties for the purchasing of airline tickets. *Tourism Management* 35: 23–31. [CrossRef]

Long, Mary, and Chareles McMellon. 2004. Exploring the determinants of retail service quality on the Internet. *Journal of Service Marketing* 18: 78–90. [CrossRef]

Madu, Christian N., and Assumpta A. Madu. 2002. Dimensions of e-quality. *International Journal of Quality & Reliability Management* 19: 246–58.

Noone, Breffni M., and Anna S. Mattila. 2009. Hotel revenue management and the Internet: The effect of price presentation strategies on customers' willingness to book. *International Journal of Hospitality Management* 28: 272–79. [CrossRef]

Nunnally, Jum. 1978. *Psychometric Methods*. New York: McGraw-Hill.

Oliver, Richard L. 2010. *Satisfaction: A Behavioral Perspective on the Consumer*, 2nd ed. Armonk: M.E. Sharpe.

Olsen, Svein O. 2002. Comparative evaluation and the relationship quality, satisfaction and repurchase loyalty. *Journal of the Academy of Marketing Science* 30: 240–49. [CrossRef]

Oskan, Jeroen, and Tjeerd Zandberg. 2016. Who will sell your rooms? Hotel distribution scenarios. *Journal of Vacation Marketing* 22: 265–78. [CrossRef]

Ozturk, Ahmet B., Anil Bilgihan, Khaldoon Nusair, and Fevzi Okumus. 2016. What keeps the mobile hotel booking users loyal? Investigating the roles of self-efficacy, compatibility, perceived ease of use, and perceived convenience. *International Journal of Information Management* 36: 1350–59. [CrossRef]

Parasuraman, A., Valarie A. Zeithaml, and Arvind Malhotra. 2005. ES-QUAL a multiple-item scale for assessing electronic service quality. *Journal of Service Research* 7: 213–33. [CrossRef]

Park, Young A., and Ulrike Gretzel. 2007. Success factors for destination marketing web sites: A qualitative meta-analysis. *Journal of Travel Research* 46: 46–63. [CrossRef]

Park, Young A., Ulrike Gretzel, and Ercan Sirakaya-Turk. 2007. Measuring web site quality for online travel agencies. *Journal of Travel & Tourism Marketing* 23: 15–30.

Petter, Stacie, Detmar Straub, and Arun Rai. 2007. Specifying formative constructs in information systems research. *MIS Quarterly* 31: 623–56. [CrossRef]

Ponte, Enrique B., Elena Carvajal-Trujillo, and Tomás Escobar-Rodriguez. 2015. Influence of trust and perceived value on the intention to purchase travel online: Integrating the effects of assurance on trust antecedents. *Tourism Management* 47: 286–302. [CrossRef]

Prahalad, Coimbatore Krishna, and Venkat Ramaswamy. 2004. Co-creation experiences: The next practice in value creation. *Journal of Interactive Marketing* 18: 5–14. [CrossRef]

Prahalad, Coimbatore Krishna, and Venkat Ramaswamy. 2013. *The Future of Competition: Co-Creating Unique Value with Customers*. Boston: Harvard Business School Press.

Ruiz-Mafe, Carla, Enrique Bigne-Alcañiz, Silvia Sanz-Blas, and José Tronch. 2018. Does social climate influence positive Ewom? A study of heavy-users of online communities. *BRQ Business Research Quarterly*. in press. [CrossRef]

Ryu, Kisang, Lee Hye-Rin, and Woo Kim. 2012. The influence of the quality of the physical environment, food, and service on restaurant image, customer perceived value, customer satisfaction, and behavioral intentions. *International Journal of Contemporary Hospitality Management* 24: 200–23. [CrossRef]

Sarmiento, José R. 2016. El impacto de los medios sociales en la estructura del sistema de distribución turístico: Análisis y clasificación de los nuevos proveedores de servicios turísticos en el entorno online. *Cuadernos de Turismo* 36: 459–83. [CrossRef]

Sauro, Jeff. 2015. SUPR-Q: A comprehensive measure of the quality of the website user experience. *Journal of Usability Studies* 10: 68–86.

Shaw, Gareth, Adrian Bailey, and Allan Williams. 2011. Aspects of service-dominant logic and its implications for tourism management: Examples from the hotel industry. *Tourism Management* 32: 217–14. [CrossRef]

Seiders, Kathleen, Glenn B. Voss, Andrea L. Godfrey, and Dhruv Grewal. 2007. SERVCON: Development and Validation of a Multidimensional Service Convenience Scale. *Journal of the Academy of Marketing Science* 35: 144–156. [CrossRef]

Sigala, Marianna, and Odysseas Sakellaridis. 2004. The impact of users' cultural characteristics on e-service quality: Implications for globalizing tourism and hospitality web sites. In *Information and Communication Technologies in Tourism*. Edited by A. Frew. Vienna: Springer Verlag, pp. 106–17.

Stangl, Brigitte, Alessandro Inversini, and Roland Schegg. 2016. Hotel's dependency on online intermediaries and their chosen distribution channel portfolios: Three country insights. *International Journal of Hospitality Management* 16: 87–96. [CrossRef]

Stockdale, Rosemary. 2007. Managing customer relationships in the self-service environment of e-tourism. *Journal of Vacation Marketing* 13: 205–19. [CrossRef]

Urban, Glen, Cinda Amyx, and Antonio Lorenzon. 2009. Online trust: State of the art, new frontiers, and research potential. *Journal of Interactive Marketing* 23: 179–90. [CrossRef]

Vargo, Stephen L., and Robert F. Lusch. 2004. Evolving to a new dominant logic for marketing. *Journal of Marketing* 68: 1–17. [CrossRef]

Vargo, Stephen L., and Robert F. Lusch. 2008. Service-dominant logic: Continuing the evolution. *Journal of the Academy of Marketing Science* 36: 1–10. [CrossRef]

Vázquez, Rodolfo, Ana B. Del Río, and Leticia Suárez. 2009. Virtual travel agencies: Analysing the e-service quality and the effect on customer satisfaction. *Universia Business Review* 24: 122–43.

Verhoef, Peter C., Scott A. Neslin, and Björn Vroomen. 2007. Multichannel customer management: Understanding the research-shopper phenomenon. *International Journal of Research in Marketing* 24: 129–48. [CrossRef]

Wang, Liang, Rob Law, Basak D. Guillet, Kam Hung, and Davis K.C. Fong. 2015. Impact of hotel website quality on online booking intentions, eTrust as a mediator. *International Journal of Hospitality Management* 47: 108–15. [CrossRef]

Webb, Timothy. 2016. From travel agents to OTAs: How the evolution of consumer booking behaviour has affected revenue management. *Journal of Revenue and Pricing Management* 13: 276–82. [CrossRef]

Yang, Zhilin, and Minjoon Jun. 2002. Consumer perception of e-service quality: From Internet purchaser and non-purchaser perspectives. *Journal of Business Strategies* 19: 19–41.

Ye, Qiang, Rob Law, Bin Gu, and Wei Chen. 2011. The influence of user-generated content on traveler behavior: An empirical investigation on the effects of e-word-of-mouth to hotel online bookings. *Computers in Human Behavior* 27: 634–39. [CrossRef]

Yüksel, Atila, Fisun Yüksel, and Yasin Bilim. 2010. Destination attachment: Effects on customer satisfaction and cognitive, affective and conative loyalty. *Tourism Management* 31: 274–84. [CrossRef]

Zeithaml, Valarie A. 1988. Consumer perceptions of price, quality, and value: A means-end model and synthesis of evidence. *The Journal of Marketing* 52: 2–22. [CrossRef]

Zeithaml, Valarie A., Leonard L. Berry, and A. Parasuraman. 1996. The behavioral consequences of service quality. *Journal of Marketing* 60: 31–46. [CrossRef]

© 2018 by the authors. Licensee MDPI, Basel, Switzerland. This article is an open access article distributed under the terms and conditions of the Creative Commons Attribution (CC BY) license (http://creativecommons.org/licenses/by/4.0/).

Article

Local Food Shopping: Factors Affecting Users' Behavioural E-Loyalty

Maria Francisca Blasco Lopez [1,*], Nuria Recuero Virto [1] and Sonia San-Martín [2]

[1] Organización de Empresas y Marketing, Complutense University, 28003 Madrid, Spain; nrecuero@ucm.es
[2] Economía y Administración de Empresas, Burgos University, 09001 Burgos, Spain; sanmargu@ubu.es
* Correspondence: fblasco@ucm.es

Received: 18 July 2018; Accepted: 16 August 2018; Published: 21 August 2018

Abstract: While most research on electronic commerce has focused on customer behaviour according to websites' functional tasks, consumers are influenced by many other factors such as website content and design, especially in online food shopping. This is the first study that aims to examine which variables best explain satisfaction and behavioural e-loyalty (to return to the website and purchase) regarding online local food shopping. It empirically tested a model with a local food e-commerce website using a sample of 305 real e-buyers. The partial least squares structural equation modeling (PLS-SEM) technique was used to estimate the structural relationships. The findings revealed that all the tasks of a website could be strategically designed to enhance users' loyalty, and stressed the importance of measuring how all website features jointly influence perceived flow and control. This study makes a significant contribution to the consumer literature that deals with local food websites, a subject which is currently under-researched, and the eventual impact on behavioural e-loyalty.

Keywords: local food; e-commerce; behavioural e-loyalty; purchase intentions; revisit intentions; satisfaction; website; PLS-SEM

1. Introduction

Online grocery shopping is expected to grow worldwide, although those websites account for only a small proportion of the e-commerce market at the present time (Grunert and Ramus 2004; Heng et al. 2018). Despite the several advantages of grocery online shopping, such as the ability to find products, compare prices, save time, shop for ready-to-eat or semi-ready-to-eat food and arrange delivery at a suitable time, among other benefits, there are still many consumers who have not yet adopted online grocery shopping as a regular habit (Hansen 2008; Quevedo-Silva et al. 2016). The demand for speciality foods is also increasing (Canavan et al. 2007). At the same time, the slow food movement is expanding in response to the modern world's eating habits (Lee et al. 2015; Heng et al. 2018).

In this changing food culture, consumers are progressively demanding more information regarding the food they eat, such as additional details about the components, the origin and the production chain (Ilbery et al. 2006; Megicks et al. 2012; Pearson et al. 2011; Seyfang 2008). These growing concerns are predictable outcomes of the competitive global food marketplace, where customers have become more specialized (Zepeda and Li 2006). In this quest, consumers are searching for alternatives in relation not only to the product offering, but also to the shopping experience and to the current dominant supermarket food supply chain (Pearson et al. 2011).

Buyers' main reasons for shopping for local food products are related to economic, social, environmental, and health issues. Specifically, it has been pointed out that these buyers have a high and positive perception of: (1) the quality, freshness, taste, and authenticity of these products; (2) the supply chain that it entails and hence, the support that it offers to local community development; and (3) the environmental, social, safety, and sustainable benefits of the production chain (Pearson et al. 2011; Sims 2009). Whereas some years ago the shopping experience was considered a functional and utilitarian activity, it has proved to have an emotional and entertaining importance (Megicks et al. 2012).

In the last two decades, the expansion of local food retailers and networks from food cooperatives, farm shops, and ecological stores to supermarket chains has been considerable in response to the trend of local food consumption and supermarkets' strategies regarding corporate social responsibility (Megicks et al. 2012; Tobler et al. 2011). The study of local food consumption has recently become a popular subject of research, where scholars have analysed consumer behaviour, environmentally responsible buying, and sustainable policy buying (Blake et al. 2010; Megicks et al. 2012; Pearson et al. 2011; Zepeda and Deal 2009).

Although there are many advantages of developing local food websites for the advancement of the supply chain, such as promoting food self-sufficiency, decreasing the environmental footprint and re-engaging consumers with the origin of their food (Pearson et al. 2011), consumers' behaviour regarding these websites remains under-researched. Research that focuses not only on local food customers' behaviour regarding the websites' functional tasks but also on the website design and content is even sparser.

Despite the fact that local food can be purchased from many different stores, it seems that frequent buyers tend to be those that live in nearby rural areas (Pearson et al. 2011). There is therefore an opportunity to examine buyers' behavioural e-loyalty regarding local food websites as the ability to find these products decreases. It is not only an issue of purely academic interest but also a possible contribution to food supply management practices.

This study serves as a first step toward the development of a model that can be used by future scholars and practitioners to gain knowledge regarding loyal local food consumers. This research provides insight into this area by addressing the relationships among website evaluation (WE) (which comprises aesthetics, content, customization, ease of use, and information quality), personal variables (perceived flow, perceived control), and relational variables (satisfaction and behavioural e-loyalty). Table 1 shows prior studies conducted in relation to the navigation experience. A partial least squares path modeling (partial least squares structural equation modeling or PLS-SEM) was used to analyse the hypotheses. Figure 1 presents the proposed model for this research.

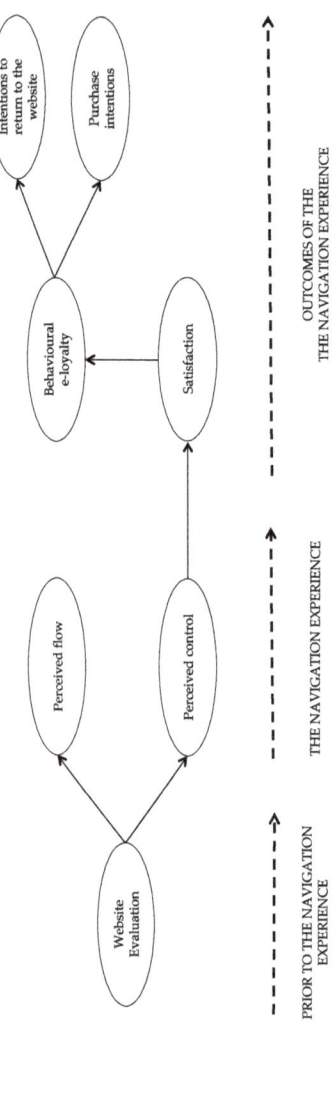

Figure 1. Proposed model.

Table 1. References conducted in relation to the navigation experience.

Reference	Variables of the Navigation Experience	Outcomes of the Navigation Experience
Koufaris (2002)	Ease of use, perceived usefulness, entertainment, control, concentration	Purchase intentions
Lee and Lin (2005)	Website design, viability, reactivity, customization	Perceived quality, satisfaction, purchase intentions
Hausman and Siekpe (2009)	Entertainment, utility, information and content	Purchase intentions, revisit intentions
Constantinides et al. (2010)	Usability, interactivity, aesthetics, marketing mix and trust	Website selection
Manganari et al. (2011)	Ease of use	Trust, satisfaction
Rose et al. (2012)	Ease of use, aesthetics, perceived benefits, connectivity, customization, ability, challenge, interaction speed, immersion	Satisfaction, trust, purchase intention
Hsu et al. (2012)	Website quality	Satisfaction, purchase intention
Ha and Stoel (2012)	Privacy and security, content and functionality, customer service, atmosphere	Satisfaction, purchase intention
Hsu et al. (2012)	Utility and perceived ease of use	Satisfaction, loyalty
Pappas et al. (2014)	Customization	Purchase intentions
Pallud and Straub (2014)	Content, made for the medium, ease of use, promotion, emotion, aesthetics, subjective norms, attitudes, facilitating conditions	Intentions to return to the website, intentions to go to the museum
Bilgihan et al. (2016)	Easiness to locate the website or app, ease of use, perceived usefulness, hedonic and utilitarian features, perceived enjoyment, personalization, social interactions and multi-device compatibility	Brand engagement, positive word of mouth (WOM), and repeat purchase

2. Literature Review

2.1. Relational Variables in Local Food E-Commerce

Loyalty is economically vital in e-commerce because attracting new customers is more expensive in online businesses than in brick-and-mortar stores (Chang et al. 2014; Luarn and Lin 2003). It has been defined as a bidimensional construct that entails the result of all marketing efforts to maintain existing customers (Pereira et al. 2016). Therefore, developing long-lasting relationships in the e-commerce context can be reflected in intentions to return to the website (Ku and Chen 2014) and purchase and repurchase intentions (San-Martín and Herrero 2012).

Intentions to return to the website denote continuance purposes, which is especially reinforced by positive interactions with the website (Huang et al. 2014). It has been stated that the success of e-commerce business relies more on users' continued usage intention rather than on their initial adoption (Chou et al. 2010; Kabadayi and Gupta 2011). Purchase intention is a dimension of behavioural intentions (Zeithaml et al. 1996), and it has been argued that it is the best predictor of action (Dedeke 2016). Specifically, consumers usually purchase and repurchase a product or service that can maximize their benefits, which is probably influenced by their satisfaction, their shopping enjoyment, and their desire to continue their exciting shopping experience (Atulkar and Kesari 2017).

Customer satisfaction is based on all cumulative experiences with a certain company that can lead to pleasure or disappointment, and it is not a result of a specific transaction (Atulkar and Kesari 2017; Chang et al. 2014; San-Martín et al. 2012; Filieri et al. 2015). In the online context, satisfaction refers to a favourable navigation experience and the perception of a well-designed website, representing also a basic key element for a successful e-commerce business relationship since it increases rate profitability and long-term sales growth in online shops (Chen et al. 2012; Pereira et al. 2016). Nevertheless, e-commerce is characterized by the absence of the physical interaction with people that leads to users' dissatisfaction due to the impersonality of the transaction (Pereira et al. 2016). In this paradigm, it is very complex to generate loyalty among users.

Several studies have analysed the effects of satisfaction on continuance intentions (Bhattacherjee 2001; Chiu et al. 2007; Zhao and Lu 2012). Ku and Chen (2014) have corroborated that satisfaction positively influences intentions to continue using the particular website. Chung et al. (2015) have also confirmed the positive impact of satisfaction on continued usage intentions. As Kabadayi and Gupta (2011) pointed out, a satisfactory perception normally results in a positive attitude toward the website.

It has been proved that individual satisfaction has a positive impact on repurchase intention (Mohamed et al. 2014). Specifically, prior studies have confirmed that satisfaction is favourably related to purchase intention (Lin and Lekhawipat 2014; Pee et al. 2018; Wen et al. 2011; Yen and Lu 2008). Hence, it has been proved that satisfied customers tend to repurchase more than dissatisfied consumers (Sánchez-García et al. 2012). In addition, it has been proved in the online context that satisfaction positively and significantly influences behavioural e-loyalty regarding search engines (Sirdeshmukh et al. 2018), about tourism e-commerce (Gonçalves et al. 2016), among female online shoppers (Chou et al. 2015), regarding luxury brands (Yoo and Park 2016), among others. Thus, it is reasonable to think that users of online local food websites that feel satisfied with the navigation experience tend to return to the website and increase their purchase intentions. Therefore,

Hypothesis 1 (H1). *The e-buyer's satisfaction positively influences their behavioural e-loyalty.*

2.2. The Impact of Perceived Flow and Control

Flow has been studied as a psychological factor that describes users' state of involvement regarding the activity of web surfing (Bilgihan 2016; Hsu et al. 2012). The creation of a positive experience for a user within a website relies on the capacity of a website to induce the consumer to feel engaged during the interaction (Ali 2016; Hoffman and Novak 1996). This state of flow can take place during the search for information of products or during other kind of utilitarian tasks that ensue in a shopping online website (Mathwick and Rigdon 2004). Hence, if using online local e-commerce can induce a state of flow in users, they should be satisfied, and predisposed to purchase and continue visiting these websites.

It has been assumed that the state of flow generates diverse positive responses among users (Mathwick and Rigdon 2004), not only emotional but also behavioural (Lee and Jeong 2012). In this regard, Hausman and Siekpe (2009) revealed that perceived flow has a positive impact on intentions to return to the website and purchase intentions. In addition, Ilsever et al. (2007) concluded that a flow experience had a positive effect on behavioural e-loyalty, understood as intentions to return to the website and repurchase. Furthermore, O'Cass and Carlson (2010) indicated that users' website-induced flow on professional sporting team websites positively influenced their satisfaction. This is in line with the conclusions indicated by Hsu et al. (2012) regarding travel agency websites, where users' perceived flow had a positive effect on their satisfaction. Based on the preceding discussion, users that have a favourable perception of flow tend to increase their behavioural loyalty and to be satisfied. Therefore,

Hypothesis 2 (H2). *The e-buyer's perception of flow positively influences their behavioural e-loyalty.*

Hypothesis 3 (H3). *The e-buyer's perception of flow positively influences their satisfaction.*

In addition, there is another variable referring to personal skills related to information and communication technologies (ICTs), that is, perceived control. In interactive technology, perceived control has been defined as the extent to which users feel that they have the skills to manage their actions while shopping on an online website (Mohd-Any et al. 2015).

Control has been determined as a predictor of consumers' satisfaction (Duman and Mattila 2005), as it reduces anxiety and enhances customers' positive emotions (Hui and Bateson 1991). Perceived control seems to be essential for online shoppers because they might be searching for more control during the service process (Smith and Bolton 2002). Results of some studies suggested that people behave more positively when they believe they have control over the environment (Ozkara et al. 2017). Hence, it is reasonable to think that if users have a perception of control, their satisfaction levels will rise. Therefore,

Hypothesis 4 (H4). *The e-buyer's perception of control positively influences their satisfaction.*

2.3. The Impact of Website Evaluation on Perceived Flow and Control

In this study, the WE is a variable that comprises several concepts (aesthetics, content, customization, ease of use, and information quality), which other authors have considered (Hausman and Siekpe 2009; Lee and Lin 2005; Pallud and Straub 2014; Rose et al. 2012; Wolfinbarger and Gilly 2003). They are all signals of website quality.

Content and ease of use refer to the task-oriented quality of a product or a service. Content is related to textual and visual information and its adjustment to the needs of the core audience, and ease of use denote users' perceptions for mainly navigating and searching information (Pallud and Straub 2014; Rose et al. 2012; Venkatesh 2000). Aesthetics is a quality signal more associated with originality and innovativeness of the website design that provides sensory stimuli and supports the development of experience feelings (Eroglu et al. 2003; Pallud and Straub 2014). Customization has been considered one of the most interesting advantages of online shopping over physical stores, because it makes it easier for users to personalize their experiences according to their preferences (Manganari et al. 2009; Wolfinbarger and Gilly 2003), by attending to customers individually and customizing the website appearance and functionality (Lee and Lin 2005; Rose et al. 2012). Information quality has also been considered as another advantage of e-commerce because users can have access to broader, richer and more updated information than in physical stores (Wolfinbarger and Gilly 2003). Customer service in e-commerce is related to the extent to which users perceive that it is easy, quick and cheap to contact the company, and that their questions are answered promptly (Liu and Arnett 2000; Hsu et al. 2012).

It has been stated that hedonic and utilitarian features of a website, as is the case with the variables included in the WE, positively impact flow (Bilgihan et al. 2015). Wu et al. (2016) recognized the positive impact of web skills on flow experience. Specifically, information quality has been identified as a factor that contributes to customers' positive perceptions of websites (Chen et al. 1999), and it directly and positively influences flow (Hausman and Siekpe 2009). Taking into account the above discussion, this study proposes that all of the characteristics included in the global construct WE positively affect the sensation of absorption and enjoyment implicit in flow.

Websites allow users to build a sense of personal control, which is directly influenced by ease of use and customization (Rose et al. 2012). Moreover, the inclusion of a higher number of interactive elements on a website can increase the users' sense of control (Hoffman and Novak 1996). Furthermore, the online shopping websites that provide users with clear and simple ways to contact customer service are more likely to encourage users, giving them perceived control with a greater sense of managing the situation (Hoffman and Novak 1996). Therefore,

Hypothesis 5 (H5). *WE positively influences an e-buyer's perception of flow.*

Hypothesis 6 (H6). *WE positively influences an e-buyer's perception of control.*

3. Research Methodology

3.1. Sampling Procedure and Data Collection

A non-probabilistic sampling technique was adopted, namely the convenience sampling technique, because it is a very useful method to identify real online purchasers and it allows for a high level of response rate (Kim and Li 2009). The online questionnaire was placed on an online survey website for approximately 44 days. The survey data were collected from 18 February to 4 April 2016. All participants were requested to participate by an email that explained the objectives of the research and included a link to the questionnaire, which was available in three languages (namely, Spanish, German and English). A total of 305 usable questionnaires from real e-buyers was obtained, which is a higher sample than in other studies conducted in similar contexts and procedures (Rose et al. 2012). The demographic details of the sample are shown in Table 2. Respondents were mainly European (287 real e-buyers; 94%, specifically from Austria, Belgium, Bulgaria, Croatia, France, Germany, Greece, Holland, Italy, Macedonia, Netherlands, Norway, Portugal, Romania, Serbia, Spain, Sweden, Switzerland, Turkey, Ukraine and United Kingdom) and non-European (namely, from Argentina, Benin, Bolivia, Chile, Costa Rica, Ivory Coast, Mexico, Tanzania, United Arab Emirates, USA and Vietnam).

3.2. Measurement of Constructs

The scale items used in this research were adapted from previous studies and rated according to a seven-point Likert scale (see Table 3). The WE was operationalized using the first-order dimensions: aesthetics, content, customization, ease of use, and information quality developed by Pallud and Straub (2014), Rose et al. (2012), and Hsu et al. (2012). Perceived control was adapted from Rose et al. (2012), and perceived flow was measured following Hsu et al. (2012). Satisfaction was adapted from Kim et al. (2011). First-order dimensions for behavioural e-loyalty (intention to return to the website and purchase intention) were adapted from Hsu et al. (2012) and Huang et al. (2014).

Table 2. Sample profile.

	n	%		n	%
Gender			**Number of visits to the website**		
Female	175	57	1–5 visits	254	83
Male	130	43	>5 visits	51	17
Age			**Time spent on the website**		
18–25	8	3	0–5 min	105	34
26–30	42	14	6–10 min	108	35
31–35	115	38	11–15 min	56	19
36–40	38	12	>16 min	36	12
41–45	30	10	**How often do you buy online?**		
46–50	25	8	1–5 times per year	98	32
51–55	23	7.5	6–10 times per year	77	25
56–60	14	4.5	>10 times per year	111	36
61–65	7	2	Never	19	6
66–69	2	1	**Household monthly income (in euros)**		
>70	1	0	<900	41	13
Education			901–1200	38	13
Postgraduate	90	29.5	1201–1500	44	15
Graduate	158	52	1501–2000	74	24
Undergraduate	30	10	2001–2000	46	15
Secondary	26	8.5	3001–4000	25	8
Primary	1	0	>4000	37	12
Occupation					
Employed	231	76			
Student	5	2			
Unemployed	16	4			
Housewife	9	3			
Other	42	14			
Retired	2	1			

The translation of the original version of the questionnaire from English to Spanish and to German received special attention. Native Spanish and German speakers ensured the translation so that all feasible nuances and connotations could be considered. Then, native Spanish and German speakers translated the scale items from Spanish to English and from German to English following the specifications of several scholars (Sireci et al. 2006). Finally, all translators evaluated the scale items in order to resolve any discrepancies.

3.3. Reliability and Validity

In order to estimate the proposed model (see Figure 2), variance-based structural equation modeling was used, also known as partial least squares structural equation modelling (PLS-SEM). This method was particularly suitable for this research because the model was a combination of first- and second-order constructs for which a covariance-based structural equation modeling would have required a higher sample size (Hair et al. 2012). Preliminary tests completed on the sample indicated the presence of non-normal data, and PLS-SEM is less strict with this type of bias (Hair et al. 2014).

Tables 3 and 4 present the findings of the measurement model reliability and convergent validity test. Cronbach's alpha values correspond to the recommendation of 0.60 (Hair et al. 2010). Composite reliability denotes the shared variance among a set of observed items measuring a construct (Fornell and Larcker 1981), where the value of at least 0.60 is considered desirable (Bagozzi and Yi 1988). This was respected for every factor. Moreover, average variance extracted (AVE) for each construct was greater than 0.50 (Fornell and Larcker 1981).

Table 3. Measurement model.

Factor	Description	Mean	Standard Deviation
Aesthetics (AE)			
1.	I find that the design of this website looks pleasant.	6.072	1.050
2.	The layout of this website is fascinating.	6.020	1.107
3.	I find the design of this website to be creative.	5.797	1.211
4.	I find that the design of this website looks aesthetic.	5.970	1.138
Content (CO)			
1.	This website offers content that is relevant to the core audience.	5.708	1.221
2.	… uses media appropriately and effectively to communicate the content.	5.702	1.288
3.	… provides the appropriate breadth and depth of content.	5.567	1.271
4.	… provides current and timely information.	5.708	1.189
Customization (CU)			
1.	This website makes me feel they are talking to me personally as a customer.	5.275	1.431
2.	The requirement to login to this shopping website makes me feel recognized as a customer.	5.266	1.538
3.	It is important to me that this shopping website feels like my personal area when I use it.	5.439	1.510
4.	I like that I am able to customize this shopping website to my own liking.	5.580	1.438
Ease of use (EO)			
1.	This website offers clear and understandable goals.	6.007	1.043
2.	… is well-structured and organized.	5.964	1.111
3.	… provides clear and understandable results and feedback regarding your progress.	5.787	1.091
4.	… allows me to easily shop for what I want.	6.010	1.070
5.	It is easy to become confident at this website shopping.	5.751	1.258
6.	Learning how to navigate through this website has not taken too long for me.	6.246	1.044
Information quality (IQ)			
1.	The website produces the most current information.	5.767	1.166
2.	… provides me with all the information I need.	5.623	1.335
3.	The information provided by the website is accurate.	5.770	1.212
4.	In general, the website provides me with high-quality information.	5.728	1.331
Intention to return to the website (IR)			
1.	I will revisit this website next time I need.	5.587	1.576
2.	It is worth returning to this website again.	5.695	1.449
3.	I am likely to return to this website next time I need.	5.590	1.547
4.	I am encouraged to revisit this website next time I need.	5.587	1.539

Table 3. *Cont.*

Factor	Description	Mean	Standard Deviation
Perceived control (PC)			
1.	I feel in control of what I am doing when I purchase from this website.	5.810	1.178
2.	I can easily control the information that is provided on this website.	5.721	1.141
3.	I feel I can control my use of information on this website.	5.698	1.146
4.	The level of information provided by this website helps me to feel in control of my purchase decision.	5.757	1.217
Perceived flow (PF)			
1.	When I navigate in this website, I felt totally captivated.	5.466	1.333
2.	When I navigate in this website, time seemed to pass very quickly.	5.318	1.444
3.	When I visit this website, nothing seemed to matter to me.	4.475	1.845
Purchase intention (PI)			
1.	It is likely that next year I will transact with this website.	4.928	1.820
2.	Given the chance, I intend to use this website.	5.213	1.715
3.	Given the chance, I predict that next year I should use this website.	5.157	1.776
Satisfaction (SA)			
1.	Overall, I was satisfied with this online commerce.	5.662	1.288
2.	The online site information content met my needs.	5.495	1.389
3.	It was easy to buy the product I chose.	5.954	1.167
4.	I was satisfied with online buying when compared to offline buying.	5.557	1.420

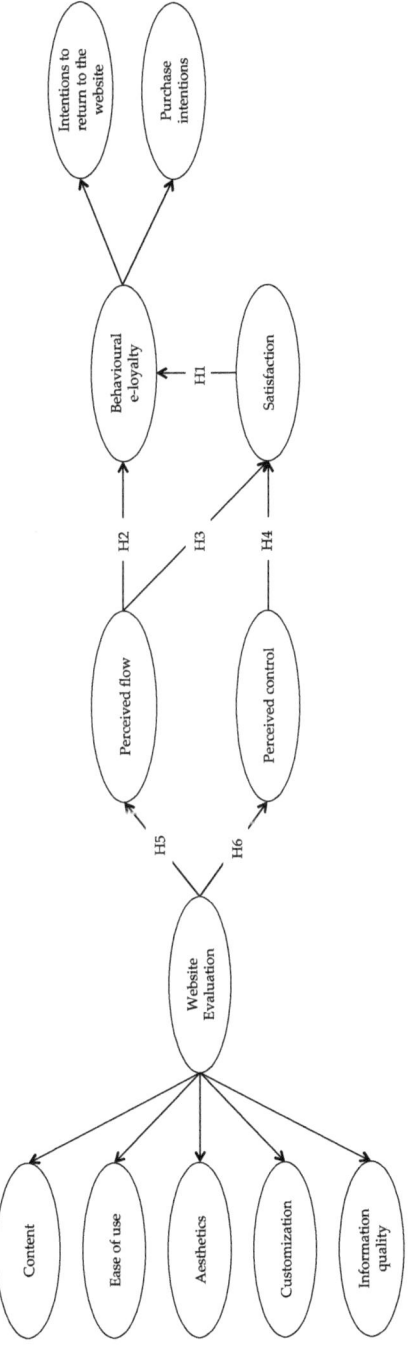

Figure 2. Research model.

Table 4. Reliability and Convergent Validity of the Final Measurement Model.

Factor	Indicator	Standardized Loading	t-Value (Bootstrap)	CA	rho_A	CR	AVE
Aesthetics	AE1	0.896	58,910	0.918	0.920	0.942	0.803
	AE2	0.907	51,329				
	AE3	0.892	63,188				
	AE4	0.890	45,549				
Content	CO1	0.878	62,306	0.913	0.914	0.939	0.793
	CO2	0.892	57,361				
	CO3	0.888	57,888				
	CO4	0.904	69,183				
Customization	CU1	0.869	48,781	0.896	0.902	0.927	0.761
	CU2	0.904	66,494				
	CU3	0.891	49,864				
	CU4	0.825	29,581				

Table 4. Cont.

Factor	Indicator	Standardized Loading	t-Value (Bootstrap)	CA	rho_A	CR	AVE
Ease of use	EO1	0.774	27,960	0.877	0.884	0.907	0.621
	EO2	0.834	39,925				
	EO3	0.818	35,686				
	EO4	0.779	27,734				
	EO5	0.818	37,089				
	EO6	0.695	14,603				
Information quality	IQ1	0.861	43,953	0.926	0.930	0.948	0.820
	IQ2	0.928	88,819				
	IQ3	0.917	54,849				
	IQ4	0.914	63,480				
Intention to return to the website	IR1	0.952	114,008	0.966	0.967	0.975	0.908
	IR2	0.928	44,796				
	IR3	0.973	182,997				
	IR4	0.958	78,820				
Perceived control	PC1	0.913	80,785	0.938	0.939	0.956	0.844
	PC2	0.930	91,755				
	PC3	0.920	89,280				
	PC4	0.912	71,321				
Perceived flow	PF1	0.909	74,597	0.893	0.897	0.933	0.824
	PF2	0.932	106,859				
	PF3	0.881	50,650				
Purchase intention	PI1	0.951	105,532	0.962	0.963	0.976	0.930
	PI2	0.970	177,271				
	PI3	0.972	190,928				
Satisfaction	SA1	0.925	82,634	0.927	0.934	0.948	0.822
	SA2	0.927	102,152				
	SA3	0.840	28,827				
	SA4	0.931	114,582				
Website evaluation	Aesthetics	0.790	24,756	0.892	0.894	0.920	0.698
	Content	0.848	40,512				
	Customization	0.833	40,261				
	Ease of use	0.867	52,389				
	Information quality	0.837	37,856				
Behavioural e-loyalty	Intention to return to the website	0.915	61,930	0.831	0.838	0.922	0.855
	Purchase intention	0.934	102,260				

Note: All loadings are significant at $p < 0.01$ level. CA = Cronbach's alpha; CR = composite reliability; AVE = average variance extracted.

In relation to convergent validity, all items were significantly ($p < 0.01$) associated to their hypothesized factors, and standardized loadings were higher than 0.60 (Bagozzi and Yi 1988). The discriminant validity of measures was analysed, proving that the shared variance between the pairs of constructs was lower than the corresponding AVE (Fornell and Larcker 1981) (see Table 5). The heterotrait-monotrait (HTMT) ratio method recently proposed by Henseler et al. (2015) was also applied to test the discriminant validity, and all ratios were less than 0.90 (Hair et al. 2017; Teo et al. 2008). Therefore, all the measures in this research provided enough evidence of reliability, convergent and discriminant validity. Reliability and convergent validity were tested both at the first- and second-order level for the two second-order constructs of the model.

Table 5. Measurement Model Discriminant Validity for Higher-Order Constructs.

	Factor	F1	F2	F3	F4	F5
F1.	Perceived control	0.919	0.805	0.897	0.838	0.665
F2.	Perceived flow	0.740	0.908	0.890	0.830	0.742
F3.	Satisfaction	0.835	0.816	0.906	0.900	0.781
F4.	Website Evaluation	0.769	0.745	0.820	0.835	0.700
F5.	Behavioural e-loyalty	0.590	0.644	0.691	0.603	0.924

Note: Diagonal values are AVE square root, values below the diagonal are latent variable correlation values, and those above the diagonal are heterotrait-monotrait (HTMT) ratios.

4. Research Findings

The results of the inner estimation for the model proposed are presented in Table 6. To establish parameters significance, bootstrapping with individual sign changes of 5000 samples was calculated (Hair et al. 2012). The endogenous latent variable satisfaction presented a R^2 higher than 0.67 and can be described as substantial. The R^2 of perceived control, perceived flow and behavioural e-loyalty can be described as moderate because the values were higher than 0.33 (Chin 1998). Positive Stone-Geisser's Q^2 were obtained using blindfolding, and therefore the predictive relevance of the model was established (Henseler et al. 2009). In addition, the goodness of model fit was assessed (Henseler et al. 2014; Henseler et al. 2016), and the standardized root mean square residual (SRMR) presented a value of 0.047 (Hu and Bentler 1999).

Table 6. Hypotheses Testing.

	Hypothesis	Standardized Beta	t-Value (Bootstrap)
H1	Satisfaction → Behavioural e-loyalty	0.497	6266
H2	Perceived flow → Behavioural e-loyalty	0.238	3161
H3	Perceived flow → Satisfaction	0.437	8306
H4	Perceived control → Satisfaction	0.512	9454
H5	Website Evaluation → Perceived flow	0.745	27,411
H6	Website Evaluation → Perceived control	0.769	28,474

Note: All loadings are significant at $p < 0.01$ level. R^2 (perceived control) = 0.590; R^2 (perceived flow) = 0.553; R^2 (satisfaction) = 0.783; R^2 (behavioural e-loyalty) = 0.493. Q^2 (perceived control) = 0.468; Q^2 (perceived flow) = 0.430; Q^2 (satisfaction) = 0.606; Q^2 (behavioural e-loyalty) = 0.404.

Table 6 presents the results of the hypotheses testing. As hypothesized, e-buyer satisfaction has a significant effect on their behavioural e-loyalty (H1: β = 0.497; $p < 0.01$). E-buyer perception of flow has a positive impact on their behavioural e-loyalty (H2; β = 0.238; $p < 0.01$) and their satisfaction (H3; β = 0.437; $p < 0.01$). E-buyer perception of control positively influences their satisfaction (H4; β = 0.512; $p < 0.01$). WE positively influences e-buyer perception of flow (H5; β = 0.745; $p < 0.01$) and e-buyer perception of control (H6; β = 0.769; $p < 0.01$). These results are presented in Figure 3.

In addition, the significance of indirect effects was assessed. Only one indirect effect was found, presented in Table 7.

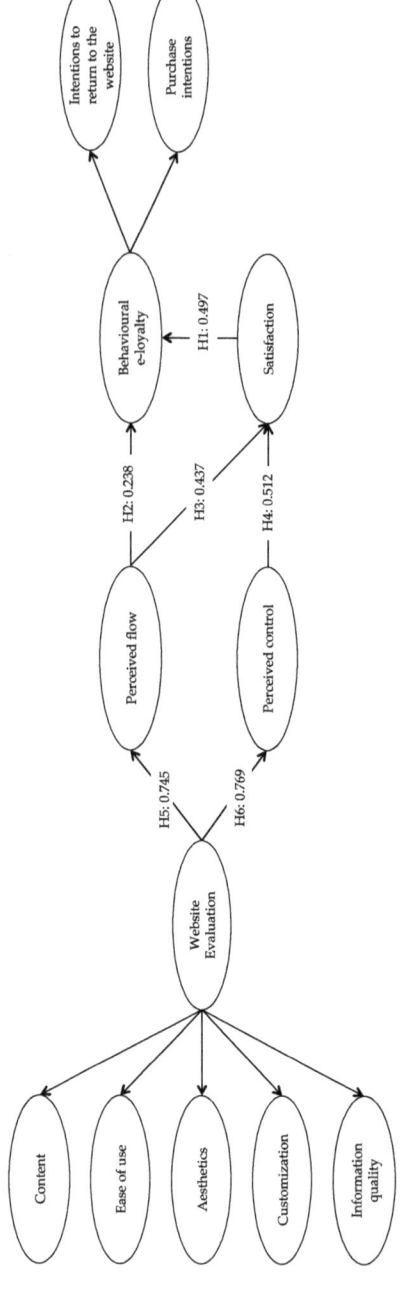

Figure 3. Estimation of the proposed model.

Table 7. Mediation effect testing.

Paths	Standardized Beta	t-Value (Bootstrap)	VAF	Partial/Full Mediation
Perceived control → Satisfaction → Behavioural e-loyalty	0.547	6786	0.926	Full

Note: All loadings are significant at $p < 0.01$ level.

These statistical results offered two major findings: (1) e-buyer satisfaction influences their behavioural e-loyalty; and (2) the construct WE has a positive effect on customers' personal perception of flow and control.

5. Discussion and Implication

Today's consumers use information and communication technologies (ICTs) for a large number of tasks, such as obtaining information and purchasing goods and services (Alcántara-Pilar et al. 2017). Literature has mainly focused on revealing users' behaviour outcomes when web surfing by analysing websites' functional features. This article initiated the research regarding the influence of online local food shopping on behavioural e-loyalty. The value and usefulness of this application was empirically tested by means of a quantitative research (using PLS-SEM) that explored the perceptions of real e-buyers from a Spanish local food e-commerce website.

This paper highlighted academic and practical contributions, as well as limitations. First, it offered a valuable foundation for understanding online local food e-commerce development by considering two loyalty interrelated concepts: intentions to return to the website and purchase intentions. Secondly, it incorporated website evaluation as a global dimension that included different quality signals: aesthetics, content, customization, ease of use, and information quality. It was observed that the main functional elements of an e-commerce website were related and interacted within the customers' behavioural outcomes.

6. Conclusions

6.1. Academic Contributions

The findings of this research make several significant contributions to the literature on food supply management, culinary consumers' behaviour, and e-commerce management. First, this study is the first to analyse the impact of local food shopping websites on users' loyalty. All the tasks of a website can be strategically designed to enhance users' intentions.

Second, the study results support the finding that users' satisfaction is an important relational predictor of behavioural e-loyalty (Chung et al. 2015; Ku and Chen 2014; Lin and Lekhawipat 2014; Mohamed et al. 2014; Wen et al. 2011; Zhao and Lu 2012). Third, the findings confirm previous results concerning the positive effect of perceived flow on the two relational variables of the proposed model (satisfaction and behavioural e-loyalty) (Hausman and Siekpe 2009; Hsu et al. 2012; O'Cass and Carlson 2010). Fourth, this research reveals there is a positive relationship between perceived control and satisfaction in the local food e-commerce context.

Fifth, this study shows the significance of measuring several features (the WE dimension) in order to understand users' perceptions of the website layout, and how all these features jointly influence e-buyer perceived flow and control. With respect to the above, most research has analysed separately the WE constructs without taking into account the overall website analysis of features and its impacts, and the global future intentions of users after an e-commerce experience. In this regard, past studies have determined the positive effect of certain website features on perceived flow (Bilgihan et al. 2015; Hausman and Siekpe 2009; Wu et al. 2016) and control (Hoffman and Novak 1996; Rose et al. 2012).

6.2. Practical Implications

The findings of this research support the current local food trend (Ilbery et al. 2006; Megicks et al. 2012; Pearson et al. 2011; Seyfang 2008; Tobler et al. 2011; Zepeda and Li 2006), suggesting that these consumers can meet their needs regarding this type of product and enhance their shopping activity as regular e-buyers. In this regard, many of these consumers complain about the restricted availability of certain products, the lack of information about where to buy the local products and the high costs due to the long supply chain (Pearson et al. 2011). Moreover, consumers compare the perceived values attributed to the other available alternatives (Pedraja and Yagüe 2004). These issues can be improved by offering additional information concerning the moment that seasonal or non-seasonal products will again be for sale (the information can even be dated and give the main reasons for the product scarcity), the supply management chain, the system of price regulation, and to what extent the product supports the sustainable community development. This information can fill consumers' demands for traditional and local food, which is perceived as authentic as well as safe, distinctive, and traceable (Sims 2009).

Another practical implication is for website designers so that they can improve users' perceptions and behavioural intentions. For example, photos that emphasize the uniqueness and attractiveness of local food have the potential to enhance not only users' willingness to purchase those products but also their intentions to return to those websites. Additionally, the information provided can be enriched using storytelling strategies based on local aspects.

Furthermore, local food is a very appealing market for tourists and, in this regard, Khanal et al. (2014) suggest that it could also very interesting for the Spanish government to invest and promote the links between the food sector and the tourism industry in order to improve the general economy. Moreover, these websites can promote the first visit to a destination as well as the continuance of local food consumption once the tourists return home.

6.3. Limitations and Future Research

This research had some limitations, which offer interesting avenues for future studies. First, this research was limited by the use of convenience sampling. The current study involved approaching users of a specific local food e-commerce. Second, in the proposed model, the WE and behavioural e-loyalty were global constructs that comprised related concepts in order to gain parsimony and understand their relations with many other variables. However, the separate effects of the proposed model were not measured.

Future research should test the model by using a probabilistic sampling method in order to improve the generalizability of the findings. Scholars could also approach various local food shopping online websites to obtain different insights into the effect of local food e-commerce on behavioural e-loyalty, and test the influence of local food brands on consumers' perceived value (Rubio et al. 2014). In addition, researchers are prompted to consider attitudinal loyalty to complete e-loyalty dimensionality and examine the effect of satisfaction on both behavioural and affective attributes of e-loyalty.

Finally, other studies could deal with the moderating effects of nationality, age, and experience on the proposed model, as other studies have demonstrated (San-Martín et al. 2012). Furthermore, it could be interesting to analyse the effect of hedonic web browsing (Rezaei et al. 2016) on behavioural e-loyalty. As well, several scholars have pointed out the relevance of trust to boost online sales (Wang et al. 2015) and predict behavioural intention toward the online shopping website (Bilgihan and Bujisic 2015; Chen and Chou 2012).

Author Contributions: M.F.B.L. co-conceived the idea for the study, contributed to the conceptual and overall development of the project and survey, provided a contextual framework for the work, and supervised all the different stages of the research and manuscript elaboration. N.R.V. co-developed the model used in this study, analysed the data, developed the findings, wrote the paper, and coordinated the efforts of the other authors. S.S.M. contributed to the conceptual and overall development of the project and survey, and supervised all the different stages of the research and the manuscript elaboration. She has extensive knowledge of the topic and links with extant literature.

Funding: This research received no external funding.

Acknowledgments: The authors would like to thank Gastronomics Spain for the support offered.

Conflicts of Interest: The authors declare no conflict of interest. The founding sponsors had no role in the design of the study; in the collection, analyses, or interpretation of data; in the writing of the manuscript; and in the decision to publish the results.

References

Alcántara-Pilar, Juan Miguel, Salvador del Barrio-García, Esmeralda Crespo-Almendros, and Lucía Porcu. 2017. Toward an understanding of online information processing in e-tourism: Does national culture matter? *Journal of Travel and Tourism Marketing* 34: 1128–42. [CrossRef]

Ali, Faizan. 2016. Hotel website quality, perceived flow, customer satisfaction and purchase intention. *Journal of Hospitality and Tourism Technology* 7: 213–28. [CrossRef]

Atulkar, Sunil, and Bikrant Kesari. 2017. Satisfaction, loyalty and repatronage intentions: Role of hedonic shopping values. *Journal of Retailing and Consumer Services* 39: 23–34. [CrossRef]

Bagozzi, Richard, and Youjae Yi. 1988. On the evaluation of structural equation models. *Journal of the Academy of Marketing Science* 16: 74–94. [CrossRef]

Bhattacherjee, Anol. 2001. An empirical analysis of the antecedents of electronic commerce service continuance. *Decision Support Systems* 32: 201–14. [CrossRef]

Bilgihan, Anil. 2016. Gen Y customer loyalty in online shopping: An integrated model of trust, user experience and branding. *Computers in Human Behavior* 61: 103–13. [CrossRef]

Bilgihan, Anil, and Milos Bujisic. 2015. The effect of website features in online relationship marketing: A case of online hotel booking. *Electronic Commerce Research and Applications* 4: 222–32. [CrossRef]

Bilgihan, Anil, Khaldoon Nusair, Fevzi Okumus, and Cihan Cobanoglu. 2015. Applying flow theory to booking experiences: An integrated model in an online service context. *Information and Management* 52: 668–78. [CrossRef]

Bilgihan, Anil, Jay Kandampully, and Tingting Zhang. 2016. Towards a unified customer experience in online shopping environments: Antecedents and outcomes. *International Journal of Quality and Service Sciences* 8: 102–19. [CrossRef]

Blake, Megan K., Jody Mellor, and Lucy Crane. 2010. Buying local food: Shopping practices, place, and consumption networks in defining food as "local". *Annals of the Association of American Geographers* 100: 409–26. [CrossRef]

Canavan, Orla, Maeve Henchion, and Seamus O'Reilly. 2007. The use of the internet as a marketing cannel for Irish speciality food. *International Journal of Retail and Distribution Management* 35: 178–95. [CrossRef]

Chang, Shu-Chun, Pei-Yu Chou, and Lo Wen-Chien. 2014. Evaluation of satisfaction and repurchase intention in online food group-buying, using Taiwan as an example. *British Food Journal* 16: 44–61. [CrossRef]

Chen, Yen-Ting, and Tsung-Yu Chou. 2012. Exploring the continuance intentions of consumers for B2C online shopping: Perspectives of fairness and trust. *Online Information Review* 36: 104–25. [CrossRef]

Chen, Qimei, Sandra J. Clifford, and William D. Wells. 1999. Attitude toward the site II: New information. *Journal of Advertising Research* 42: 33–45. [CrossRef]

Chen, Zhao, Kwek Choon Ling, Guo XiaoYing, and Tang Chun Meng. 2012. Antecedents of online customer satisfaction in China. *International Business Management* 6: 168–75. [CrossRef]

Chin, Wynne W. 1998. Issues and opinions on structural equation modeling. *MIS Quarterly* 22: 7–16.

Chiu, Chao-Min, Chao-Sheng Chiu, and Hae-Ching Chang. 2007. Examining the integrated influence of fairness and quality on learners' satisfaction and Web-based learning continuance intention. *Information Systems Journal* 17: 271–87. [CrossRef]

Chou, Pao-Hua, Pi-Hsiang Li, Kuang-Ku Chen, and Menq-Jiun. 2010. Integrating web mining and neural network for personalized e-commerce automatic service. *Expert Systems with Applications* 37: 2898–910. [CrossRef]

Chou, Shihyu, Chi-Wen Chen, and Jiun-You Lin. 2015. Female online shoppers: Examining the mediating roles of e-satisfaction and e-trust on e-loyalty development. *Internet Research* 25: 542–61. [CrossRef]

Chung, Namho, Hyunae Lee, Seung Jae Lee, and Chulmo Koo. 2015. The influence of tourism website on tourists' behavior to determine destination selection: A case study of creative economy in Korea. *Technological Forecasting and Social Change* 96: 130–43. [CrossRef]

Constantinides, Efthymios, Carlota Lorenzo-Romero, and Miguel A. Gómez. 2010. Effects of web experience on consumer choice: A multicultural approach. *Internet Research* 20: 188–209. [CrossRef]

Dedeke, Adenekan. 2016. Travel web-site design: Information task-fit, service quality and purchase intention. *Tourism Management* 54: 541–54. [CrossRef]

Duman, Teoman, and Anna S. Mattila. 2005. The role of affective factors on perceived cruise vacation value. *Tourism Management* 26: 311–23. [CrossRef]

Eroglu, Segvin A., Karen A. Machleit, and Lenita M. Davis. 2003. Empirical testing of a model of online store atmospherics and shopper responses. *Psychology and Marketing* 20: 139–50. [CrossRef]

Filieri, Raffaele, Salma Alguezaui, and Fraser McLeay. 2015. Why do travelers trust TripAdvisor? Antecedents of trust towards consumer-generated media and its influence on recommendation adoption and word of mouth. *Tourism Management* 51: 174–85. [CrossRef]

Fornell, Claes, and David F. Larcker. 1981. Structural equation models with unobservable variables and measurement error. *Journal of Marketing Research* 18: 39–50. [CrossRef]

Gonçalves, Helia, Maria de Fátoma Salgueiro, and Paulo Rita. 2016. Online purchase determinants of loyalty: The mediating effect of satisfaction in tourism. *Journal of Retailing and Consumer Services* 30: 279–91. [CrossRef]

Grunert, Klaus G., and Kim Ramus. 2004. Consumers' willingness to buy food through the internet: A review of the literature and a model for future research. *British Food Journal* 107: 381–403. [CrossRef]

Ha, Sejin, and Leslie Stoel. 2012. Online apparel retailing: Roles of e-shopping quality and experiential e-shopping motives. *Journal of Service Management* 23: 197–215. [CrossRef]

Hair, Joseph F., William C. Black, Barry J. Babin, and Rolph Anderson. 2010. *Multivariate Data Analysis*. Upper Saddle River: Prentice Hall.

Hair, Joseph F., Markco Sarstedt, Christian Ringle, and Jeannette A. Mena. 2012. An assessment of the use of partial least squares structural equation modeling in marketing research. *Journal of the Academy of Marketing Science* 40: 414–33. [CrossRef]

Hair, Joseph F., Markco Sarstedt, Lukas Hopkins, and Volker G. Kuppelwieser. 2014. Partial least squares structural equation modeling (PLS-SEM): An emerging tool in business research. *European Business Review* 26: 106–21. [CrossRef]

Hair, Joseph F., G. Tomas M. Hult, Christian Ringle, and Markco Sarstedt. 2017. *A Primer on Partial Least Squares Structural Equation Modeling (PLS-SEM)*. Thousand Oaks: Sage.

Hansen, Torben. 2008. Consumer values, the theory of planned behaviour and online grocery shopping. *International Journal of Consumer Studies* 32: 128–13. [CrossRef]

Hausman, Angela V., and Jeffrey Sam Siekpe. 2009. The effect of web interface features on consumer online purchase intentions. *Journal of Business Research* 62: 5–13. [CrossRef]

Heng, Yan, Zhifeng Gao, Yuan Jiang, and Xuqi Chen. 2018. Exploring hidden factors behind online food shopping from Amazon reviews: A topic mining approach. *Journal of Retailing and Consumer Services* 42: 161–68. [CrossRef]

Henseler, Jörg, Christian M. Ringle, and Rudolf R. Sinkovics. 2009. The use of partial least squares path modeling in international marketing. *Advances in International Marketing* 20: 277–320.

Henseler, Jörg, Theo K. Dijkstra, Markco Sarstedt, Christian M. Ringle, Adamantios Diamantopoulos, Detmar W. Straub, David J. Ketchen, Joseph F. Hair, G. Tomas M. Hult, and Roger J. Calantone. 2014. Common beliefs and reality about PLS comments on Rönkkö and Evermann (2013). *Organizational Research Methods* 17: 182–209. [CrossRef]

Henseler, Jörg, Christian M. Ringle, and Markco Sarstedt. 2015. A new criterion for assessing discriminant validity in variance-based structural equation modelling. *Journal of the Academy of Marketing Science* 43: 115–35. [CrossRef]

Henseler, Jörg, Geoffrey Hubona, and Paulina A. Ray. 2016. Using PLS path modelling in new technology research: Updated guidelines. *Industrial Management and Data Systems* 116: 2–120. [CrossRef]

Hoffman, Donna L., and Thomas P. Novak. 1996. Marketing in hypermediacomputer-mediated environments: Conceptual foundations. *Journal of Marketing* 60: 50–68. [CrossRef]

Hsu, Chia-Lin, Kuo Chien Chang, and Mu-Chen Chen. 2012. The impact of website quality on customer satisfaction and purchase intention: Perceived playfulness and perceived flow as mediators. *Information Systems and e-Business Management* 10: 549–70. [CrossRef]

Hu, Li-tze, and Peter M. Bentler. 1999. Cutoff criteria for fit indexes in covariance structure analysis: Conventional criteria versus new alternatives. *Structural Equation Modeling* 6: 1–55. [CrossRef]

Huang, Lan-Ying, Ying-Jiun Hsieh, and Yen-Chun Jim Wu. 2014. Gratifications and social network service usage: The mediating role of online experience. *Information and Management* 51: 774–82. [CrossRef]

Hui, Michael K., and John E. G. Bateson. 1991. Perceived control and the effects of crowding and consumer choice on the service experience. *Journal of Consumer Research* 18: 174–84. [CrossRef]

Ilbery, Brian, David Watts, Sue Simpson, Andrew Gilg, and Jo Little. 2006. Mapping local foods: Evidence from two English regions. *British Food Journal* 18: 213–25. [CrossRef]

Ilsever, Joe, Dianne Cyr, and Michael Parent. 2007. Extending models of flow and e-loyalty. *Journal of Information Science and Technology* 4: 3–22.

Kabadayi, Sertan, and Reetika Gupta. 2011. Managing motives and design to influence web site revisits. *Journal of Research in Interactive Marketing* 5: 153–69. [CrossRef]

Khanal, Bhoj Raj, Christopher Gan, and Susanne Becken. 2014. Tourism inter-industry linkages in the Lao PDR economy: An input–output analysis. *Tourism Economics* 20: 171–94. [CrossRef]

Kim, Yeong Gug, and Gang Li. 2009. Customer satisfaction with and loyalty towards online travel products: A transaction cost economics perspective. *Tourism Economics* 15: 825–46. [CrossRef]

Kim, Myung-Ja, Namho Chung, and Choong-Ki Lee. 2011. The effect of perceived trust on electronic commerce: Shopping online for tourism products and services in South Korea. *Tourism Management* 32: 256–65. [CrossRef]

Koufaris, Marios. 2002. Applying the technology acceptance model and flow theory to online consumer behavior. *Information Systems Research* 13: 205–23. [CrossRef]

Ku, Edward C. S., and Chun-Der Chen. 2014. Cultivating travellers' revisit intention to e-tourism service: The moderating effect of website interactivity. *Behaviour and Information Technology* 34: 465–78. [CrossRef]

Lee, Seonjeong A., and Miyoung Jeong. 2012. Effects of e-servicescape on consumers' flow experiences. *Journal of Hospitality and Tourism Technology* 3: 47–59. [CrossRef]

Lee, Gwo-Guang, and Hsiu-Fen Lin. 2005. Customer perceptions of e-service quality in online shopping. *International Journal of Retail and Distribution Management* 33: 161–76. [CrossRef]

Lee, Kuan Huei, Jan Packer, and Noel Scott. 2015. Travel lifestyle preferences and destination activity choices of Slow Food members and non-members. *Tourism Management* 46: 1–10. [CrossRef]

Lin, Chinho, and Watcharee Lekhawipat. 2014. Factors affecting online repurchase intention. *Industrial Management and Data Systems* 114: 597–611. [CrossRef]

Liu, Chang, and Kirk P. Arnett. 2000. Exploring the factors associated with Web site success in the context of electronic commerce. *Information and Management* 38: 23–33. [CrossRef]

Luarn, Pin, and Hsin-Hui Lin. 2003. A customer loyalty model for e-serve context. *Journal of Electronic Commerce Research* 4: 156–67.

Manganari, Emmanouela E., George J. Siomkos, and Adam P. Vrechopoulos. 2009. Store atmosphere in web retailing. *European Journal of Marketing* 43: 1140–53. [CrossRef]

Manganari, Emmanouela E., George J. Siomkos, Irini D. Rigopoulou, and Adam P. Vrechopoulos. 2011. Virtual store layout effects on consumer behaviour: Applying an environmental psychology approach in the online travel industry. *Internet Research* 21: 326–46. [CrossRef]

Mathwick, Charla, and Edward Rigdon. 2004. Play, flow, and the online search experience. *Journal of Consumer Research* 31: 324–32. [CrossRef]

Megicks, Phil, Juliet Memer, and Robert J. Angell. 2012. Understanding local food shopping: Unpacking the ethical dimension. *Journal of Marketing Management* 28: 264–189. [CrossRef]

Mohamed, Norshidah, Ramlah Hussein, Nurul Hidayah, Ahmad Zamzuri, and Hanif Haghshenas. 2014. Insights into individual's online shopping continuance intention. *Industrial Management and Data Systems* 114: 1453–176. [CrossRef]

Mohd-Any, Amrul Asraf, Heidi Winklhofer, and Christine Ennew. 2015. Measuring users' value experience on a travel website (e-Value): What value is co-created by the user? *Journal of Travel Research* 54: 496–510. [CrossRef]

O'Cass, Aron, and Jamie Carlson. 2010. Examining the effects of website-induced flow in professional sporting team websites. *Internet Research* 20: 115–34. [CrossRef]

Ozkara, Behcet Yalin, Mujdat Ozmen, and Jong Woo Kim. 2017. Examining the effect of flow experience on online purchase: A novel approach to the flow theory based on hedonic and utilitarian value. *Journal of Retailing and Consumer Services* 37: 119–31. [CrossRef]

Pallud, Jessie, and Detmar W. Straub. 2014. Effective website design for experience-influenced environments: The case of high culture museums. *Information and Management* 51: 359–73. [CrossRef]

Pappas, Ilias O., Adamantia G. Pateli, Michail N. Giannakos, and Vassilious Chrissikopoulos. 2014. Moderating effects of online shopping experience on customer satisfaction and repurchase intentions. *International Journal of Retail & Distribution Management* 42: 187–204. [CrossRef]

Pearson, David, Joanna Henryks, Alex Trott, Philip Jones, Gavin Parker, David Dumaresq, and Rob Dyball. 2011. Local Food: Understanding consumer motivations in innovative retail formats. *British Food Journal* 113: 886–99. [CrossRef]

Pedraja, Marta, and M. Jesus Yagüe. 2004. Perceived quality and price: Their impact on the satisfaction of restaurant customers. *International Journal of Contemporary Hospitality Management* 16: 373–79. [CrossRef]

Pee, Loo Geok, James Jiang, and Gary Klein. 2018. Signaling effect of website usability on repurchase intention. *International Journal of Information Management* 39: 228–41. [CrossRef]

Pereira, Hélia G., Maria de Fátima Salgueiro, and Paulo Rita. 2016. Online purchase determinants of loyalty: The mediating effect of satisfaction in tourism. *Journal of Retailing and Consumer Services* 30: 279–91. [CrossRef]

Quevedo-Silva, Filipe, Otavio Freire, Dario de Oliveira, Marcelo Moll, Guiliana Isabella, and Luisa Brito. 2016. Intentions to purchase food through the internet: Developing and testing a model. *British Food Journal* 118: 572–87. [CrossRef]

Rezaei, Sajad, Faizan Ali, Muslim Amin, and Sreenivasan Jayashree. 2016. Online impulse buying of tourism products. *Journal of Hospitality and Tourism Technology* 7: 60–83. [CrossRef]

Rose, Susan, Moira Clark, Philip Samouel, and Neil Hair. 2012. Online customer experience in e-retailing: An empirical model of antecedents and outcomes. *Journal of Retailing* 88: 308–22. [CrossRef]

Rubio, Natalia, Javier Oubiña, and Nieves Villaseñor. 2014. Brand awareness–Brand quality inference and consumer's risk perception in store brands of food products. *Food Quality and Preference* 32: 289–98. [CrossRef]

Sánchez-García, Isabel, Rik Pieters, Marcel Zeelenberg, and Enrique Bigné. 2012. When satisfied consumers do not return: Variety seeking's effect on short- and long-term intentions. *Psychology and Marketing* 29: 15–24. [CrossRef]

San-Martín, Héctor, and Ángel Herrero. 2012. Influence of the user's psychological factors on the online purchase intention in rural tourism: Integrating innovativeness to the UTAUT framework. *Tourism Management* 33: 341–50. [CrossRef]

San-Martín, Sonia, Jana Prodanova, and Nadia Jiménez. 2012. The impact of age in the generation of satisfaction and WOM in mobile shopping. *Journal of Retailing and Consumer Services* 23: 1–8. [CrossRef]

Seyfang, Gill. 2008. Avoiding Asda? Exploring consumer motivations in local organic food networks. *Local Environment* 13: 187–201. [CrossRef]

Sireci, Stephen G., Yongwei Yang, James Harter, and Eldin J. Ehrlich. 2006. Evaluating guidelines for test adaptations: A methodological analysis of transalation quality. *Journal of Cross-Cultural Psychology* 37: 557–67. [CrossRef]

Sims, Rebecca. 2009. Food, place and authenticity: Local food and the sustainable tourism experience. *Journal of Sustainable Tourism* 17: 321–36. [CrossRef]

Sirdeshmukh, Deepak, Norita B. Ahmad, M. Sajid Khan, and Nicholas J. Ashill. 2018. Drivers of user loyalty intention and commitment to a search engine: An exploratory study. *Journal of Retailing and Consumer Services* 44: 71–81. [CrossRef]

Smith, Amy K., and Ruth N. Bolton. 2002. The effect of customer's emotional responses to service failures on their recovery effort evaluations and satisfaction judgment. *Journal of the Academy of Marketing Science* 30: 5–23. [CrossRef]

Teo, Thompson, Shirish Srivastava, and Li Jiang. 2008. Trust and electronic government success: An empirical study. *Journal of Management Information Systems* 25: 99–132. [CrossRef]

Tobler, Christina, Vivianne H. M. Visschers, and Michael Siegrist. 2011. Eating green. Consumers' willingness to adopt ecological food consumption behaviors. *Appetite* 57: 674–82. [CrossRef] [PubMed]

Venkatesh, Viswanath. 2000. Determinants of perceived ease of use: Integrating control, intrinsic motivation, and emotion into the technology acceptance model. *Information Systems Research* 11: 342–65. [CrossRef]

Wang, Liang, Rob Law, Basak Denizci, Kam Hung, and Davis Ka Chio Fong. 2015. Impact of hotel website quality on online booking intentions: ETrust as a mediator. *International Journal of Hospitality Management* 47: 108–15. [CrossRef]

Wen, Chao, Victor Prybutok, and Chenyan Xu. 2011. An integrated model for customer online repurchase intention. *Journal of Computer Information Systems* 52: 14–23. [CrossRef]

Wolfinbarger, Mary, and Mary C. Gilly. 2003. Etailq: Dimensionalizing, measuring and predicting etail quality. *Journal of Retailing* 79: 183–98. [CrossRef]

Wu, Ing-Long, Kuei-Wan Chen, and Mai-Lun Chiu. 2016. Defining key drivers of online impulse purchasing: A perspective of both impulse shoppers and system users. *International Journal of Information Management* 36: 284–96. [CrossRef]

Yen, Chia-Hiu, and Hsi-Peng Lu. 2008. Factors influencing online auction repurchase intention. *Internet Research* 18: 7–25. [CrossRef]

Yoo, Jungmin, and Minjung Park. 2016. The effects of e-mass customization on consumer perceived value, satisfaction, and loyalty toward luxury brands. *Journal of Business Research* 69: 5775–84. [CrossRef]

Zeithaml, Valane, Leonard Berry, and Ananthanarayanan Parasuraman. 1996. The behavioral consequences of service quality. *Journal of Marketing* 60: 31–46. [CrossRef]

Zepeda, Lydia, and David Deal. 2009. Organic and local food consumer behaviour: Alphabet theory. *International Journal of Consumer Studies* 33: 697–705. [CrossRef]

Zepeda, Lydia, and Jinghan Li. 2006. Who buys local food? *Journal of Food Distribution Research* 37: 385–94. [CrossRef]

Zhao, Ling, and Yaobin Lu. 2012. Enhancing perceived interactivity through network externalities: An empirical study on micro-blogging service satisfaction and continuance intention. *Decision Support Systems* 53: 825–34. [CrossRef]

© 2018 by the authors. Licensee MDPI, Basel, Switzerland. This article is an open access article distributed under the terms and conditions of the Creative Commons Attribution (CC BY) license (http://creativecommons.org/licenses/by/4.0/).

Article

Do Brands Matter in Unlisted Firms? An Empirical Study of the Association between Brand Equity and Financial Performance

Anne Schmitz * and Nieves Villaseñor-Román

Marketing Department, Autónoma University of Madrid, 28049 Madrid, Spain; nieves.villasenor@uam.es
* Correspondence: anne.schmitz@uam.es

Received: 5 September 2018; Accepted: 20 October 2018; Published: 25 October 2018

Abstract: In spite of the importance of the brand management in marketing studies and practice, there is a scarcity of prior research on the links between brand equity and financial performance, particularly in unlisted (unquoted) firms. The study contributes to prior research along a number of dimensions. It provides evidence on the relevance of brands for unlisted firms of several industries, by showing that brand equity is associated with financial performance even in non-quoted firms without world-recognized brands. Second, the study analyzes the association between brands and accounting-based measures of performance, across different windows and financial indicators. Finally, the evidence on earnings persistence is particularly relevant, as it potentially sheds light on the existing debate on the association between brand equity and stock markets. To the extent that firms with greater brand equity have more persistent earnings, current earnings contain greater information about future earnings, which show the relevance of brand management in the strategic planning of unlisted firms.

Keywords: brand equity; financial performance; unlisted firms; earnings

1. Introduction

Brands differentiate firms from the competition. The conceptualizations of consumer-based brand equity have mainly derived from cognitive psychology and information economics (Rahman et al. 2018). The dominant stream of research has been grounded in cognitive psychology, focusing on memory structure (Christodoulides and De Chernatony 2010). Aaker (1991) identified the conceptual dimensions of brand equity as brand awareness, brand associations, perceived quality, brand loyalty, and other proprietary brand assets such as patents, trademarks and channel relationships. The former four dimensions of brand equity represent consumer perceptions and reactions to the brand, while proprietary brand assets are not pertinent to consumer-based brand equity. Keller (1993) defined the consumer-based brand equity as 'the differential effect of brand knowledge on consumer response to the marketing of the brand' and brand knowledge is a key antecedent of customer based brand equity. It is in turn conceptualized as a brand node in memory to which a variety of associations have been linked. Brand knowledge is then decomposed into two separate constructs: brand awareness and brand image (associations).

From the perspective of cognitive psychology, the customer based brand equity occurs when consumers hold some favorable, strong, and unique brand associations in memory, which in turn leads to incremental utility or valued added. Thus, investing in brand equity is expected to lead to differential consumer response that may positively affect firm value (through greater consumer retention, price tolerance, or word-of-mouth recommendations, for example).

While Aaker's brand equity model has been more frequently adopted in existing research, particularly empirical studies (Yoo and Donthu 2001), two research gaps remain unexplored in his model. First, the interrelationships between the four brand components are not considered. Second, Aaker's model does not integrate the effectiveness of marketing programs into the consumer-based brand equity concept (Keller and Lehmann 2006). In his customer-based brand equity definition, Keller highlights the importance of marketing programs in linking consumers' awareness, desired thoughts, feelings, perceptions, and opinions to a brand (Huang and Cai 2015). In addition, while Aaker's model places the four dimensions at the same level, Keller's customer-based customer equity stated that consumers' knowledge of a brand including awareness and perceptions will result in their attitudes and behaviors favorable to that brand. Keller argued that customer-based customer equity can largely be captured by four blocks that form a hierarchy pyramid, which are from the bottom (the lowest level) to the top (the highest level) as follows: brand identity, brand meaning, brand responses and brand relationships (Keller 2002).

Despite this appealing theoretical notion, a number of recent studies have tested the links between brand equity (and its components) and firm value, failing to provide a unifying body of evidence on this issue (Madden et al. 2006; Rego et al. 2009; Johansson et al. 2012; Larkin 2013; Narteh 2018; Kim et al. 2018).[1]

As noted in Ittner et al. (2009), a potential weakness of this prior work is that it hinges crucially on the often untested assumption that brand equity leads to enhanced firm performance, and thus much is still not known about the short- and long-window consequences of enhanced brand equity. Furthermore, Johansson et al. (2012) find that the strength of the relationship between brand equity and financial performance differs according to the measure applied and how each captures the equity.[2] Indeed, there is a scarcity of prior research on the links between brand equity and financial performance, particularly in unlisted firms, even though there is some preliminary research focused on small and medium-sized enterprises (Anees-ur-Rehman et al. 2018).

This lack of evidence is potentially explained because prior literature on brand equity and the determinants of performance indicators have developed separately, with the possible exception of a limited number of accounting-based studies. This prior research in accounting attempts to clarify whether brand names are economic assets and should therefore be recognized in the balance sheet,[3] that is, whether they are associated with firm performance. In this paper, we build on this prior research in accounting that suggests that brands are intangible assets that influence a firm's value and results (e.g., Barth et al. 1998) and study the association between brand equity and financial performance. As noted above, understanding how precisely brand equity impacts on firm performance is particularly relevant for unlisted firms. These firms represent a unique challenge because of data availability issues, but also a perfect setting for a test of brand equity and firm performance.

Tests conducted on unlisted firms do not suffer from the confounding effects that are pervasive in market-based research, particularly when studying intangible assets, such as brand equity (Ohlson 1998; Ittner et al. 2009). Our setting thus allows us to provide new evidence that permits understanding the interrelationships between brand equity and financial indicators. This is a key to better distributing marketing efforts towards the construction of a brand equity that serves to optimize firm profitability. In addition, by focusing on unlisted firms we can explore brand equity in firms that do not have worldwide recognized brands (such as those surveyed by Interbrand, Brand Z, or Brand Asset Valuator and generally analyzed in prior research).

If investment in brand equity leads to greater consumer retention, inelasticity to price increases, and lower volatility of sales, it is expected that it will lead to greater firm profitability, and greater

---

[1] In particular, the study of the links between customer satisfaction and stock market pricing has attracted much controversy, providing mixed views and conflicting evidence (see, e.g., Aksoy et al. 2008; Ittner et al. 2009; Jacobson and Mizik 2009; Tuli and Bharadwaj 2009).
[2] The authors work with listed companies and two brand equity proprietary metrics models, Interbrand and EquiTrend.
[3] By definition, this implies that brand equity is associated with earnings. An asset is a resource controlled by the entity as a result of past events and from which future economic benefits are expected to flow (IASB International Accounting Standards Board).

earnings persistence. We study if this is the case by looking at the association between brand equity and financial performance for a sample of Spanish unlisted firms.

Brand equity is measured from perspectives of Aaker (1991) and Keller (1993), both models have elements in common but are different in the building of customer-based customer equity. In our main tests, we use the models of Ittner and Larcker (1998) and Ittner et al. (2009) to study the association between financial performance as measured by a number of accounting-based measures and brand equity. This study represents progress in the research on the positive effects of brand equity in the strategic planning and financial performance of unlisted firms.

The remainder of the paper is structured as follows. The next section reviews the literature and presents our predictions. Another section details the methods and presents the results. Finally, the last section concludes.

2. Literature Review and Hypotheses Development

The debate on whether marketing investments constitute intangible assets and how to value them has been present in the accounting literature for decades (e.g., Abdel-Khalik 1975; Hirschey and Weygandt 1985) and in the marketing literature more recently (e.g., Madden et al. 2006; Rego et al. 2009; Johansson et al. 2012). In the last few years, in the multidisciplinary literature calls for greater emphasis on the reporting and disclosure of non-financial measures, such as on customer satisfaction, have been motivated by the widespread perception that marketing efforts are key drivers of firm value (Srinivasan and Hanssens 2009; Livne et al. 2011).

In particular, recent research emphasizes the importance of brand equity. The concept of brand equity has its origins in cognitive psychology (Aaker 1991, 1996; Keller 1993, 2002) as a measure of the long-term results achieved by the investment made in the creation and strengthening of brands. Brand equity represents the consumers' perceptions and attitudes towards it. As noted in Campo et al. (2013), perceptions are, in turn, a function both of organic sources, such as word-of-mouth recommendations, and of induced sources, like the brand positioning created by the firm and its marketing communication. Prior literature indicates that brand equity is a good measure of the effectiveness of brand investments. In particular, Keller (2003) interprets brand equity as a bridge between the marketing efforts dedicated in the past to the creation of a brand and their future results.

Although definitions of brands differ, the underlying notion is that a brand is a distinctive name with which consumers have a high level of awareness and a willingness to pay either higher than otherwise average prices or make higher than otherwise purchase frequency. Some of the benefits of a brand name would be: greater loyalty, less vulnerability to competitive marketing actions and economic crises, larger margins, less (more) elastic response to price increases (decreases), greater trade cooperation and support, increased marketing communication effectiveness, or greater supply chain power.

As argued in Barth et al. (1998), the net effect of all these positive consequences would be that brand equity provides a firm with a higher level of operating earnings over time (relative to otherwise unbranded firms). However, not all expenses incurred in promoting a brand result in brand equity. Advertising efforts can misfire with dire consequences, and it is less obvious what the benefits of brand equity are in smaller, unlisted firms, which do not have world-renowned brands, bringing into question how brand equity increases operating performance and value for these firms.

Recent research in marketing has started to address related issues, by studying the links between marketing and firm value (Srinivasan and Hanssens 2009), and more specifically, between brand equity and stock performance. For example, brand equity has been introduced as a mediator between different marketing variables (corporate social responsibility) and financial performance (Malik and Kanwal 2018). However, despite some evidence on the positive effect of brand equity on a firm's market performance and risk (Madden et al. 2006; Rego et al. 2009), these prior studies generally provide mixed results and inconclusive evidence on the links between brand equity and financial measures. Although the studies that indicate a positive association between brand equity and stock returns or profit efficiency are important for understanding the link between branding and shareholder value, they do not unequivocally demonstrate how precisely branding affects performance directly, thereby leading to positive market consequences. Furthermore, results also show considerable heterogeneity across industries (Mizik and Pavlov 2017).

We expect that brand equity improves financial performance by increasing the loyalty of existing customers, reducing price elasticities, lowering marketing costs thorough positive word-of-mouth, enhancing firm reputation and lowering transaction costs. Thus, we expect that brand equity leads to greater consumer satisfaction, engagement and loyalty, and thus, to smoother, more predictable streams of earnings. While not directly looking at brand equity, but studying the influence of marketing efforts on profitability, prior research by Krasnikov et al. (2009) is consistent with the view that marketing efforts can affect profitability. These authors show that firms that deploy consumer relationship management have greater profit efficiency.

Given the above discussion, we test the following hypothesis:

Hypothesis 1 (H1). *Brand equity is positively associated with firm financial performance in unlisted firms.*

This hypothesis is tested using two different indicators of customer-based customer equity. The first indicator based on the four dimensions of Aaker (1991) and the second indicator based on the approach of Keller (1993). This is to establish whether the relationship between customer-based customer equity and financial performance is independent or not of the indicators used to measure brand equity.

3. Methods and Data

We study the association between brand equity and firm performance, and also whether firms that invest more in brand equity benefit from smoother earnings streams, by looking at earnings persistence. In this section, we first describe our proxy of brand equity, then we explain the models used to test our hypotheses.

3.1. Measuring Brand Equity

There are two proxies used to measure customer-based customer equity. Both are measured with a set of items from a survey of marketing managers of Spanish service firms. The items come from previously validated scales. All items are measured using a Likert scale of 11 points from 0 (totally disagree) to 10 (totally agree). Specifically, the items are: awareness (in its market, its brands are well known); image (among their clients, their brand image is very good); perceived quality (among their customers, the perceived quality of their brand is very good); and loyalty (their customers are very loyal to their brand).

The first proxy is a variable that derives from the scale of Aaker (1991), which is calculated as an average score of items that reflect the four components of the concept: awareness, image, perceived quality, and loyalty. The second proxy is based on the model of Keller (1993), which is calculated as an average score of items that reflect the two main components of the knowledge concept: awareness and image.

3.2. Association between Brand Equity, Firm Performance and Earnings Persistence

We predict that firms that invest in brand equity will benefit from better performance. Prior work by Johansson et al. (2012) provides evidence consistent with this claim, although their evidence is indirect and focuses only on quoted firms. To ascertain the association between brand equity and firm performance, we run the following simple model, based on the work of Ittner and Larcker (1998) and Ittner et al. (2009):

$$Perfomance = \alpha + \beta \text{ Brand Equity} + \delta \text{ Controls} + \varepsilon \quad (1)$$

where, Performance is a proxy of firm performance, defined as accounting return-on-assets measured as the decile rank of earnings before interest and tax expenses scales by lagged assets. It is also calculated a proxy of Aaker's brand equity and a proxy of Keller's brand equity. In sensitivity analyses we also use as indicators of brand equity its individual components as well as an average score of quality and loyalty. Finally, controls is a vector of control variables derived from Ittner and Larcker (1998) and Ittner et al. (2009) that may affect financial performance. In particular, in our first specification, we control for firm size, measured as the natural logarithm of total assets; age, measured as the number of years since the firm was first incorporated; and leverage as the ratio of total liabilities to total assets.

If brand equity is positively associated with enhanced firm performance, we expect that β will be significantly positive in model (1), indicating that those firms that invest more in brand equity have greater performance as measured by firm profitability.

3.3. Sample Selection and Data

To conduct our analysis we base our work on a sample of Spanish unquoted service firms that responded to a questionnaire on brand equity. Our brand equity proxies come from this questionnaire, which is described in detail in the section above. The 95% of firms of the sample declare that their corporate brand contributes to improve the firm value but only the 39.8% of firms measure some components of the customer-based customer equity and the 36% of firms affirm to assess the economic or monetary value of their corporate brand.

Accounting data comes from Orbis. The sample consisted of 201 firms, including companies with more than 50 employees (see Table 1).

Table 1. Population and sample.

Industries	Number of Companies	% of Companies	Average Operating Incomes (Thousands of Euros Per Year)	Average Number of Employees	Number of Companies in the Sample	Percentage of Companies in the Sample
Accommodation and food service activities	1166	20.30	11,709.95	198	61	30.35
Administrative and support service activities	513	8.93	40,707.47	498	14	6.97
Arts, entertainment and recreation	104	1.81	15,906.07	141	4	1.99
Education	175	3.05	7442.72	132	9	4.48
Financial and insurance activities	181	3.15	106,268.56	187	5	2.49
Information and communication	714	12.43	103,321.54	360	16	7.96
Professional, scientific and technical activities	1167	20.31	26,354.54	212	41	20.40
Real estate activities	73	1.27	56,323.79	130	3	1.49
Retail trade, except of motor vehicles and motorcycles	214	3.72	296,873.21	1470	8	3.98
Supplies, sewerage, waste management and remediation activities	210	3.66	149,430.98	367	4	1.99
Transportation and storage	1049	18.26	48,112.45	309	31	15.42
Other services	179	3.12	7605.33	170	5	2.49

For this sample, we collect all financial data. We require the availability of at least three years of consecutive data to calculate earnings persistence measures (from t-2 to t). This results in a final sample of 182 firms, and 1338 firm-year observations, albeit sample sizes change slightly in some of our tests.

Table 2 provides descriptive statistics of the main variables of interest. We provide descriptive statistics for both the separate elements and two average scores; Aaker's brand equity and Keller's brand equity. We also present evidence on an average score of brand equity, which aggregate perceived quality and loyalty. Table 2 also contains descriptive evidence on the financial proxies of interest and controls. The sample is composed of healthy firms. The mean firm is profitable, with a mean (median) ROA of 0.04 (0.04), has low leverage and an age of 19 years. The evidence reported in Table 2 indicates that there are a number of extreme values in the distribution of ROA and validates the use of a decile rank measure to assess financial performance.

Table 2. Descriptive evidence.

	Obs.	Min.	Quartile1	Mean	Median	Std.	Quartile3	Max.
Awareness	1338	2.0	6.0	7.4	8.0	1.7	8.0	10
Image	1338	4.0	7.0	7.8	8.0	1.3	9.0	10
Quality	1338	5.0	7.0	7.9	8.0	1.1	9.0	10
Loyalty	1338	3.0	6.0	7.3	7.0	1.4	8.0	10
A's BE	1338	4.5	6.8	7.6	7.5	1.1	8.5	10
Keller's BE	1338	3.5	6.5	7.6	7.5	1.3	8.5	10
Q+L quaEQ_QL	1338	5.0	7.0	7.6	7.5	1.1	8.5	10
IC	1338	0.0	3.3	4.7	4.7	1.9	6.0	9.3
ROA	1237	−1.68	0.00	0.04	0.04	0.15	0.08	0.66
ROA_{t-1}	1237	−1.27	0.00	0.05	0.04	0.14	0.09	0.66
P	1237	1.00	3.00	5.01	5.00	2.77	7.00	10.00
Age	1237	1	10	19	17	16	24	130
Size	1237	0.10	8.26	9.10	9.06	1.30	9.83	16.10
Leverage	1237	0.00	0.01	0.17	0.09	0.21	0.27	1.21

Notes: BE: Brand Equity. Q+L: Brand Equity as average of quality and loyalty. IC: Composite measure of industry competition. The composite measure of industry competition is obtained from the survey. ROA is earnings before interest and tax expenses scaled by lagged assets. A's BE: Aaker's brand equity. P: Perform is a decile rank transformation of ROA. Age is the number of years since the firm was incorporated. Size is the natural logarithm of firm total sales. Leverage is the ratio of firm total liabilities to total assets. Obs.: Observations. Min.: Minimum. Std.: Standard Deviation. Max.: Maximum.

Table 3 contains the correlation matrix. As expected, all components of brand equity are positively associated with firm performance, with all correlations being statistically significant. Also, as expected, there are high correlations between the individual components of brand equity and between the individual components and the aggregate measure (Aaker's brand equity). The strongest individual correlation is between quality and perform (correlation = 0.150, p-value $<$ 0.01). ROA is highly correlated to lagged ROA, indicating a high persistence of financial performance, consistent with the arguments in Ittner et al. (2009). All other correlations are as expected, and below 0.05. Indeed, the highest one is between age and size (correlation = 0.324, p-value $<$ 0.01), which is as expected, as with age, firms tend to grown larger.

Table 3. Correlation matrix.

	P	A	I	Q	L	A's BE	IC	P_{-1}	Age	Size
Awareness	0.079									
	0.01									
Image	0.101	0.624								
	0.00	0.00								
Quality	0.150	0.531	0.729							
	0.00	0.00	0.00							
Loyalty	0.096	0.547	0.580	0.496						
	0.00	0.00	0.00	0.00						
Aaker's BE	0.124	0.843	0.874	0.803	0.793					
	0.00	0.00	0.00	0.00	0.00					
IC	0.119	0.017	−0.045	0.081	0.105	0.045				
	0.00	0.54	0.11	0.00	0.00	0.12				

Table 3. Cont.

	P	A	I	Q	L	A's BE	IC	P.₁	Age	Size
ROA$_{t-1}$	0.554	0.047	0.049	0.103	0.068	0.077	0.057			
	0.00	0.10	0.09	0.00	0.02	0.01	0.04			
Age	−0.111	0.139	0.127	0.150	0.048	0.139	0.024	−0.052		
	0.00	0.00	0.00	0.00	0.09	0.00	0.40	0.07		
Size	0.008	0.126	0.056	0.095	0.027	0.094	0.136	0.016	0.324	
	0.77	0.00	0.05	0.00	0.34	0.00	0.00	0.58	0.00	
Leverage	−0.225	−0.098	−0.074	−0.101	−0.157	−0.130	−0.050	−0.131	0.000	−0.094
	0.00	0.00	0.01	0.00	0.00	0.00	0.08	0.00	0.99	0.00

Notes: See Table 2 for variable definitions. P: Perform. A: Awareness. I: Image. Q: Quality. L: Loyalty. A's BE: Aaker's brand equity.

4. Results

4.1. Association between Brand Equity and Financial Performance

In our main tests, we regress performance on measures of brand equity and controls. Table 4 reports results of running model (1) using the individual components of brand equity first, and then, the aggregate scores. We run model (1) using data-panel techniques and clustering the standard errors both at the firm and year level, following Petersen (2009). This is the same method used in Ittner et al. (2009) to correct for both serial and cross-sectional dependence. Considering the brand equity components used, perceived quality is significant, which is consistent with the evidence reported in the correlation table (coefficient = 0.405, p-value < 0.01 for quality). Between the two aggregate scores, Aaker's brand equity presents highly significant results, while hardly any of Keller's brand equity reaches an acceptable level of significance. Herein, we conduct all analyzes with the scale of Aaker's brand equity model.

Table 4. Relation between brand equity (and components) and performance.

	Coeff / t-stat	Coeff / t-stat	Coeff / t-stat	Coeff / t-stat	Coeff / t-stat	Coeff / t-stat	Coeff / t-stat
Intercept	3.865 *** / 4.07	3.038 *** / 2.78	4.416 *** / 5.52	4.416 *** / 5.52	3.825 *** / 4.16	2.292 *** / 2.18	3.981 *** / 4.54
Aaker's brand equity	0.323 ** / 2.19						
Keller's brand equity		0.215 / 1.68					
BE as average of quality and loyalty			0.381 ** / 2.59				
Awareness				0.146 / 1.33			
Image					0.214 / 1.80		
Quality						0.405 *** / 2.99	
Loyalty							0.206 / 1.68
Observations	1338	1338	1338	1338	1338	1338	1338
R-square	0.02	0.01	0.01	0.01	0.01	0.02	0.01

Notes: Coeff. t-stat: t-statistic coefficient. BE: brand equity. ***, and ** indicate coefficients are significant at the 1% and 5%.

Table 5 presents results from our main tests. The evidence is presented in four columns. The first column incorporates industry competition as an additional control, the second column contains the full model, as based on Ittner and Larcker (1998), where we also incorporate age, size and leverage as controls for firm performance. Finally, we run two additional variations of the model, including lagged performance and industry dummies. As before, all standard errors are clustered at the firm and year level. Our main variable of interest is Aaker's brand equity. If firms that have greater brand equity have superior financial performance, we predict Aaker's brand equity to be significantly positive.

The results from Table 4 Panel B confirm this intuition. Aaker's brand equity is consistently positive and significant across all model specifications. The last two specifications contain lagged performance as a control. As predicted, the coefficient on this variable is positive and significant, confirming the importance of controlling for prior year performance, and consistent with prior research that indicates that performance is very persistent (see, e.g., Penman 1992). In the last specification, where we include industry dummies, R-square rises to 0.404, indicating an adequate fit of the model. Also note that, in this model, industry competition is no longer significant, validating its use as a control for differences across industries. Overall, the results reported in Panels A and B of Table 4 strongly indicate a positive association between brand equity and financial performance, as measured by firm return on assets.

Table 5. Brand equity and performance, and controls.

	Coeff t-stat	Coeff t-stat	Coeff t-stat	Coeff t-stat
Intercept	2.381 **	3.401 **	3.587 ***	2.865 ***
	2.22	2.32	3.22	2.95
Aaker's brand equity	0.298 **	0.276 **	0.186 **	0.192 **
	2.11	2.00	1.96	2.08
Industry competition	0.169 **	0.157 **	0.119 **	0.030
	2.39	2.19	2.47	0.58
Age		−0.024 **	−0.017 **	−0.008
		−2.52	−2.42	−1.17
Size		0.015	0.010	−0.001
		0.11	0.10	−0.01
Leverage		−2.812 ***	−2.010 ***	−1.321 ***
		−4.46	−3.86	−2.93
ROA_{t-1}			10.28 ***	9.63 ***
			6.88	7.88
Industry dummies				Included
Observations	1237	1237	1237	1237
R-square	0.03	0.09	0.35	0.40

Notes: ***, and ** indicate coefficients are significant at the 1% and 5% or better levels, using a two-tail test. See Table 1 for variable definitions. Coeff. t-stat.: t-statistic coefficient.

4.2. Sensitivity Analyses

To check the robustness of our findings, we conduct a number of sensitivity analyses. First of all, we repeat our main analyses focusing on an alternative performance indicator: earnings persistence. Finally, we use alternative definitions of performance. In this section, we explain each of these robustness checks in turn.

4.3. Analysis of Earnings Persistence

To further understand how brand equity affects financial performance, we look at the association between brand equity and earnings persistence. As argued in Frankel and Litov (2009), understanding the factors that drive earnings persistence is of practical importance, since such knowledge is key for earnings prediction and thus, for equity valuation. To test whether brand equity is one such factor, we modify the simple method described in Frankel and Litov (2009) and Dichev and Tang (2009) and regress current earnings on 1-year lagged earnings and brand equity, as follows:

$$Performance_t = \alpha + \beta 1\ ROA_{t-1} + \beta 2\ \text{Aaker's brand equity} + \beta 3\ ROA_{t-1} * \text{Aaker's brand equity} + \varepsilon_t \quad (2)$$

where ROA is defined as earnings before interest and tax expenses deflated by lagged total assets and Aaker's brand equity has already been defined. The coefficient of interest in model (2) is β3 which captures the incremental persistence of earnings in firms that invest in brand equity. This coefficient is expected to be significantly positive, indicating that firms that invest in brand equity have more persistent earnings streams. Given our prior prediction, we expect β2 will be also positive, indicating that, overall, greater investment in brand equity is associated with greater firm performance. As additional specifications, we add control variables to model (2) following prior research, and consistent with model (1) above. The results from this analysis are reported in Table 6.

Table 6. Sensitivity analyses. Brand equity and persistence of performance.

	Coeff t-stat	Coeff t-stat	Coeff t-stat
Intercept	4.583 *** 4.85	4.670 *** 3.64	4.042 *** 3.67
Aaker's brand equity	0.032 0.26	0.029 0.24	0.012 0.10
ROA_{t-1}	−13.219 −1.55	−11.291 −1.43	−11.442 0.118
Aaker's brand equity*ROA_{t-1}	3.378 *** 3.14	3.035 *** 3.03	2.954 *** 3.14
Industry Competition		0.101 ** 2.43	0.021 0.47
Age		−0.015 ** −2.28	−0.007 −1.04
Size		0.014 0.14	0.01 0.15
Leverage		−1.943 *** −4.01	−1.362 *** −3.13
Industry dummies			Included
Observations	1237	1237	1237
R-square	0.34	0.37	0.41

Note: ***, and ** indicate coefficients are significant at the 1% and 5% or better levels.

We report three specifications, one with only the main variables of interest, one with controls, and a final one with industry dummies. As before, we use the panel data estimation technique, clustering the standard errors at the firm and year levels. Our main coefficient of interest is β3 that captures the incremental persistence of earnings in firms that have greater brand equity. If brand equity leads to greater earnings persistence, this coefficient is expected to be significantly positive. The results from this test confirm that brand equity is positively associated with earnings persistence. The interaction is significantly positive across all three specifications (coefficient = 3.378, p-value < 0.01 in column 1, coefficient = 3.035, p-value < 0.01 in column 2, and coefficient = 2.954, p-value < 0.01 in column 3).

4.4. Alternative Definition of Performance

In our final sensitivity analysis, we repeat our main analyses using three alternative definitions of performance, the first one is future profitability (defined as before, but measured in t + 1), and the second and third ones are measures of profitability incorporated after interest charges (profit before tax) and bottom line earnings (net income). Results from this test are reported on Table 7 and are consistent with our previous finding, confirming the positive association between brand equity and financial performance.

Table 7. Sensitivity analyses. Alternative definitions of performance.

	Perform1	Perform2	Perform3
	Coeff t-stat	Coeff t-stat	Coeff t-stat
Intercept	3.494 *** 3.51	3.570 *** 4.15	4.067 *** 4.55
Aaker's brand equity	0.227 ** 1.91	0.185 ** 1.92	0.158 1.74
Industry Competition	0.030 0.53	0.045 0.88	0.037 0.66
Age	−0.010 −1.23	−0.011 −1.39	−0.014 −1.55
Size	−0.049 −0.45	0.031 0.30	0.036 0.36
Leverage	−1.130 *** −2.97	−2.465 *** −4.07	−2.777 *** −5.16
ROA_{t-1}	6.956 *** 7.07	7.802 *** 8.01	8.022 *** 4.13
Industry dummies	Included	Included	Included
Observations	1081	1237	1236
R-square	0.33	0.44	0.40

Notes: ***, and ** indicate coefficients are significant at the 1% and 5% or better levels, using a two-tail test. See Table 1 for variable definitions. Coeff. t-stat.: t-statistic coefficient.

5. Discussion

We study the association between brand equity and financial performance in unlisted (non-quoted) firms. This association has not been explored in detail in prior work, albeit some recent research indicates that a positive association exists between brand equity and measures of market value and performance of the listed firms and with global strong brands. Our results indicate that unlisted firms that invest more in brand equity have stronger financial performance, more earnings persistence and greater future profitability. This is consistent with brand equity serving to create value for firms and with the importance of brand equity in the strategic planning of unlisted firms.

We show that brand equity is strongly and positively associated with financial performance, both over long and short windows. The positive relationship between brand equity and financial performance is stronger and more significant when measured with the model of Aaker (1991) than when modeled of Keller (1993). Our results indicate that, considering the four components of brand equity, it is quality that shows the strongest association with financial performance. These results are robust to the inclusion of a number of additional control variables and alternative definitions of financial performance. We also show that firms with greater equity show greater earnings persistence, as measured using models consistent with Frankel and Litov (2009) and Dichev and Tang (2009).

Our study contributes to prior research along a number of dimensions. First, it provides evidence on the relevance of brands for unlisted firms, by showing that brand equity is associated with financial performance even in firms that are not quoted and do not have world-recognized brands. Moreover, this association is stronger when the brand equity component of perceived quality is included. In particular, we find that the quality component is mainly related to these positive economic consequences. Second, we contribute to the literature that links brand equity and firm value, by providing evidence on the association between brands and accounting-based measures of performance, across different windows and financial indicators. Finally, the evidence on earnings persistence is particularly relevant, as it potentially sheds light on the existing debate on the association between brand equity and stock markets. To the extent that firms with greater brand equity have more persistent earnings, current earnings contain greater information about future earnings, thus potentially leading to stronger association between brand measures and market returns. In addition, the results add to the growing literature in accounting on the determinants of earnings volatility and earnings predictability. This is relevant as a number of prior studies hinge on the prediction of earnings. Valuation research typically uses projections of earnings to derive estimates of firm and equity value. These studies are concerned with understanding what firm characteristics may help in the projection of future fundamentals and, particularly, of future earnings (Dichev and Tang 2009). Analysts and other market participants are continuously looking for information that may help them more accurately predict earnings. The results reported in this paper would suggest that brands are a key component of this information.

Author Contributions: A.S. wrote part of the paper and N.V.-R. has participated in the design of the research. All authors read and approved the final manuscript.

Funding: Financial support of the project ECO2015-69103-R.

Acknowledgments: The authors acknowledge the contribution of Beatriz García-Osma in relation to the data analysis and the research design.

Conflicts of Interest: The authors declare no conflict of interest.

References

Aaker, David A. 1991. *Managing Brand Equity*. New York: The Free Press.
Aaker, David A. 1996. *Building Strong Brands*. New York: The Free Press.
Abdel-Khalik, A. Rashad. 1975. Advertising effectiveness and accounting policy. *The Accounting Review* 50: 657–70.
Aksoy, Lerzan, Bruce Cooil, Christopher Groening, and Timothy L. Keiningham. 2008. The long-term stock market valuation of customer satisfaction. *Journal of Marketing* 72: 105–22. [CrossRef]
Anees-ur-Rehman, Muhammad, Ho Yin Wong, Parves Sultan, and Bill Merrilees. 2018. How brand-oriented strategy affects the financial performance of B2B SMEs. *Journal of Business & Industrial Marketing* 33: 303–15.
Barth, Mary E., Michael B. Clement, George Foster, and Ron Kasznik. 1998. Brand values and capital market valuation. *Review of Accounting Studies* 3: 41–68. [CrossRef]
Campo, Sara, Alejandro Gómez, and María Jesús Yagüe. 2013. *The Impact of Destination Brand Personality on Destination Brand Equity*. Madrid: Autónoma University Madrid.
Christodoulides, George, and Leslie De Chernatony. 2010. Consumer-based brand equity conceptualization and measurement. *International Journal of Market Research* 52: 43–66.
Dichev, Ilia D., and Vicki Wei Tang. 2009. Earnings volatility and earnings predictability. *Journal of Accounting and Economics* 47: 160–81. [CrossRef]
Frankel, Richard, and Lubomir Litov. 2009. Earnings persistence. *Journal of Accounting and Economics* 47: 182–90. [CrossRef]
Hirschey, Mark, and Jerry J. Weygandt. 1985. Amortization policy for advertising and research and development expenditures. *Journal of Accounting Research* 23: 326–35. [CrossRef]
Huang, Zhuowei Joy, and Liping A. Cai. 2015. Modeling consumer-based brand equity for multinational hotel brands–When hosts become guests. *Tourism Management* 46: 431–43. [CrossRef]
IASB (International Accounting Standards Board). 2010. *Conceptual Framework for Financial Reporting*. London: IASB.
Ittner, Christopher D., and David F. Larcker. 1998. Are nonfinancial measures leading indicators of financial performance? An analysis of customer satisfaction. *Journal of Accounting Research* 36: 1–34. [CrossRef]
Ittner, Christopher, David Larcker, and Daniel Taylor. 2009. The stock market's pricing of customer satisfaction. *Marketing Science* 25: 826–35. [CrossRef]
Jacobson, Robert, and Natalie Mizik. 2009. The financial markets and customer satisfaction: Reexaming possible financial market mispricing of customer satisfaction. *Marketing Science* 28: 810–19. [CrossRef]
Johansson, Johny K., Claudiu V. Dimofte, and Sanal K. Mazvancheryl. 2012. The performance of global brands in the 2008 financial crisis: A test of two brand value measures. *International Journal of Research in Marketing* 29: 235–45. [CrossRef]
Keller, Kevin Lane. 1993. Conceptualizing, measuring, and managing customer-based brand equity. *Journal of Marketing* 57: 1–22. [CrossRef]
Keller, Kevin Lane. 2002. *Building Customer-Based Brand Equity: A Blueprint for Creating Strong Brands*. Cambridge: Marketing Science Institute.

Keller, Kevin Lane. 2002. *Building, Measuring, and Managing Brand Equity*, 2nd ed. Upper Saddle River: Prentice Hall.

Keller, Kevin Lane. 2003. *Strategic Brand Management*. Upper Saddle River: Prentice-Hall.

Keller, Kevin Lane, and Donald R. Lehmann. 2006. Brands and branding: Research findings and future priorities. *Marketing Science* 25: 740–59. [CrossRef]

Kim, Renee B., Jong Min Park, and Dong Hyun Yoon. 2018. Marketing Accountability of Korea Corporate: The Relationship between Branding Investments and Financial Performance. *Engineering Economics* 29: 332–40. [CrossRef]

Krasnikov, Alexander, Satish Jayachandran, and V. Kumar. 2009. The impact of customer relationship management implementation on cost and profit efficiencies: Evidence from the U.S. commercial banking industry. *Journal of Marketing* 73: 61–76. [CrossRef]

Larkin, Yelena. 2013. Brand perception, cash flow stability, and financial policy. *Journal of Financial Economics* 110: 232–53. [CrossRef]

Livne, Gilad, Ana Simpson, and Eli Talmor. 2011. Do Customer Acquisition Cost, Retention and Usage Matter to Firm Performance and Valuation? *Journal of Business Finance & Accounting* 38: 334–63.

Madden, Thomas J., Frank Fehle, and Susan Fournier. 2006. Brands matter: An empirical demonstration of the creation of shareholder value through branding. *Journal of the Academy of Marketing Science* 34: 224–335. [CrossRef]

Malik, Muhammad Shoukat, and Lubna Kanwal. 2018. Impact of Corporate Social Responsibility Disclosure on Financial Performance: Case Study of Listed Pharmaceutical Firms of Pakistan. *Journal of Business Ethics* 150: 69–78. [CrossRef]

Mizik, Natalie, and Eugene Pavlov. 2017. Assessing the Financial Impact of Brand Equity with Short Time-Series Data. In *Handbook of Market Research*. Edited by Christian Homburg, Martin Klarmann and Arnd Vomberg. Cham: Springer.

Narteh, Bedman. 2018. Brand equity and financial performance: The moderating role of brand likeability. *Marketing Intelligence & Planning* 36: 381–95.

Ohlson, James A. 1998. Discussion of "Brand values and capital market valuation". *Review of Accounting Studies* 3: 69–71. [CrossRef]

Penman, Stephen H. 1992. Return to fundamentals. *Journal of Accounting, Auditing and Finance* 7: 465–83. [CrossRef]

Petersen, M. A. 2009. Estimating standard errors in finance panel data sets: Comparing approaches. *The Review of Financial Studies* 22: 435–80. [CrossRef]

Rahman, Mahabubur, M. Ángeles Rodríguez-Serrano, and Mary Lambkin. 2018. Brand management efficiency and firm value: An integrated resource based and signalling theory perspective. *Industrial Marketing Management* 72: 112–26. [CrossRef]

Rego, Lopo L., Matthew T. Billett, and Neil A. Morgan. 2009. Consumer-based brand equity and firm risk. *Journal of Marketing* 73: 47–60. [CrossRef]

Srinivasan, Shuba, and Dominique M. Hanssens. 2009. Marketing and firm value: Metrics, methods, findings, and future directions. *Journal of Marketing Research* 66: 293–312. [CrossRef]

Tuli, Kapil R., and Sundar G. Bharadwaj. 2009. Customer satisfaction and stock returns risk. *Journal of Marketing* 73: 184–97. [CrossRef]

Yoo, Boonghee, and Naveen Donthu. 2001. Developing and validating a multidimensional consumer-based brand equity scale. *Journal of Business Research* 52: 1–14. [CrossRef]

© 2018 by the authors. Licensee MDPI, Basel, Switzerland. This article is an open access article distributed under the terms and conditions of the Creative Commons Attribution (CC BY) license (http://creativecommons.org/licenses/by/4.0/).

Review

A Systematic Mapping Study on Customer Loyalty and Brand Management

Andrea Moretta-Tartaglione, Ylenia Cavacece *, Giuseppe Russo and Giuseppe Granata

Department of Economics and Law, University of Cassino and Southern Lazio, 03043 Cassino, Italy; a.moretta@unicas.it (A.M.T.); giuseppe.russo@unicas.it (G.R.); g.granata@unicas.it (G.G.)
* Correspondence: ylenia.cavacece@unicas.it

Received: 10 November 2018; Accepted: 4 January 2019; Published: 11 January 2019

Abstract: Customer loyalty is a topic of great interest for marketing scholars due to its importance in gaining sustainable competitive advantages and financial outcomes. Literature is prolific of works regarding customer loyalty and brand management. In order to improve the quantity and quality of research publications, research themes mapping of published studies is required. The aim of this paper is to provide scholars with a systematization and mapping of the contributions on this topic to develop an effective research road map for future research. A bibliometric analysis and a mapping study have been conducted on 337 publications on customer loyalty and brand management from 2000 to 2018. The results present the most cited works on the topic, an evaluation map showing the most frequent and cited words and six clusters of words based on their co-occurrence. From the analysis of the clusters, the most relevant research findings, trends, and issues emerge, suggesting interesting theoretical and practical implications.

Keywords: customer loyalty; brand; satisfaction; commitment; trust; engagement; bibliometric analysis; mapping study

1. Introduction

Customer loyalty is one of the most debated topics in marketing literature of last decades. The great interest in customer loyalty can be attributed to its importance in achieving sustainable competitive advantages and financial outcomes (Grönroos 2009). Customer loyalty refers to positive attitudes of customers toward a company or brand that result in repeated repurchasing behaviors and in a lower customer sensitivity to the price and the offerings of competitors (Anderson and Srinivasan 2003). Loyal customers are more profitable than a new one, since they spend more with the firm and have lower servicing costs (Richard and Zhang 2012). Hence, managing and enhancing customer loyalty becomes a strategic imperative for firms.

Brand acquires great importance in improving customer loyalty through the effective management of the brand awareness and brand image (Han et al. 2008). The emotional attachment towards a brand creates affective commitment that encourages consumers to constantly rely on a specific brand's offering (Gustafsson et al. 2005; Lee et al. 2007), repurchase the same brand, spread good words, and not visit competitor's stores (Han et al. 2018). These behaviors ultimately result in customer loyalty (Evanschitzky et al. 2006; Fullerton 2005; Iglesias et al. 2011; Mattila 2001).

The interest in customer loyalty has resulted in a large number of contributions on this topic. Literature shows interesting advancements in its understanding and conceptualization. However, to date, further efforts are required of scholars (Nguyen et al. 2018; Shahid Iqbal et al. 2018; Sitorus and Yustisia 2018). The reason is that customer loyalty is a complex and multifaceted concept involving dynamic interactions and exchanges (Dick and Basu 1994). It is a multidimensional construct and some difficulties emerge in identifying its dimensions and operationalize them. First of all, customer loyalty can be defined as a combination of attitudinal and behavioral dimensions that create difficulties in analyzing it (Richard and Zhang 2012). Second, a large amount of research has been devoted to investigating its antecedents and consequences (Han et al. 2008; Pan et al. 2012) because loyalty is related to other complex variables like consumer involvement, trust, satisfaction, commitment, and engagement (Ball et al. 2004; Huang et al. 2006; Hajli et al. 2017). Moreover, in last years, the evolution of consumers and the development of social media have profoundly changed the consumers' behaviors and the way that they interact with other consumers and with the firm itself (Dolan et al. 2016; Gensler et al. 2013; Pentina et al. 2013).

For scholars, therefore, it is not easy to identify the directions to which address their efforts aimed at contributing to the advancement of the research on this topic. This paper aims to provide an overview of the research findings and trends by mapping the research field in clusters able to guide the researcher to the most influential works, results, and issues that need more insights.

With this end, this paper offers a bibliometric analysis and a mapping study of the works on customer loyalty and brand management.

Traditionally, researchers have analyzed earlier findings using two methods: the qualitative approach of a structured literature review and the quantitative approach of meta-analysis (Schmidt 2008). In last years, thanks to the introduction of online databases with citation data (e.g., Web Of Science) and the proliferation of software for conducting bibliometric analyses (e.g., SciMAT and BibExcel), bibliometric methods have spread.

Bibliometric methods use a quantitative approach for the description, evaluation, and monitoring of published research. These methods, by using a systematic, transparent, and reproducible review process, allow the overcoming of the limits of narrative literature reviews, which often lack rigor and are exposed to bias by the researcher (Tranfield et al. 2003).

As highlighted by Zupic and Čater (2015), bibliometric methods have been widely used to map the fields of strategic management since 1999. In the field of customer loyalty, Siemieniako (2018) provides a bibliometric analysis of scientific works published in the Scopus database in the period from 2003 to 2017; the analysis is focused only on the customer loyalty in the business-to-business context. With regard to the topic of brand management, some bibliometric analyses have been conducted, particularly on the consumer brand relationships (Fetscherin and Heinrich 2015), on brand personality (Llanos-Herrera and Merigo 2018; Radler 2018), and on corporate branding (Fetscherin and Usunier 2012). This work contributes to the previous knowledge by analyzing customer loyalty for both the B2B and B2C contexts, with a focus on the relationships between customer loyalty and brand management.

Among the different bibliometric methods, this paper adopts the science mapping, which allow for mapping the cognitive structure and evolution of scientific fields and disciplines (Noyons et al. 1999) producing a spatial representation of them (Calero Medina and Leeuwen 2012; Small 1999). Based on the citation index, the most important papers on customer loyalty and brand management have been identified and analyzed to display the structural and dynamic aspects of scientific research (Börner et al. 2003; Morris and Van der Veer Martens 2008). In a second phase, the different works have been clustered on the basis of the words co-occurrence and each cluster has been analyzed to facilitate the identification of the relationships between each dimension involved.

This work is organized, as follows: first, the method used is described; second, results are illustrated and then discussed; finally, conclusions, theoretical and practical implications are provided.

2. Materials and Methods

This work is based on a bibliometric analysis and mapping study of the contributions about customer loyalty and brand management.

Document information was recovered from the Web of Science's (WOS) SCI-Expanded by Thomson Reuters. This database was chosen because it offers a significant advantage being multidisciplinary and including social sciences literature (Norris and Oppenheim 2007).

The analysis was carried out by searching for the Topic: (customer loyalty AND brand management), refined by: Web of Science Categories = (Business or Management) AND Document Types = (Article or Review or Book Chapter), using Indexes = Sci-Expanded, SSCI, A&HCI, CPCI-S, CPCI-SSH, BKCI-S, BKCI-SSH, ESCI, CCR-Expanded, IC (Waltman 2016). The search was conducted during September 2018 within the Timespan = 2000–2018 because a substantial presence of works on the subject was detected only starting from 2000 (only four works were found in all the '90s).

Results have been collected in a unique database containing the variables of authors, language, year of publication, type of research, country, keywords, and cited references in each of the publications included in the search.

First, a bibliometric analysis was conducted to identify the total publications by year, the sum of times cited by year, the most cited authors, and productive countries. A top ten of the most cited publications was created. Subsequently, the scientific mapping study was carried out using the software SciMAT, developed by the "SECABA" group from the University of Granada, which allows the construction of scientific maps as well as a better visualization of the evolution within a scientific area (Cobo et al. 2012). SciMAT provides different modules that help the analyst conduct a science mapping workflow: a module that is dedicated to the management of the knowledge base and its entities, a module responsible for conducting the science mapping analysis, and a module to visualize the generated results and maps (Cobo et al. 2012).

To perform the analysis, the following configuration in SciMAT was established: word as the unit of analysis, co-occurrence analysis as the tool to build the networks, equivalence index as the similarity measure to normalize the networks, Jaccard index as the evolution measure, Inclusion index as the overlapping measure, the H-Index to detect the relevance, and the simple centers algorithm as the clustering algorithm to detect the clusters (Castillo-Vergara et al. 2018). The analysis provides an evaluation map for the topic "customer loyalty and brand management" with the most occurring words and their relevance in the publications analyzed. The relevance of the words was established on the basis of three measures: documents count, H-Index, and sum citations. For each relevant word of the analysis, a cluster of the related words was created, graphically showing the relevance of each word in the cluster and the links between each one.

3. Results

3.1. Bibliometric Analysis

The search on Web of Science yielded 337 publications on customer loyalty and brand management. Publications started from 2000 and grew exponentially, reaching a pick in 2017. Because the search was conducted in September 2018, data related to the year 2018 are not complete but looking at the trend, it is assumed a confirmation of growth also for this year (Figure 1). Citations of works about customer loyalty and brand management date back to 2002 and then grew over the years, showing a constant growth rate (Figure 1).

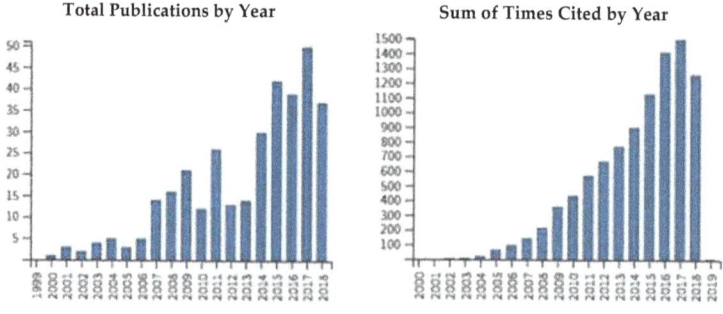

Figure 1. Publications and citations distribution by year.

Among the most productive authors, we find Heiner Evanschitzky, Sunil Gupta, and Peter C. Verhoef and most of the works have been published in the United States (Figure 2).

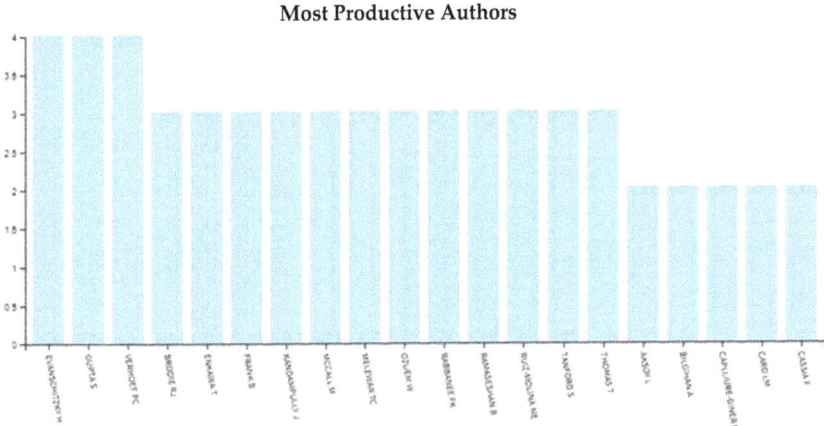

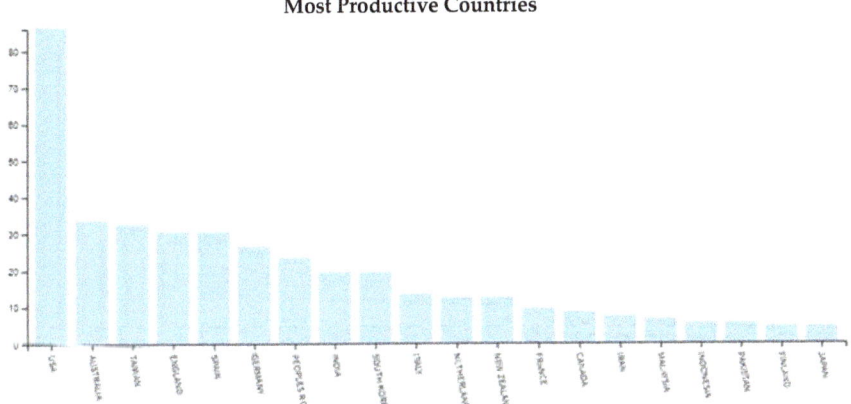

Figure 2. Most productive Authors and Countries.

The study of customer loyalty and brand management is transversal to different fields of study in the research areas of management and business, belonging to both the B2C and B2B contexts; the main ones are listed in the Table 1.

Table 1. Fields of study.

Field of Study	Most Relevant Works
Retail	(Chiou et al. 2010; Baltas et al. 2010)
e-Commerce	(Jin et al. 2008; Ng 2013; Chen et al. 2009)
Social media	(Gamboa and Gonçalves 2014; Van Doorn et al. 2010; Zhang and Luo 2016)
Service sector	(Cassia et al. 2017; Han et al. 2008; Caruana 2002)
Hospitality & Tourism	(Chen and Myagmarsuren 2010; Horng et al. 2012; Huang et al. 2006)

Table 2 shows a top ten of the most cited works about customer loyalty and brand management. From the analysis of these works, it is possible to identify the most relevant research topics in the literature on customer loyalty. First of all, it should be noted that there is a strong interest from the scientific community in the attempts of identification and operationalization of the dimensions of customer loyalty and their links with other variables related to the consumer, like satisfaction and engagement, or to the company, like reputation and brand image. Particularly, the work of McAlexander et al. (2002) tries to conceptualize customer loyalty as integration in a brand community and it received 894 citations since its publication. A great interest is also shown by scholars towards customer engagement behaviors (CEBs), defined as the customers' behavioral manifestation toward a brand or firm, beyond purchase, that results from motivational drivers (Van Doorn et al. 2010). The attention is on the antecedents, impediments, and firm consequences of customer engagement (Verhoef et al. 2010).

Table 2. Top 10 of the most cited works on customer loyalty and brand.

Authors	Publication Year	Title	Total Citations	Average per Year
McAlexander, J.H.; Schouten, J.W.; Koenig, H.F.	2002	Building brand community	894	52.59
Van Doorn, J.; Lemon, K.N.; Mittal, V.; Nass, S.; Pick, D.; Pirner, P.; Verhoef, P.C.	2010	Customer Engagement Behavior: Theoretical Foundations and Research Directions	518	57.56
Ganesh, J.; Arnold, M.J.; Reynolds, K.E.	2000	Understanding the customer base of service providers: An examination of the differences between switchers and stayers	429	22.58
Rauyruen, P.; Miller, K.E.	2007	Relationship quality as a predictor of B2B customer loyalty	297	24.75
Johnson, M.D.; Herrmann, A.; Huber, F.	2006	The evolution of loyalty intentions	278	21.38
Yi, Y.J.; Jeon, H.	2003	Effects of loyalty programs on value perception, program loyalty, and brand loyalty	245	15.31
Cooil, B.; Keiningham, T.L.; Aksoy, L.; Hsu, M.	2007	A longitudinal analysis of customer satisfaction and share of wallet: Investigating the moderating effect of customer characteristics	243	20.25
Verhoef, P.C.; Reinartz, W.J.; Krafft, M.	2010	Customer Engagement as a New Perspective in Customer Management	220	24.44
Cretu, A.E.; Brodie, R.J.	2007	The influence of brand image and company reputation where manufacturers market to small firms: A customer value perspective	220	18.33
Yi, Y.J.; La, S.	2004	What influences the relationship between customer satisfaction and repurchase intention? Investigating the effects of adjusted expectations and customer loyalty	210	14

In the same way, many authors have found useful for their research the study of Ganesh et al. (2000), which provides insights for a deeper understanding of the customer base in order to target the customer retention and loyalty-building efforts to the right customers. Another study of interest concerns the dimensions of relationship quality that can explain the influence of relationships on customer loyalty in terms of behavioral aspects (purchase intentions) and attitudinal loyalty (Rauyruen and Miller 2007); trust, commitment, satisfaction, and service quality are considered among the most important relationship quality dimensions. From the analysis of the selected publications, it also emerges a great scientific interest about the drivers of customer loyalty intentions toward the brand as variables that mediate the effects of value on intentions (Johnson et al. 2006). Other debated themes are the relationship between customer satisfaction and customer retention as the primary measure of loyalty (Cooil et al. 2007) and the influences of brand image and company reputation on customers' perceptions of quality, customer value, and customer loyalty (Cretu and Brodie 2007).

Finally, other most cited works investigate how loyalty influences the relationship between customer satisfaction and repurchase intention (Yi and La 2004), and how reward schemes of a loyalty program influence the perceived value of the program and how value perception of the loyalty program affects customer loyalty (Yi and Jeon 2003).

3.2. Mapping Study

From the scientific mapping study, an evaluation map emerged showing six relevant nodes. These nodes represent the most frequent words in the analyzed documents, as well as the most cited and relevant ones that are based on H-Index. As Figure 3 shows, customer satisfaction is the most frequent, relevant, and cited topic in the works on customer loyalty and brand management, followed by consumer trust, brand community, consumer perceptions, consumer behavior, and competitive advantage.

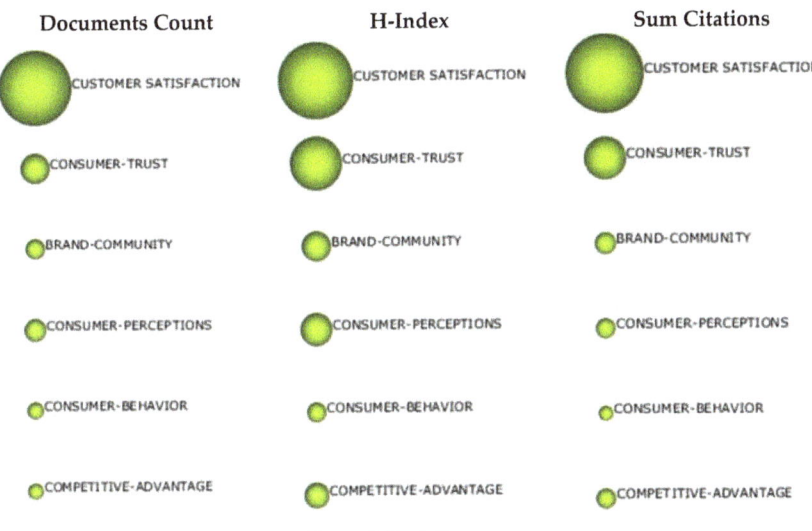

Figure 3. Evolution map.

At each node, the software identified a cluster of related words.

The first cluster shows a high correlation between the words customer satisfaction and customer loyalty (Figure 4). Customer satisfaction, as a measure of the perceived quality, is considered to be the basis for the customer loyalty to the firm, and, in most cases to the brand, able to predict behavioral intentions of customers such as purchasing intentions. The majority of works in this area adopt a quantitative method proposing empirical models able to operationalize and measure these constructs. Customer loyalty, satisfaction, and intentions are generally operationalized as second order constructs and the correlations between them are generally analyzed through the method of the structural equation modelling.

The second cluster detects a high correlation in the papers that were analyzed between the words consumer trust and consumer commitment (Figure 4). Particularly, in most cases, trust is considered to be an antecedent of consumer commitment. Several works attribute the increasing in trust and commitment to the Customer Relationship Management (CRM) policies of the firm aimed at influencing the perceived value of consumers. Others consider commitment and trust key elements of relationship marketing, and not only consequences, because they encourage marketers to work at preserving relationship investments. CRM, by increasing consumer commitment and trust, creates positive effects on the firm performance. These issues are mostly studied in the e-commerce context.

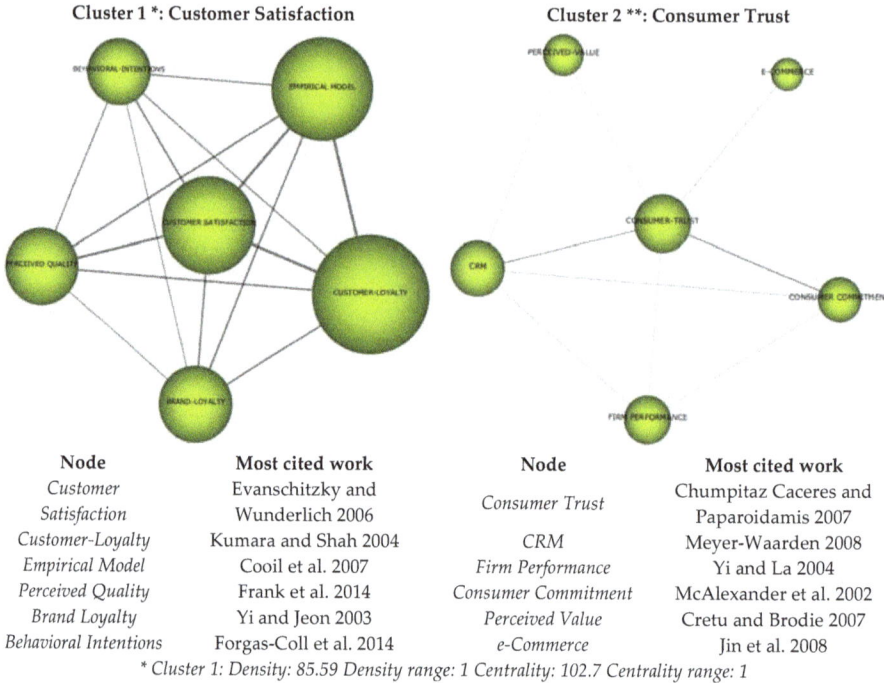

Figure 4. Cluster 1 and cluster 2 (Chumpitaz Caceres and Paparoidamis 2007; Kumara and Shah 2004).

The central node of the third cluster is the brand community (Figure 5). A brand community is generally defined as a customer–customer–brand triad (Muniz and O'guinn 2001). The social aggregation of brand users and their relationships to the brand itself spread widely thanks to social media that favor interactions and information sharing. Participation in a brand community represents one of the main expressions of customer engagement that in these contexts is manifested through behaviors, such as the word-of-mouth. The interactions between consumers and companies within the brand communities often take the form of value co-creation paths. Value co-creation was introduced by the Service-Dominat logic (Vargo and Lusch 2004, 2008), which defines it as the creation of a joint value through the application of competences and the integration of resources between the firm and the customer.

In cluster 4, consumer-perception is the concept around which many other topics are analyzed (Figure 5). Consumers' perceptions about a company are mainly determined by the brand image but also by the brand equity. Brand equity represents the customer's subjective and intangible perceptions and attitudes about the brand and it tends to represent the emotional and irrational aspects of the market offering that connect the customer with the brand. Consumers' perceptions are also affected by the corporate social responsibility of the firm, which positively influences the benefit and the value perceived by the consumer in the company's offer, the judgment of fairness in the price differential charged for it, and his/her buying intention, in a context where the socially responsible firm practices a price higher than the competition. Positive consumers' perceptions about a firm or a brand represent a determinant of the purchase intentions, thus increasing the customer value.

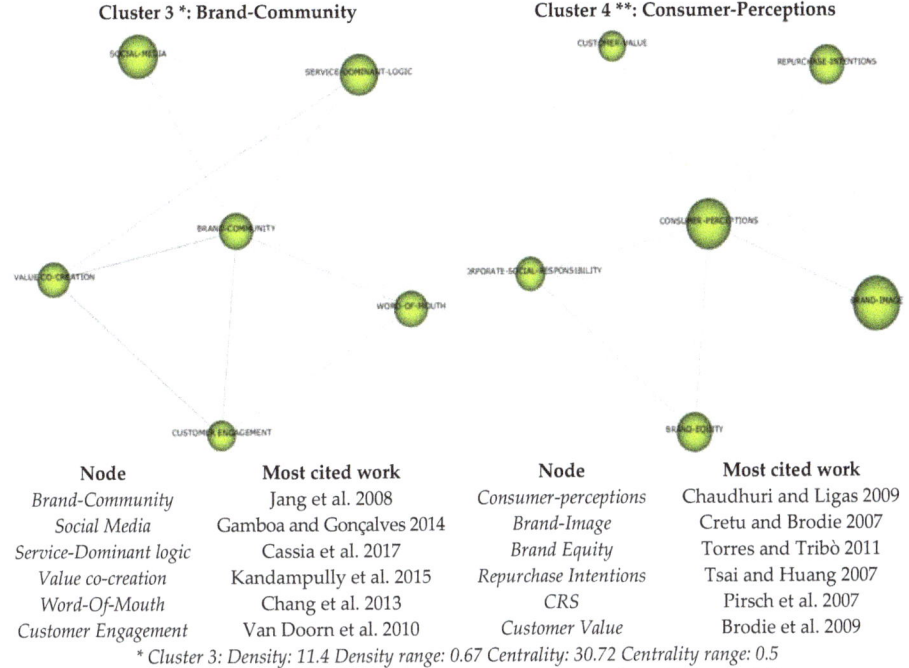

Figure 5. Cluster 3 and cluster 4.

Cluster 5 is focused on the consumer behaviors that depend on the customer involvement and the customer experience with the brand (Figure 6). Customer involvement motivates consumers to identify with product/service offerings, their consumption patterns, and consumption behavior. Involvement creates an urge within consumers to look for and think about the product/service category and the varying options before making decisions on brand preferences and the final act of purchase. It determinates the amount of physical and mental effort that a consumer puts into a purchase decision, thus influencing the decision-making process of consumers, particularly the purchasing decisions. These decisions also influence the choice of the store, for this reason these variables are studied above all in the retail context.

Finally, in cluster 6 the central node is represented by the competitive advantage of the firm (Figure 6). The achievement of a sustainable competitive advantage depends on the ability of the firm to increase the switching costs for the customers to dissuade them from switching to a competitor's product, brand, or services and thus enhancing the customer retention. Greater customer retention as well as lower customer sensitivity to company's prices have positive effects on customer equity in terms of the total combined customer lifetime values of the company's customers. Finally, firm reputation is one of the most important intangible resources for competitive advantage, because it possesses rarity, value, non-substitutability, and imperfect immutability. Firm reputation influences the perception of the company that is held by consumers, favorably influences new products amongst consumers making purchasing decisions that are more likely to take a risk on a new product if they already know and trust a company with a strong reputation.

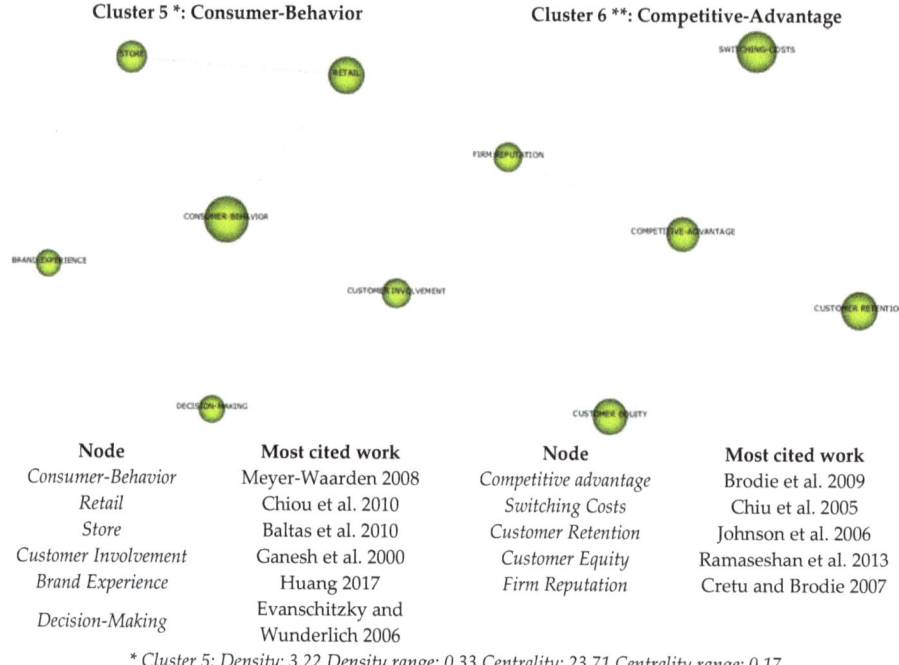

Figure 6. Cluster 5 and cluster 6.

4. Discussion

4.1. Towards a Better Understanding of Customer Loyalty

Customer loyalty, which generally refers to the strong commitment to repurchase a preferred product or service (Kim et al. 2018b), is one of the most debated topics in management and marketing literature. The interest of scholars about customer loyalty started from 2000 and it is still growing in the scientific community. By analyzing the contributions in this research area, it emerges that the interest of scholars is focused on the analysis of the attitudinal and behavioral dimensions of customer loyalty (Oliver 2014), its antecedents and consequences (Kim et al. 2018c), the evolution of the concept after social changes and ITCs advancements (Yoshida et al. 2018), and on the different strategies that are implemented by companies for its enhancement (Han et al. 2018).

Attitudinal loyalty refers to the customer attachment to a product, brand, or organization (McManus and Guilding 2008), price tolerance (Sánchez et al. 2011), and purchase intention (Kim and Ko 2012). These variables allow for estimating consumers' future behaviors on the basis of their attitudes (Kim and Lee 2009; Kim and Ko 2010).

The behavioral component of loyalty focuses on repeated purchases (Richard and Zhang 2012), positive word-of-mouth (Hajli et al. 2017), and customer equity (Kim and Ko 2012).

Among the principal antecedents of customer loyalty, authors recognize customer satisfaction, commitment, and trust. Customer satisfaction is the principal variable that is related to customer loyalty, since several authors state that satisfied customers tend to remain loyal to a firm or brand (Schultz and Bailey 2000; Caruana 2002; Chumpitaz and Paparoidamis 2004; Smith and Wright 2004; Huang et al. 2006; Richard and Zhang 2012). Customer satisfaction is defined as the positive evaluation of the consumption experience (Anderson et al. 2004), which derives by the difference between the prior expectations and the perceptions after consumption (Tu et al. 2012). Several studies show the positive correlation between satisfaction and loyalty (Chen 2008; Chang and Hung 2013; Nesset and Helgesen 2014; Akamavi et al. 2015) and the results of some empirical analyses indicate that customer satisfaction exerts stronger effects on the behavioral loyalty (Rajaguru 2016; Koklic et al. 2017; Shahid Iqbal et al. 2018). Both cognitive and affective satisfaction are considered when they are related to customer loyalty (Coursaris and Osch 2016; Gallarza et al. 2016).

Satisfaction enhances commitment because satisfied customers are more favorable to continue the relationship (Ranaweera and Menon 2013; Jeong and Oh 2017), enjoying benefits like reduced search cost and lower perceived risks (Hess and Story 2005). Relationship commitment is defined as the development of a relationship based on cooperative sentiments, strong preference for existing partners, and propensity for relation continuity (Han et al. 2018).

According to Hajli et al. (2017), consumer trust is another dimension that is able to improve the relationship quality, thus positively affecting customer relationship commitment and customer loyalty (Huang et al. 2006; Ng 2013). Consumer trust refers to the credibility and reliability of the company that determine the conviction in consumers that the company will provide the promised product or service as expected (Sirdeshmukh et al. 2002). In sum, from the literature emerges that customers' loyalty towards a firm or brand increases as trust, commitment, and satisfaction levels increase (Sitorus and Yustisia 2018).

In past decade, the interest of scholars focused on another dimension strongly related to those described above, which is customer engagement. Customer engagement is defined as the intensity of the customer's participation in the relationship with the organization (Patterson et al. 2006). Several authors have considered as consequences of customer engagement the dimensions of trust (Casaló et al. 2007; Hollebeek 2011), satisfaction (Bowden 2009a), commitment (Chan and Li 2010), and loyalty (Bowden 2009a, 2009b). Bowden (2009a) describes engagement as an iterative process that starts with customer satisfaction, transits for commitment and trust, and culminates in customer loyalty.

Related to the concept of customer engagement, value co-creation is proposed as a process for engaging customers in creating value (Prahalad and Ramaswamy 2004) transforming them from passive customers to active players (Vargo and Lusch 2004). Value co-creation is defined by Service-Dominant logic as the application of competences and the integration of resources between users and providers during service delivery (Vargo and Lusch 2004, 2008).

Studies on customer engagement have increased with the development of the social media (Gummerus et al. 2012; Sashi 2012; Zhang and Luo 2016) that facilitate the interactions (Wirtz et al. 2013), collaboration (Laroche et al. 2012), and participation (Algesheimer et al. 2005) between customers and other members of the communities and firms. Moreover, social media favor behaviors of engaged customers, like word-of-mouth, recommendations, activities in support of other consumers, blogging, and product reviews (Van Doorn et al. 2010; Zhang and Luo 2016), which are connected to the customer behavioral loyalty. In the last few years, the concept of social media engagement has developed as the consumer's behavioral manifestations that have a social media focus, beyond purchase, resulting from motivational drivers (Van Doorn et al. 2010; Dolan et al. 2016). Several researches show that social media engagement enhances customer loyalty in terms of both loyalty intentions (Calder et al. 2009; Jahn and Kunz 2012; Hollebeek et al. 2014; Lim et al. 2015) and behavioral loyalty manifestations (Brodie et al. 2013; Dolan et al. 2016).

Some authors state that satisfaction by itself does not determines customer loyalty if it is not accompanied by switching barriers that make the alternative offerings less attractive (Jones et al. 2000; Balabanis et al. 2006; López-Miguens and Vázquez 2017). Picón et al. (2014) found that perceived switching costs are significant mediators in the relationship between satisfaction and loyalty. Other works demonstrate that switching costs have direct and positive effects on customer loyalty (Chang and Chen 2008; Ghazali et al. 2016; Teng 2018).

Finally, from the analysis, it emerges the important role of companies in managing effective strategies of Customer Relationship Management to maintain and increase the quality of the relationship. The quality of the relationship, in terms of its intensity and tightness, influences customer loyalty (Palmatier et al. 2006; Yadav et al. 2013). According to Palmatier et al. (2006), the relationship quality is based on the dimensions of trust, commitment, and satisfaction, which represent the dimensions to enhance through branding activities and value co-creation paths in order to achieve customer loyalty (Hajli et al. 2017). By enhancing loyalty, CRM allows firm to achieve a sustainable competitive advantage (Grönroos 2009). Companies gain considerable benefits from retaining an existing customer (Brunner et al. 2008). The ability to maintain long-term customer relationships contribute to an increase in the revenue and a reduction of the costs to companies (Gallo 2014), such as the high costs of acquiring a new customer (Edvardsson et al. 2000; Smith and Wright 2004).

In conclusion, customer loyalty is a very complex area of study because it includes several interrelated and mutually dependent variables. The efforts of the scientific community up to now have been directed to the identification of these variables, the relationships between them, and their influence on customer loyalty. Table 3 summarizes the variables that have were studied by the analyzed works and their role in explaining the customer loyalty and its dimensions.

Table 3. Variables and dimensions of customer loyalty.

The Explanation of Customer Loyalty		
Customer loyalty as attitudinal	Customer attachment	(McManus and Guilding 2008; Kim and Ko 2010; Kim and Lee 2009)
	Price tolerance	(Sánchez et al. 2011; Anderson and Srinivasan 2003; Yi and La 2004)
	Repurchase intentions	(Tsai and Huang 2007; Kim and Ko 2012; Tsai and Huang 2007)
	Disinterest towards competitors' offerings	(Evanschitzky et al. 2006; Evanschitzky et al. 2012; Kang et al. 2015)
Customer loyalty as behavioral	Repeated purchases	(Forgas-Coll et al. 2014; Richard and Zhang 2012; Evanschitzky et al. 2006)
	Positive word-of-mouth	(Meyer-Waarden 2008; Hajli et al. 2017; Chang et al. 2013)
	Customer equity	(Ramaseshan et al. 2013; Kim and Ko 2012)
	Decision-making	(Evanschitzky and Wunderlich 2006; Sashi 2012; Zhang et al. 2014)
The Dimensions of Customer Loyalty		
Antecedents of customer loyalty	Perceived quality	(Frank et al. 2014; Chen 2008; Gallarza et al. 2016)
	Perceived value	(Cretu and Brodie 2007; Yi and Jeon 2003; Han et al. 2011)
	Customer satisfaction	(Evanschitzky and Wunderlich 2006; Picón et al. 2014; Gronholdt et al. 2000)
	Consumer trust	(Lee et al. 2007; Sirdeshmukh et al. 2002; Sitorus and Yustisia 2018)
	Relationship quality	(Rauyruen and Miller 2007; Hajli et al. 2017; Huang et al. 2006)
	Relationship commitment	(Jeong and Oh 2017; Hess and Story 2005; Evanschitzky et al. 2006)
	Customer involvement	(Ganesh et al. 2000; Park et al. 2007; Yi and Jeon 2003)
	Consumer-perceptions	(Chaudhuri and Ligas 2009; Cretu and Brodie 2007; Zins 2001)
	Corporate Social Responsibility	(Pirsch et al. 2007; Mandhachitara and Poolthong 2011; Bolton and Mattila 2015)
	Customer engagement	(Van Doorn et al. 2010; Verhoef et al. 2010; Patterson et al. 2006)
	Value co-creation	(Kandampully et al. 2015; Prahalad and Ramaswamy 2004; Hajli et al. 2017)
	Firm Reputation	(Cretu and Brodie 2007; Jin et al. 2008; Ageeva et al. 2018)
	Switching Costs	(Chiu et al. 2005; Picón et al. 2014; Ghazali et al. 2016)
Consequences of customer loyalty	Customer Retention	(Johnson et al. 2006; Ganesh et al. 2000; Cooil et al. 2007)
	Firm performance	(Yi and La 2004; Smith and Wright 2004; Ciunova-Shuleska et al. 2017)
	Customer Value	(Brodie et al. 2009; Cretu and Brodie 2007; Wu and Li 2018)
	Competitive advantage	(Brodie et al. 2009; Grönroos 2009; Villanueva et al. 2007)
	Costs reduction	(Edvardsson et al. 2000; Smith and Wright 2004; Gallo 2014)

4.2. Customer Loyalty and Brand Management

Brand management plays a fundamental role in the development of customer loyalty. Sometimes, consumers are not loyal to the company in general, but rather to a specific brand. Brand loyalty is commonly connoted as "the biased (non-random) behavioral response (purchase), expressed over time by some decision-making unit with respect to one or more alternative brands out of a set of brands and is a function of psychological processes" (Jacoby 1971, p. 25).

Several works show that customer satisfaction improves brand loyalty (Gronholdt et al. 2000; Lee et al. 2009; Nam et al. 2011; Sahin et al. 2011). According to Han et al. (2018), the correlation between satisfaction and brand loyalty is mediated by the relationship commitment. Committed customers feel an emotional attachment towards a brand and they have behaviors like repurchasing, positive recommendations, and disinterest towards competitors' offerings (Evanschitzky et al. 2006); all of these dimensions can be related to the behavioral brand loyalty (Saleem and Raja 2014).

Brand loyalty also depends on the ability of firms to build a strong brand identity through corporate communication strategies, because, as highlighted by Melewar et al. (2017), the more favorable the brand identity is perceived by consumers, the more favorable the attitude consumers have towards the brand strategy.

In last years, in the context of social media, the concept of (online) brand community emerged as the "specialized, non-geographically bound community, based on a structured set of social relationships among admirers of a brand" (Muniz and O'guinn 2001, p. 412). The commitment to a brand community characterizes customers with a strong brand identification, self-identification, and satisfaction with the brand (Park et al. 2007), who purchase the same brand consistently (Algesheimer et al. 2005). Moreover, the committed participation and interactions with other members improves consumers' brand experience and value, leading to enhance their brand commitment (Jang et al. 2008; Kim et al. 2008a) and brand loyalty (Zhou et al. 2012). According to several authors, brand communities also boost the brand engagement (Sprott et al. 2009; Mollen and Wilson 2010; Vivek et al. 2012; Hollebeek et al. 2014), defined by Hollebeek (2011, p. 6) as "the level of a customer's motivational, brand-related, and context-dependent state of mind characterized by specific levels of cognitive, emotional, and behavioral activity in brand interactions."

The commitment to a brand community also has positive effects on brand equity, defined as "the differential effect that brand knowledge has on consumer response to the marketing of that brand" (Keller 1993, p. 8). Several contributions have shown that brand equity includes perceived quality, brand image, and brand loyalty (Dioko and So 2012; Horng et al. 2012; Hsu et al. 2012; Kimpakorn and Tocquer 2010; Manthiou et al. 2014; Nam et al. 2011; Oh and Hsu 2014; Šerić et al. 2014; Xu and Chan 2010). Brand image is a set of perceptions of a consumer that identifies the representation of the brand in his/her mind (Dobni and Zinkhan 1990). Some studies indicate that brand image influences brand loyalty through perceived quality (Chen and Myagmarsuren 2010; Sean Hyun and Kim 2011; Im et al. 2012; Kladou and Kehagias 2014). Perceived quality can be understood as the comparison between firm's performance and customer's expectations (Parasuraman et al. 1988); when the disconfirmation is negative, dissatisfaction is created, when it is positive, customer satisfaction is generated, thus increasing customer loyalty. The concept of perceived quality is strongly related to that of perceived value, which is defined as the consumer's overall evaluation of the benefits that are attained from a product or service in return of the perceived cost, in terms of monetary and non-monetary price (Monroe 2002). The perceived value, in addition to increase customer satisfaction, encourages the consumers' repurchases (Han et al. 2011), promotes re-patronage intentions, and discourages switching behaviors (Wathne et al. 2001), thus improving customer loyalty (Nguyen et al. 2018).

Therefore, from this study, it emerges that also in the case of brand management there are many variables and dimensions related to the brand that are able to affect customer loyalty. The study of these variables and their relationships is fundamental for understanding how to manage the brand in order to increase customer loyalty. The various variables and dimensions of the brand studied by scholars in relation to the customer loyalty are shown in Table 4, reporting the most relevant works for each of them.

Table 4. Brand variables and dimensions affecting customer loyalty.

Variables and Dimensions Affecting Customer Loyalty	Most Relevant Works
Brand loyalty	(Yi and Jeon 2003; Nam et al. 2011; Han et al. 2018)
Brand engagement	(Mollen and Wilson 2010; Vivek et al. 2012; Hollebeek et al. 2014)
Brand community	(Jang et al. 2008; McAlexander et al. 2002; Muniz and O'guinn 2001)
Brand commitment	(Park et al. 2007; Jang et al. 2008; Kim et al. 2008a)
Brand equity	(Torres and Tribó 2011; Hsu et al. 2012; Manthiou et al. 2014)
Brand image	(Cretu and Brodie 2007; Han et al. 2008; Kladou and Kehagias 2014)
Brand experience	(Huang 2017; Iglesias et al. 2011; Sahin et al. 2011)

5. Conclusions

The research on customer loyalty has produced interesting results in terms of clarification of its dimensions. As attitudinal dimensions, scholars have identified the involvement and attachment to a firm or brand and the price tolerance, while as behavioral dimensions, the repurchasing behavior, positive recommendations, and word-of-mouth. However, it emerges that more studies are needed for measuring the combined effects of the two class of dimensions on loyalty.

Customer satisfaction, commitment, trust, and engagement have been detected as the principal variables that are related to loyalty. Relationships between these variables have been investigated through the definition of empirical models and quantitative analyses, which show positive correlations between them. All of the variables exert positive effects on customer loyalty, and at the same time, loyalty has a positive influence on all them. These results suggest overcoming the distinction between loyalty antecedents and consequences in favor of a consideration of the different variables in a positive circle in which the improvement of one variable triggers a chain reaction of improvements. All of the psychological processes comprise cognitive and emotional aspects and both enhance the behavioral loyalty. Hence, companies must pay more attention to the emotional content in the relationships.

Brand management becomes more and more important for the loyalty improvements. In fact, new concepts have been introduced, like brand loyalty, brand engagement, brand equity, and brand communities. Brand is recognized as the principal factor that is able to create commitment and engage customers. Particular attention is devoted to the online brand communities as environments where new forms of consumers-to-consumers communication emerge, allowing for new forms of brand identification and brand experiences that enhance the brand value and the consumers' attachment to the brand. Brand communities thus become the most important tool for CRM strategies. The participation of companies in brand communities allow them to acquire the necessary information, share and emphasize contents, target the consumers, and increase the brand equity. According to the results of Zhou et al. (2012), companies should support brand community providing resources (e.g., funds, staff, and place), cultivating a cohesive brand community and providing not only material assistance, but also care and rewards to the brand community. Moreover, companies should propose some activities for the members of the community according to the style, personality, feeling, and values of the brand.

Generally, all social media are indicated as places where the relationships with customers are managed, as they provide more opportunities of interaction and information sharing allowing the customer engagement and activating value co-creation paths with them. Through social media, firms can facilitate the social interactions of customers for branding co-creation, knowledge sharing, and customer empowerment (Andersen 2005; Ramaswamy 2009).

From these considerations, useful suggestions for future research emerge. First, despite the variables influencing customer loyalty have been well identified by previous works, there is a need for further empirical research on the relationships between them. A confusion about how these variables influence each other before exerting their effect on customer loyalty is still detected. New studies should be carried out in the social media that offer a large amount of information and evidences about the attitudes and behaviors of consumers that could be studied, for example, with sentiment and content analyses. Second, to keep up with the latest advancements in marketing, future research should focus on those variables that allow for studying the role of consumers as active co-creators of a higher value in a perspective of mutual benefit with the firm. Topics, such as customer engagement and value co-creation, should therefore acquire a dominant position in future studies.

Author Contributions: Although the paper is the result of a synergic work, it is attributed to A.M.T. the Sections 3.1 and 4.2, to Y.C. the Sections 3.2 and 4.1, to G.R. the Sections 1 and 2, and to G.G. the Section 5.

Funding: This research received no external funding.

Conflicts of Interest: The authors declare no conflict of interest.

References

Ageeva, Elena, T. C. Melewar, Pantea Foroudi, Charles Dennis, and Zhongqi Jin. 2018. Examining the influence of corporate website favorability on corporate image and corporate reputation: Findings from fsQCA. *Journal of Business Research* 89: 287–304. [CrossRef]

Akamavi, Raphaël K., Elsayed Mohamed, Katharina Pellmann, and Yue Xu. 2015. Key determinants of passenger loyalty in the low-cost airline business. *Tourism Management* 46: 528–45. [CrossRef]

Algesheimer, René, Utpal M. Dholakia, and Andreas Herrmann. 2005. The social influence of brand community: Evidence from European car clubs. *Journal of Marketing* 69: 19–34. [CrossRef]

Andersen, Poul Houman. 2005. Relationship marketing and brand involvement of professionals through web-enhanced brand communities: The case of Coloplast. *Industrial Marketing Management* 34: 39–51. [CrossRef]

Anderson, Rolph E., and Srini S. Srinivasan. 2003. E-satisfaction and e-loyalty: A contingency framework. *Psychology and Marketing* 20: 123–38. [CrossRef]

Anderson, Eugene W., Claes Fornell, and Sanal K. Mazvancheryl. 2004. Customer satisfaction and shareholder value. *Journal of Marketing* 68: 172–85. [CrossRef]

Balabanis, George, Nina Reynolds, and Antonis Simintiras. 2006. Bases of e-store loyalty: Perceived switching barriers and satisfaction. *Journal of Business Research* 59: 214–24. [CrossRef]

Ball, Dwayne, Pedro Simões Coelho, and Alexandra Machás. 2004. The role of communication and trust in explaining customer loyalty: An extension to the ECSI model. *European Journal of Marketing* 38: 1272–93. [CrossRef]

Baltas, George, Paraskevas C. Argouslidis, and Dionysis Skarmeas. 2010. The role of customer factors in multiple store patronage: A cost—Benefit approach. *Journal of Retailing* 86: 37–50. [CrossRef]

Bolton, Lisa E., and Anna S. Mattila. 2015. How Does Corporate Social Responsibility Affect Consumer Response to Service Failure in Buyer–Seller Relationships? *Journal of Retailing* 91: 140–53. [CrossRef]

Börner, Katy, Chaomei Chen, and Kevin W. Boyack. 2003. Visualizing knowledge domains. *Annual Review of Information Science and Technology* 37: 179–255. [CrossRef]

Bowden, Jana Lay-Hwa. 2009a. The process of customer engagement: A conceptual framework. *Journal of Marketing Theory and Practice* 17: 63–74. [CrossRef]

Bowden, Jana Lay-Hwa. 2009b. Customer engagement: A framework for assessing customer–brand relationships: The case of the restaurant industry. *Journal of Hospitality Marketing and Management* 18: 574–96. [CrossRef]

Brodie, Roderick J., James RM Whittome, and Gregory J. Brush. 2009. Investigating the service brand: A customer value perspective. *Journal of Business Research* 62: 345–55. [CrossRef]

Brodie, Roderick J., Ana Ilic, Biljana Juric, and Linda Hollebeek. 2013. Consumer engagement in a virtual brand community: An exploratory analysis. *Journal of Business Research* 66: 105–14. [CrossRef]

Brunner, Thomas A., Markus Stöcklin, and Klaus Opwis. 2008. Satisfaction, image and loyalty: New versus experienced customers. *European Journal of Marketing* 42: 1095–105. [CrossRef]

Calder, Bobby J., Edward C. Malthouse, and Ute Schaedel. 2009. An experimental study of the relationship between online engagement and advertising effectiveness. *Journal of Interactive Marketing* 23: 321–31. [CrossRef]

Calero Medina, C. M., and Thed N. van Leeuwen. 2012. Seed Journal Citation Network Maps: A Method Based on Network Theory. *Journal of the American Society for Information Science and Technology* 63: 1226–34. [CrossRef]

Caruana, Albert. 2002. Service loyalty: The effects of service quality and the mediating role of customer satisfaction. *European Journal of Marketing* 36: 811–29. [CrossRef]

Casaló, Luis, Carlos Flavián, and Miguel Guinalíu. 2007. The impact of participation in virtual brand communities on consumer trust and loyalty: The case of free software. *Online Information Review* 34: 775–92. [CrossRef]

Cassia, Fabio, Nicola Cobelli, and Marta Ugolini. 2017. The effects of goods-related and service-related B2B brand images on customer loyalty. *Journal of Business & Industrial Marketing* 32: 722–32.

Castillo-Vergara, Mauricio, Alejandro Alvarez-Marin, and Dario Placencio-Hidalgo. 2018. A bibliometric analysis of creativity in the field of business economics. *Journal of Business Research* 85: 1–9. [CrossRef]

Chan, Kimmy Wa, and Stella Yiyan Li. 2010. Understanding consumer-to-consumer interactions in virtual communities: The salience of reciprocity. *Journal of Business Research* 63: 1033–40. [CrossRef]

Chang, Hsin Hsin, and Su Wen Chen. 2008. The impact of customer interface quality, satisfaction and switching costs on e-loyalty: Internet experience as a moderator. *Computers in Human Behavior* 24: 2927–44. [CrossRef]

Chang, Li-Yen, and Shao-Chih Hung. 2013. Adoption and loyalty toward low cost carriers: The case of Taipei–Singapore passengers. *Transportation Research Part E: Logistics and Transportation Review* 50: 29–36. [CrossRef]

Chang, Aihwa, Sara H. Hsieh, and Timmy H. Tseng. 2013. Online Brand community response to negative brand events: The role of group eWOM. *Internet Research* 23: 486–506. [CrossRef]

Chaudhuri, Arjun, and Mark Ligas. 2009. Consequences of Value in Retail Markets. *Journal of Retailing* 85: 406–19. [CrossRef]

Chen, Ching-Fu. 2008. Investigating structural relationships between service quality, perceived value, satisfaction, and behavioral intentions for air passengers: Evidence from Taiwan. *Transportation Research Part A: Policy and Practice* 42: 709–17. [CrossRef]

Chen, Ching-Fu, and Odonchimeg Myagmarsuren. 2010. Exploring relationships between Mongolian destination brand equity, satisfaction and destination loyalty. *Tourism Economics* 16: 981–94. [CrossRef]

Chen, Jin, Cheng Zhang, and Yunjie Xu. 2009. The Role of Mutual Trust in Building Members' Loyalty to a C2C Platform Provider. *International Journal of Electronic Commerce* 14: 147–71. [CrossRef]

Chiou, Jyh-Shen, Lei-Yu Wu, and Min-Chieh Chuang. 2010. Antecedents of retailer loyalty: Simultaneously investigating channel push and consumer pull effects. *Journal of Business Research* 63: 431–38. [CrossRef]

Chiu, Hung-Chang, Yi-Ching Hsieh, Yu-Chuan Li, and Monle Lee. 2005. Relationship Marketing and Consumer Switching Behavior. *Journal of Business Research* 58: 1681–89. [CrossRef]

Chumpitaz, Ruben, and Nicholas G. Paparoidamis. 2004. Service quality and marketing performance in business-to-business markets: Exploring the mediating role of client satisfaction. *Managing Service Quality* 14: 235–48. [CrossRef]

Chumpitaz Caceres, Ruben, and Nicholas G. Paparoidamis. 2007. Service Quality, Relationship Satisfaction, Trust, Commitment and Business-to-Business Loyalty. *European Journal of Marketing* 41: 836–67. [CrossRef]

Ciunova-Shuleska, Anita, Nikolina Palamidovska-Sterjadovska, C. Nedu Osakwe, and J. Omotoso. 2017. The impact of customer retention orientation and brand orientation on customer loyalty and financial performance in SMEs: Empirical evidence from a Balkan country. *Journal for East European Management Studies* 22: 83–104. [CrossRef]

Cobo, Manolo J., Antonio Gabriel López-Herrera, Enrique Herrera-Viedma, and Francisco Herrera. 2012. SciMAT: A new science mapping analysis software tool. *Journal of the American Society for Information Science and Technology* 63: 1609–30. [CrossRef]

Cooil, Bruce, Timothy L. Keiningham, Lerzan Aksoy, and Michael Hsu. 2007. A longitudinal analysis of customer satisfaction and share of wallet: Investigating the moderating effect of customer characteristics. *Journal of Marketing* 71: 67–83. [CrossRef]

Coursaris, Constantinos K., and Wietske van Osch. 2016. A Cognitive-affective model of perceived user satisfaction (CAMPUS): The complementary effects and interdependence of usability and aesthetics in IS design. *Information & Management* 53: 252–64.

Cretu, Anca E., and Roderick J. Brodie. 2007. The influence of brand image and company reputation where manufacturers market to small firms: A customer value perspective. *Industrial Marketing Management* 36: 230–40. [CrossRef]

Dick, Alan S., and Kunal Basu. 1994. Customer loyalty: Toward an integrated conceptual framework. *Journal of Academy Marketing Science* 22: 99–113. [CrossRef]

Dioko, Leonardo Don AN, and Siu-Ian Amy So. 2012. Branding destinations versus branding hotels in a gaming destination: Examining the nature and significance of co-branding effects in the case study of Macao. *International Journal of Hospitality Management* 31: 554–63. [CrossRef]

Dobni, Dawn, and George M. Zinkhan. 1990. In search of brand image: A foundation analysis. *Adv. Cons. Res* 17: 110–19.

Dolan, Rebecca, Jodie Conduit, John Fahy, and Steve Goodman. 2016. Social media engagement behaviour: A uses and gratifications perspective. *Journal of Strategic Marketing* 24: 261–77. [CrossRef]

Edvardsson, Bo, Michael D. Johnson, Anders Gustafsson, and Tore Strandvik. 2000. The effects of satisfaction and loyalty on profits and growth: Products versus services. *Total Quality Management* 11: 917–27. [CrossRef]

Evanschitzky, Heiner, and Maren Wunderlich. 2006. An examination of moderator effects in the four-stage loyalty model. *Journal of Service Research* 8: 330–345. [CrossRef]

Evanschitzky, Heiner, Gopalkrishnan R. Iyer, Hilke Plassmann, Joerg Niessing, and Heribert Meffert. 2006. The relative strength of affective commitment in securing loyalty in service relationships. *Journal of Business Research* 59: 1207–13. [CrossRef]

Evanschitzky, Heiner, Balasubramanian Ramaseshan, David M. Woisetschläger, Verena Richelsen, Markus Blut, and Christof Backhaus. 2012. Consequences of customer loyalty to the loyalty program and to the company. *Journal of the Academy of Marketing Science* 40: 625–38. [CrossRef]

Fetscherin, Marc, and Daniel Heinrich. 2015. Consumer brand relationships research: A bibliometric citation meta-analysis. *Journal of Business Research* 68: 380–90. [CrossRef]

Fetscherin, Marc, and Jean-Claude Usunier. 2012. Corporate branding: An interdisciplinary literature review. *European Journal of Marketing* 46: 733–53. [CrossRef]

Forgas-Coll, Santiago, Ramon Palau-Saumell, Javier Sánchez-García, and Eva Maria Caplliure-Giner. 2014. The role of trust in cruise passenger behavioral intentions: The moderating effects of the cruise line brand. *Management Decision* 52: 1346–67. [CrossRef]

Frank, Björn, Boris Herbas Torrico, Takao Enkawa, and Shane J. Schvaneveldt. 2014. Affect versus cognition in the chain from perceived quality to customer loyalty: The roles of product beliefs and experience. *Journal of Retailing* 90: 567–86. [CrossRef]

Fullerton, Gordon. 2005. The impact of brand commitment on loyalty to retail service brands. *Canadian Journal of Administrative Sciences* 22: 97–110. [CrossRef]

Gallarza, Martina G., Maria Eugenia Ruiz-Molina, and Irene Gil-Saura. 2016. Stretching the value-satisfaction-loyalty chain by adding value dimensions and cognitive and affective satisfactions: A causal model for retailing. *Management Decision* 54: 981–1003. [CrossRef]

Gallo, Amy. 2014. The Value of Keeping the Right Customers. *Harvard Business Review*, October 29.

Gamboa, Ana Margarida, and Helena Martins Gonçalves. 2014. Customer loyalty through social networks: Lessons from Zara on Facebook. *Business Horizons* 57: 709–17. [CrossRef]

Ganesh, Jaishankar, Mark J. Arnold, and Kristy E. Reynolds. 2000. Understanding the customer base of service providers: An examination of the differences between switchers and stayers. *Journal of Marketing* 64: 65–87. [CrossRef]

Gensler, Sonja, Franziska Völckner, Yuping Liu-Thompkins, and Caroline Wiertz. 2013. Managing brands in the social media environment. *Journal of Interactive Marketing* 27: 242–56. [CrossRef]

Ghazali, Ezlika, Bang Nguyen, Dilip S. Mutum, and Amrul Asraf Mohd-Any. 2016. Constructing online switching barriers: Examining the effects of switching costs and alternative attractiveness on e-store loyalty in online pure-play retailer. *Electronic Markets* 26: 157–71. [CrossRef]

Gronholdt, Lars, Anne Martensen, and Kai Kristensen. 2000. The relationship between customer satisfaction and loyalty: Cross-industry differences. *Total Quality Management* 11: 509–14. [CrossRef]

Grönroos, Christian. 2009. Marketing as promise management: Regaining customer management for marketing. *Journal of Business & Industrial Marketing* 24: 351–59.

Gummerus, Johanna, Veronica Liljander, Emil Weman, and Minna Pihlström. 2012. Customer engagement in a Facebook brand community. *Management Research Review* 35: 857–77. [CrossRef]

Gustafsson, Anders, Michael D. Johnson, and Inger Roos. 2005. The effects of customer satisfaction, relationship commitment dimensions, and triggers on customer retention. *Journal Marketing* 69: 210–18. [CrossRef]

Hajli, Nick, Mohana Shanmugam, Savvas Papagiannidis, Debra Zahay, and Marie-Odile Richard. 2017. Branding co-creation with members of online brand communities. *Journal of Business Research* 70: 136–44. [CrossRef]

Han, Xiaoyun, Robert J. Kwortnik Jr., and Chunxiao Wang. 2008. Service loyalty: An integrative model and examination across service contexts. *Journal of Service Research* 11: 22–42.

Han, Heesup, Yunhi Kim, and Eui-Keun Kim. 2011. Cognitive, affective, conative, and action loyalty: Testing the impact of inertia. *International Journal of Hospitality Management* 30: 1008–19. [CrossRef]

Han, Heesup, Hong Ngoc Nguyen, Hakjun Song, Bee-Lia Chua, Sanghyeop Lee, and Wansoo Kim. 2018. Drivers of brand loyalty in the chain coffee shop industry. *International Journal of Hospitality Management* 72: 86–97. [CrossRef]

Hess, Jeff, and John Story. 2005. Trust-based commitment: Multidimensional consumer-brand relationships. *Journal of Consumer Marketing* 22: 313–22. [CrossRef]

Hollebeek, Linda D. 2011. Demystifying customer brand engagement: Exploring the loyalty nexus. *Journal of Marketing Management* 27: 785–07. [CrossRef]

Hollebeek, Linda D., Mark S. Glynn, and Roderick J. Brodie. 2014. Consumer brand engagement in social media: Conceptualization, scale development and validation. *Journal of Interactive Marketing* 28: 149–65. [CrossRef]

Horng, Jeou-Shyan, Chih-Hsing Liu, Hsin-Yu Chou, and Chang-Yen Tsai. 2012. Understanding the impact of culinary brand equity and destination familiarity on travel intentions. *Tourism Management* 33: 815–24. [CrossRef]

Hsu, Cathy H. C., Haemoon Oh, and A. George Assaf. 2012. A customer-based brand equity model for upscale hotels. *Journal of Travel Research* 51: 81–93. [CrossRef]

Huang, Chao-Chin. 2017. The impacts of brand experiences on brand loyalty: Mediators of brand love and trust. *Management Decision* 55: 915–34. [CrossRef]

Huang, Heng-Hsiang, Chou Kang Chiu, and Ching Kuo. 2006. Exploring customer satisfaction, trust and destination loyalty in tourism. *Journal of American Academy of Business* 10: 156–59.

Sean Hyun, Sunghyup, and Wansoo Kim. 2011. Dimensions of brand equity in the chain restaurant industry. *Cornell Hospitality Quarterly* 52: 429–37. [CrossRef]

Iglesias, Oriol, Jatinder J. Singh, and Joan M. Batista-Foguet. 2011. The role of brand experience and affective commitment in determining brand loyalty. *Journal of Brand Management* 18: 570–82. [CrossRef]

Im, Holly Hyunjung, Samuel Seongseop Kim, Statia Elliot, and Heejoo Han. 2012. Conceptualizing the brand equity dimensions from a consumer-based brand equity perspective. *Journal of Travel & Tourism Marketing* 29: 385–403.

Jacoby, Jacob. 1971. A model of multi-brand loyalty. *Journal of Advertising Research* 11: 25–31.

Jahn, Benedikt, and Werner Kunz. 2012. How to transform consumers into fans of your brand. *Journal of Service Management* 23: 344–61. [CrossRef]

Jang, Heehyoung, Lorne Olfman, Ilsang Ko, Joon Koh, and Kyungtae Kim. 2008. The influence of on-line brand community characteristics on community commitment and brand loyalty. *International Journal of Electronic Commerce* 3: 57–80. [CrossRef]

Jeong, Miyoung, and Haemoon Oh. 2017. Business-to-business social exchange relationship beyond trust and commitment. *International Journal of Hospitality Management* 65: 115–24. [CrossRef]

Jin, Byoungho, Jin Yong Park, and Jiyoung Kim. 2008. Cross-cultural examination of the relationships among firm reputation, e-satisfaction, e-trust, and e-loyalty. *International Marketing Review* 25: 324–37. [CrossRef]

Johnson, Michael D., Andreas Herrmann, and Frank Huber. 2006. The evolution of loyalty intentions. *Journal of Marketing* 70: 122–32. [CrossRef]

Jones, Michael A., David L. Mothersbaugh, and Sharon E. Beatty. 2000. Switching barriers and repurchase intentions in services. *Journal of Retailing* 76: 259–74. [CrossRef]

Kandampully, Jay, Tingting Zhang, and Anil Bilgihan. 2015. Customer loyalty: A review and future directions with a special focus on the hospitality industry. *International Journal of Contemporary Hospitality Management* 27: 379–414. [CrossRef]

Kang, Jun, Thomas Brashear Alejandro, and Mark D. Groza. 2015. Customer–company identification and the effectiveness of loyalty programs. *Journal of Business Research* 68: 464–71. [CrossRef]

Keller, Kevin Lane. 1993. Conceptualizing, Measuring, and Managing Customer-Based Brand Equity. *Journal of Marketing* 57: 1–22. [CrossRef]

Kim, Angella Ji-Young, and Eun-Ju Ko. 2010. The impact of design characteristics on brand attitude and purchase intention: Focus on luxury fashion brands. *Journal of the Korean Society of Clothing and Textiles* 34: 252–65. [CrossRef]

Kim, Angella Ji-Young, and Eun-Ju Ko. 2012. Do social media marketing activities enhance customer equity? An empirical study of luxury fashion brand. *Journal of Business Research* 65: 1480–86. [CrossRef]

Kim, H. J., and H. Z. Lee. 2009. The effect of well-being, consumer value orientations, perceived value and brand preference on purchase intention of environment-friendly cosmetics. *Journal of the Korean Society for Clothing Industry* 15: 327–48.

Kim, Jae Wook, Jiho Choi, William Qualls, and Kyesook Han. 2008a. It takes a marketplace community to raise brand commitment: The role of online communities. *Journal Marketing Management* 3: 409–31. [CrossRef]

Kim, Moon-Koo, Myeong-Cheol Park, Jong-Hyun Park, Jimin Kim, and Eunhye Kim. 2018b. The role of multidimensional switching barriers on the cognitive and affective satisfaction-loyalty link in mobile communication services: Coupling in moderating effects. *Computers in Human Behavior* 87: 212–23. [CrossRef]

Kim, Seongseop Sam, Ja Young Jacey Choe, and James F. Petrick. 2018c. The effect of celebrity on brand awareness, perceived quality, brand image, brand loyalty, and destination attachment to a literary festival. *Journal of Destination Marketing & Management* 9: 320–29.

Kimpakorn, Narumon, and Gerard Tocquer. 2010. Service brand equity and employee brand commitment. *Journal of Services Marketing* 24: 378–88. [CrossRef]

Kladou, Stella, and John Kehagias. 2014. Assessing destination brand equity: An integrated approach. *Journal of Destination Marketing & Management* 3: 2–10.

Koklic, Mateja Kos, Monika Kukar-Kinney, and Spela Vegelj. 2017. An investigation of customer satisfaction with low-cost and full-service airline companies. *Journal of Business Research* 80: 188–96. [CrossRef]

Kumara, V., and Denish Shah. 2004. Building and sustaining profitable customer loyalty for the 21st century. *Journal of Retailing* 80: 317–30. [CrossRef]

Laroche, Michel, Mohammad Reza Habibi, Marie-Odile Richard, and Ramesh Sankaranarayanan. 2012. The effects of social media based brand communities on brand community markers, value creation practices, brand trust and brand loyalty. *Computers in Human Behavior* 28: 1755–67. [CrossRef]

Lee, Kuan-Yin, Hui-Ling Huang, and Yin-Chiech Hsu. 2007. Trust, satisfaction and commitment: On loyalty to international retail service brands. *Asia Pacific Management Review* 12: 161–69.

Lee, Yong-Ki, Ki-Joon Back, and Jin-Young Kim. 2009. Family restaurant brand personality and its impact on customer's emotion, csatisfaction, and brand loyalty. *Journal of Hospitality Tourism Research* 33: 305–28. [CrossRef]

Lim, Joon Soo, YoungChan Hwang, Seyun Kim, and Frank A. Biocca. 2015. How social media engagement leads to sports channel loyalty: Mediating roles of social presence and channel commitment. *Computers in Human Behavior* 46: 158–67. [CrossRef]

Llanos-Herrera, Gonzalo R., and Jose M. Merigo. 2018. Overview of brand personality research with bibliometric indicators. *Kybernetes*. [CrossRef]

López-Miguens, Mª Jesús, and Encarnación González Vázquez. 2017. An integral model of e-loyalty from the consumer's perspective. *Computers in Human Behavior* 72: 397–411. [CrossRef]

Mandhachitara, Rujirutana, and Yaowalak Poolthong. 2011. A model of customer loyalty and corporate social responsibility. *Journal of Services Marketing* 25: 122–33. [CrossRef]

Manthiou, Aikaterini, Juhee Kang, and Thomas Schrier. 2014. A visitor-based brand equity perspective: The case of a public festival. *Tourism Review* 69: 264–83. [CrossRef]

Mattila, Anna S. 2001. Emotional bonding and restaurant loyalty. *Cornell Hospitality Quarterly* 42: 73–79. [CrossRef]

McAlexander, James H., John W. Schouten, and Harold F. Koenig. 2002. Building brand community. *Journal of Marketing* 66: 38–54. [CrossRef]

McManus, Lisa, and Chris Guilding. 2008. Exploring the potential of customer accounting: A synthesis of the accounting and marketing literatures. *Journal of Marketing Management* 24: 771–95. [CrossRef]

Melewar, T. C., Pantea Foroudi, Suraksha Gupta, Philip J. Kitchen, and Mohammad M. Foroudi. 2017. Integrating identity, strategy and communications for trust, loyalty and commitment. *European Journal of Marketing* 51: 572–604. [CrossRef]

Meyer-Waarden, Lars. 2008. The influence of loyalty programme membership on customer purchase behaviour. *European Journal of Marketing* 42: 87–114. [CrossRef]

Mollen, Anne, and Hugh Wilson. 2010. Engagement, telepresence and interactivity in online consumer experience: Reconciling scholastic and managerial perspectives. *Journal of Business Research* 63: 919–25. [CrossRef]

Monroe, Kent B. 2002. *Pricing*, 3rd ed. New York: McGraw-Hill.

Morris, Steven A., and Betsy Van der Veer Martens. 2008. Mapping research specialties. *Annual Review of Information Science and Technology* 42: 213–95. [CrossRef]

Muniz, Albert M., and Thomas C. O'guinn. 2001. Brand community. *Journal of Consumer Research* 27: 412–32. [CrossRef]

Nam, Janghyeon, Yuksel Ekinci, and Georgina Whyatt. 2011. Brand equity, brand loyalty and consumer satisfaction. *Annals of Tourism Research* 38: 1009–30. [CrossRef]

Nesset, Erik, and Øyvind Helgesen. 2014. Effects of switching costs on customer attitude loyalty to an airport in a multi-airport region. *Transportation Research Part A: Policy and Practice* 67: 240–53. [CrossRef]

Ng, Celeste See-Pui. 2013. Intention to purchase on social commerce websites across cultures: A cross-regional study. *Information Management* 50: 609–20. [CrossRef]

Nguyen, Ha Thu, Hoang Nguyen, Nhan Duc Nguyen, and Anh Chi Phan. 2018. Determinants of Customer Satisfaction and Loyalty in Vietnamese Life-Insurance Setting. *Sustainability* 10: 1151. [CrossRef]

Norris, Michael, and Charles Oppenheim. 2007. Comparing alternatives to the Web of Science for coverage of the social sciences' literature. *Journal of Informetrics* 1: 161–69. [CrossRef]

Noyons, E., H. Moed, and A. Van Raan. 1999. Integrating research performance analysis and science mapping. *Scientometrics* 46: 591–604. [CrossRef]

Oh, Haemoon, and Cathy HC Hsu. 2014. Assessing equivalence of hotel brand equity measures in cross-cultural contexts. *International Journal of Hospitality Management* 36: 156–66. [CrossRef]

Oliver, Richard L. 2014. *Satisfaction: A Behavioral Perspective on the Consumer*. Abingdon: Routledge.

Palmatier, Robert W., Rajiv P. Dant, Dhruv Grewal, and Kenneth R. Evans. 2006. Factors influencing the effectiveness of relationship marketing: A meta-analysis. *Journal of Marketing* 70: 136–53. [CrossRef]

Pan, Yue, Simon Sheng, and Frank T. Xie. 2012. Antecedents of customer loyalty: An empirical synthesis and reexamination. *Journal of Retailing and Consumer Service* 19: 150–58. [CrossRef]

Parasuraman, Ananthanarayanan, Valarie A. Zeithaml, and Leonard L. Berry. 1988. Servqual: A multiple-item scale for measuring consumer perceptions. *Journal of Retailing* 64: 12.

Park, Do-Hyung, Jumin Lee, and Ingoo Han. 2007. The effect of on-line consumer reviews on consumer purchasing intention: The moderating role of involvement. *International Journal of Electronic Commerce* 11: 125–48. [CrossRef]

Patterson, Paul, Ting Yu, and Ko De Ruyter. 2006. Understanding Customer Engagement in Services. Advancing Theory, Maintaining Relevance. Paper presented at the ANZMAC 2006 Conference, Brisbane, Australia, December 4–6.

Pentina, Iryna, Bashar S. Gammoh, Lixuan Zhang, and Michael Mallin. 2013. Drivers and outcomes of brand relationship quality in the context of online social networks. *International Journal of Electronic Commerce* 17: 63–86. [CrossRef]

Picón, Araceli, Ignacio Castro, and José L. Roldán. 2014. The relationship between satisfaction and loyalty: A mediator analysis. *Journal of Business Research* 67: 746–51. [CrossRef]

Pirsch, Julie, Shruti Gupta, and Stacy Landreth Grau. 2007. A framework for understanding corporate social responsibility programs as a continuum: An exploratory study. *Journal of Business Ethics* 70: 125–40. [CrossRef]

Prahalad, Coimbatore K., and Venkat Ramaswamy. 2004. Co-creation experiences: The next practice in value creation. *Journal of Interactive Marketing* 18: 5–14. [CrossRef]

Radler, Viktoria Maria. 2018. 20 Years of brand personality: A bibliometric review and research agenda. *Journal of Brand Management* 25: 370–83. [CrossRef]

Rajaguru, Rajesh. 2016. Role of value for money and service quality on behavioural intention: A study of full service and low cost airlines. *Journal of Air Transportation Management* 53: 114–22. [CrossRef]

Ramaseshan, Balasubramanian, Fazlul K. Rabbanee, and Laine Tan Hsin Hui. 2013. Effects of customer equity drivers on customer loyalty in B2B context. *Journal of Business & Industrial Marketing* 28: 335–46.

Ramaswamy, Venkat. 2009. Leading the transformation to co-creation of value. *Strategy & Leadership* 37: 32–37.

Ranaweera, Chatura, and Kalyani Menon. 2013. For better or for worse? *European Journal of Marketing* 47: 1598–621. [CrossRef]

Rauyruen, Papassapa, and Kenneth E. Miller. 2007. Relationship quality as a predictor of B2B customer loyalty. *Journal of Business Research* 60: 21–31. [CrossRef]

Richard, James E., and Annie Zhang. 2012. Corporate image, loyalty, and commitment in the consumer travel industry. *Journal of Marketing Management* 28: 568–93. [CrossRef]

Sahin, Azize, Cemal Zehir, and Hakan Kitapçı. 2011. The effects of brand experiences, trust and satisfaction on building brand loyalty: An empirical research on global brands. *Procedia-Social and Behavioral Sciences* 24: 1288–301. [CrossRef]

Saleem, Hamad, and Naintara Sarfraz Raja. 2014. The impact of service quality on customer satisfaction, customer loyalty and brand image: Evidence from hotel industry of Pakistan. *Journal of Business Management* 16: 117–22. [CrossRef]

Sánchez, José Ángel López, María Leticia Santos Vijande, and Juan Antonio Trespalacios Gutiérrez. 2011. The effects of manufacturer's organizational learning on distributor satisfaction and loyalty in industrial markets. *Industrial Marketing Management* 40: 624–35. [CrossRef]

Sashi, C. M. 2012. Customer engagement, buyer-seller relationships, and social media. *Management Decision* 50: 253–72. [CrossRef]

Schmidt, Frank. 2008. Meta-Analysis: A Constantly Evolving Research Integration Tool. *Organizational Research Methods* 11: 96–113. [CrossRef]

Schultz, Don E., and Scott E. Bailey. 2000. Customer/brand loyalty in an interactive marketplace. *Journal of Advertising Research* 40: 41–52. [CrossRef]

Šerić, Maja, Irene Gil-Saura, and María Eugenia Ruiz-Molina. 2014. How can integrated marketing communications and advanced technology influence the creation of customer-based brand equity? Evidence from the hospitality industry. *International Journal of Hospitality Management* 39: 144–56. [CrossRef]

Shahid Iqbal, Muhammad, Masood Ul Hassan, and Ume Habibah. 2018. Impact of self-service technology (SST) service quality on customer loyalty and behavioural intention: The mediating role of customer satisfaction. *Cogent Business & Management* 5: 1423770.

Sirdeshmukh, Deepak, Jagdip Singh, and Barry Sabol. 2002. Customer Trust, Value and Loyalty in Relational Exchanges. *Journal of Marketing* 66: 15–37. [CrossRef]

Siemieniako, Dariusz. 2018. Bibliometric Analysis of Scientific Research on Customer Loyalty in the Business-to-Business Context. *Handel Wewnętrzny* 5: 257–67.

Sitorus, Tigor, and Milawati Yustisia. 2018. The influence of service quality and customer trust toward customer loyalty: The role of customer satisfaction. *International Journal for Quality Research* 12: 639–54.

Small, Henry. 1999. Visualizing science by citation mapping. *Journal of the American Society for Information Science and Technology* 50: 799–813. [CrossRef]

Smith, Rodney E., and William F. Wright. 2004. Determinants of customer loyalty and financial performance. *Journal of Management Accounting Research* 16: 183–205. [CrossRef]

Sprott, David, Sandor Czellar, and Eric Spangenberg. 2009. The importance of a general measure of brand engagement on market behavior: Development and validation of a scale. *Journal of Marketing Research* 46: 92–104. [CrossRef]

Teng, Ching-I. 2018. Managing gamer relationships to enhance online gamer loyalty: The perspectives of social capital theory and self-perception theory. *Computers in Human Behavior* 79: 59–67. [CrossRef]

Torres, Anna, and Josep A. Tribó. 2011. Customer satisfaction and brand equity. *Journal of Business Research* 64: 1089–96. [CrossRef]

Tranfield, David, David Denyer, and Palminder Smart. 2003. Towards a methodology for developing evidence-informed management knowledge by means of systematic review. *British Journal of Management* 14: 207–22. [CrossRef]

Tsai, Hsien-Tung, and Heng-Chiang Huang. 2007. Determinants of e-repurchase intentions: An integrative model of quadruple retention drivers. *Information & Management* 44: 231–39.

Tu, Yu-Te, Chin-Mei Wang, and Hsiao-Chien Chang. 2012. Corporate brand image and customer satisfaction on loyalty: An empirical study of Starbucks coffee in Taiwan. *J. Soc. Dev. Sci.* 3: 24–32.

Van Doorn, Jenny, Katherine N. Lemon, Vikas Mittal, Stephan Nass, Doreén Pick, Peter Pirner, and Peter C. Verhoef. 2010. Customer Engagement Behavior: Theoretical Foundations and Research Directions. *Journal of Service Research* 13: 253–66. [CrossRef]

Vargo, Stephen L., and Robert F. Lusch. 2004. Evolving to a new dominant logic. *Journal of Marketing* 68: 1–17. [CrossRef]

Vargo, Stephen L., and Robert F. Lusch. 2008. Service-Dominant Logic: Continuing the Evolution. *Journal of the Academy of Marketing Science* 36: 1–10. [CrossRef]

Verhoef, Peter C., Werner J. Reinartz, and Manfred Krafft. 2010. Customer Engagement as a New Perspective in Customer Management. *Journal of Service Research* 13: 247–52. [CrossRef]

Villanueva, Julian, Pradeep Bhardwaj, Sridhar Balasubramanian, and Yuxin Chen. 2007. Customer relationship management in competitive environments: The positive implications of a short-term focus. *Quantitative Marketing and Economics* 5: 99–129. [CrossRef]

Vivek, Shiri D., Sharon E. Beatty, and Robert M. Morgan. 2012. Consumer engagement: Exploring customer relationships beyond purchase. *Marketing Theory and Practice* 20: 122–46. [CrossRef]

Waltman, Ludo. 2016. A review of the literature on citation impact indicators. *Journal of Informetrics* 109: 365–91. [CrossRef]

Wathne, Kenneth H., Harald Biong, and Jan B. Heide. 2001. Choice of supplier in embedded markets: Relationship and marketing program effects. *Journal of Marketing* 65: 54–66. [CrossRef]

Wirtz, Jochen, Anouk Den Ambtman, Josée Bloemer, Csilla Horváth, Balasubramanian Ramaseshan, Joris Van De Klundert, Zeynep Gurhan Canli, and Jay Kandampully. 2013. Managing brands and customer engagement in online brand communities. *Journal of Service Management* 24: 223–44. [CrossRef]

Wu, Ya-Ling, and Eldon Y. Li. 2018. Marketing mix, customer value, and customer loyalty in social commerce: A stimulus-organism-response perspective. *Internet Research* 28: 74–104. [CrossRef]

Xu, Jing, and Andrew Chan. 2010. A conceptual framework of hotel experience and customer based brand equity: Some research questions and implications. *International Journal of Contemporary Hospitality Management* 22: 174–93.

Yadav, Manjit S., Kristine De Valck, Thorsten Hennig-Thurau, Donna L. Hoffman, and Martin Spann. 2013. Social commerce: A contingency framework for assessing marketing potential. *Journal of Interactive Marketing* 27: 311–23. [CrossRef]

Yi, Youjae, and Hoseong Jeon. 2003. Effects of loyalty programs on value perception, program loyalty, and brand loyalty. *Journal of the Academy of Marketing Science* 31: 229–40. [CrossRef]

Yi, Youjae, and Suna La. 2004. What influences the relationship between customer satisfaction and repurchase intention? Investigating the effects of adjusted expectations and customer loyalty. *Psychology & Marketing* 21: 351–73.

Yoshida, Masayuki, Brian S. Gordon, Makoto Nakazawa, Shigeki Shibuya, and Naoyuki Fujiwara. 2018. Bridging the gap between social media and behavioral brand loyalty. *Electronic Commerce Research and Applications* 28: 208–18. [CrossRef]

Zhang, Mingli, and Nuan Luo. 2016. Understanding relationship benefits from harmonious brand community on social media. *Internet Research* 26: 809–26. [CrossRef]

Zhang, Sha Sandy, Jenny van Doorn, and Peter S. H. Leeflang. 2014. Does the importance of value, brand and relationship equity for customer loyalty differ between Eastern and Western cultures? *International Business Review* 23: 284–92. [CrossRef]

Zhou, Zhimin, Qiyuan Zhang, Chenting Su, and Nan Zhou. 2012. How do brand communities generate brand relationships? Intermediate mechanisms. *Journal of Business Research* 65: 890–95. [CrossRef]

Zins, Andreas H. 2001. Relative attitudes and commitment in customer loyalty models: Some experiences in the commercial airline industry. *International Journal of Service Industry Management* 12: 269–94. [CrossRef]

Zupic, Ivan, and Tomaž Čater. 2015. Bibliometric methods in management and organization. *Organizational Research Methods* 18: 429–72. [CrossRef]

© 2019 by the authors. Licensee MDPI, Basel, Switzerland. This article is an open access article distributed under the terms and conditions of the Creative Commons Attribution (CC BY) license (http://creativecommons.org/licenses/by/4.0/).

MDPI
St. Alban-Anlage 66
4052 Basel
Switzerland
Tel. +41 61 683 77 34
Fax +41 61 302 89 18
www.mdpi.com

Administrative Sciences Editorial Office
E-mail: admsci@mdpi.com
www.mdpi.com/journal/admsci

www.ingramcontent.com/pod-product-compliance
Lightning Source LLC
LaVergne TN
LVHW071443100526
838202LV00088B/6788